BLACK UNIONISM IN THE INDUSTRIAL SOUTH

NUMBER ELEVEN:
Texas A&M Southwestern Studies

Robert A. Calvert and María Cristina García
General Editors

BLACK UNIONISM IN THE INDUSTRIAL SOUTH

Ernest Obadele-Starks

Texas A&M University Press
COLLEGE STATION

The paper used in this book meets the minimum requirements
of the American National Standard for Permanence
of Paper for Printed Library Materials, z39.48-1984.
Binding materials have been chosen for durability.

Library of Congress Cataloging-in-Publication Data

Obadele-Starks, Ernest,   1959–
    Black unionism in the industrial South / Ernest Obadele-Starks.
        p.   cm. — (Texas A&M southwestern studies ; no. 11)
    Includes bibliographical references and index.
    ISBN 0-89096-912-4 (cloth)
        1. Trade-unions—Afro-American membership—History—20th century.
    2. Race discrimination—Southern States—History—20th century.
    3. Southern States—Economic conditions.   4. Equality—Southern States.
    I. Title.   II. Series.
    HD6490.R22U66   1999
    331.6'396073—dc21   99-34233
                                                                              CIP

CONTENTS

ILLUSTRATIONS

FIGURES

MAPS

TABLES

ACKNOWLEDGMENTS

As always, few academic studies can succeed without the comments of colleagues and scholars. I am indebted to numerous entities and individuals. First and foremost I would like to thank Eric Arnesen who took time out from his own busy academic life to read the entire manuscript. He provided leads to sources and offered critical comments which helped me improve the manuscript. I also owe much thanks to George Green for his useful commentary. Robert Calvert shared his vast knowledge of Texas historical literature and provided the inspirational support that all researchers need when they pursue an endeavor such as this one. I also owe a debt of gratitude to Eileen Boris, Michael Botson, Albert Broussard, Carol Higham, Alex Lichenstein, Merline Pitre, Merl Reed, Amilcar Shabazz, Cary Wintz, and Emilio Zamora, for reading either all or segments of the manuscript.

Numerous other individuals made vital contributions to this work. Allison "Bud" Alton, Lynne Baker, Leona Mercedes Black, Jane Boley, Maurice Easterwood, Don Hahs, William H. Harris, LeRoy Hoskins, Louis Marchiafava, Mark Martin, Kelly McElmurry, Mack (Brother Mack) Merritt, Clarena Richardson, Barbara Rust, David Sanders, Herman Simpson, Angela Schnuerle, Rachel Valdez, Tara Wenger, Michele Whitley, and my labor history senior seminar either chased down data for minor details or offered their historical insight on some aspect of the book.

Of course, scholarly works are rarely completed without archival and financial assistance. To that end, I want to acknowledge the staff members at the Houston Metropolitan Research Center, the Center for American History, the Texas State Archives, the University of Texas at Arlington Special Collections, the Rosenberg Library, the Tyrrell Historical Library, the Texas Land Office, the U.S. National Archives in Washington, D.C., and the U.S. National Archives Regional Office in Fort Worth, Texas. This project could not have made it to completion without the generous funding of the University Scholarly Enhancement Program at Texas A&M University, the Cullen Research Grant Program at the University of Houston, the Murray Miller

Research Grant Program at the University of Houston, and the African American Studies Research Fellowship Program also at the University of Houston.

My immediate and extended family has played the most important part in this journey. Aerial J'nae Starks, your arrival into this world on October 15, 1998, was the greatest event of my life. Your descension from the heavens confirmed the power of prayer. Many of those prayers came from my parents, Mary Flowers-Starks and Ernest Kent Starks, Sr. Words cannot describe the love that flows between parents and children. Your combined, unwavering, and unconditional love, has meant more to me than you will ever know. The network that the two of you have established within the Starks clan is, in my opinion, unrivaled. Thus, the emotional support I have received from my siblings and their families is nothing more than an extension of the love that you have conveyed over the years toward each of us. I am forever grateful to all them: David Ussery, Marcia Starks-Ussery, Jason Ussery, Jasmine Ussery, Michael Kevin Starks, Sylvia Wells-Starks, Michael Kevin Starks, Jr., Wayne Kelly, Tamyra Starks-Kelly, Wayne Kelly, Jr., Shania Nicole Kelly, and Angela Michelle Starks. Finally, I want to extend my warmest thanks to Gina Marie Flowers, who provided large bowls of warm oatmeal during the initial stages of my research, and also to Beverly Jean Tate and Britain Flowers, and the entire Drinks contingency: Maurice, Mary, LaKesha, Skyja, Nicole, Maurice, Jr., and Naquitta.

INTRODUCTION

When Ignitiuos Kirk (I. K.) Black arrived in Houston from Lagonia, Louisiana, in February, 1921, and settled into an inexpensive boarding house, he undoubtedly had his wife, Sarah Walker Black, and his twelve-year-old daughter, Leona Mercedes Black, on his mind. The railroad brakeman and part-time sugarcane farmer left his family behind as he searched for stable employment in the Bayou City. Black arrived to the sight of bright flames jetting from towering refineries near a newly constructed ship channel, merchant ships docked at the city's port, longshoremen unloading tons of cargo, the clamoring sounds of locomotives transporting cargo to nearby and distant markets, and the construction of new housing settlements near factories and manufacturing plants. More important, Black stood before a bustling industrial complex in a city deeply entrenched in the tradition of Jim Crow and white supremacy.[1]

Despite Houston's racial climate, an expanding Texas economy motivated workers such as Black to take calculated risks and seek new work opportunities along the Upper Texas Gulf Coast. His decision to vacate his home and journey across the state line had less to do with the deteriorating racial conditions in Louisiana or expectations for better race relations in Texas, but more to do with the prospects of increased work opportunities and better wages offered by an expanding industrial region. It was not long before Black hired on with the Sinclair Refinery in Houston and sent for his wife, daughter, and nephew Roosevelt. Fortunately for Black, an expanding Upper Texas Gulf Coast economy allowed him to accept yet another job with the Texas & Pacific Railroad shortly after he lost his position with Sinclair. Despite his good fortune, Black faced the obstacles that most blacks confronted in southern workplaces. From the start of his employment with the railroad in 1922 until his retirement in 1946, he grappled with the constraints of a brutally discriminatory labor movement. Regardless of his job assignment, his employers refused to increase his wages or to match his with those of his white coworkers.[2]

Black's experience typified those of numerous black workers confronting the regime of Jim Crow in the union movement. Fortunately for Black, black railroad workers rallied their ranks and organized themselves into several pockets of resistance. As Black settled into retirement in the late 1940s, black unionists had entered a new era of struggle. The post–World War II period brought on changes in industrialization, government labor policy, and race relations. These changes fostered many new outlooks on race, class, and unionization. The struggles, strategies, and resistance that black railroad unionists put forth helped set the stage for further protest as the country entered the critical years of the civil rights movement.

This study is about black unionism in the industrial South. It examines the responses and strategies of black unionists to race and class domination along the Upper Texas Gulf Coast, a region that served as a model of industrialization in the post–Civil War South. The Upper Texas Gulf Coast, an area consisting of Chambers, Galveston, Harris, and Jefferson Counties, became a focal point of southern industrial expansion from the latter part of the nineteenth century through the first half of the twentieth. During these years, the Upper Texas Gulf Coast became one of the largest industrial centers in the United States.

Following the Civil War, the region became a primary center for cotton distribution and other southern-grown staples. As the *Galveston Daily News* reported about Houston in 1865, "everybody must be making money, the city continually full of goods . . . railroads and wagon[s] . . . leaving every hour freighted to the utmost capacity." The newspaper also predicted that the city would "have a steadily increasing commerce of no ordinary magnitude." Shippers enjoyed benefits from a revitalized economy and provided work opportunities for longshoremen at numerous docks and wharves. Cotton and timber production along with government bonds gave rise to a booming railroad industry. New tracks connected the region with other areas of the country and created a network of domestic trade that made the Upper Texas Gulf Coast an important railroad center. The discovery of oil at the Spindletop oil field near Beaumont, Texas, in 1901 ushered in a new era of industrial growth and played a vital role in the region's economic transformation. The region quickly became the focal point of oil refining and employment for the entire country when it witnessed the construction of new refineries. The oil boom along the Upper Texas Gulf Coast cleared the way for the growth of secondary industries and specialized manufacturers such as the Hughes Tool Com-

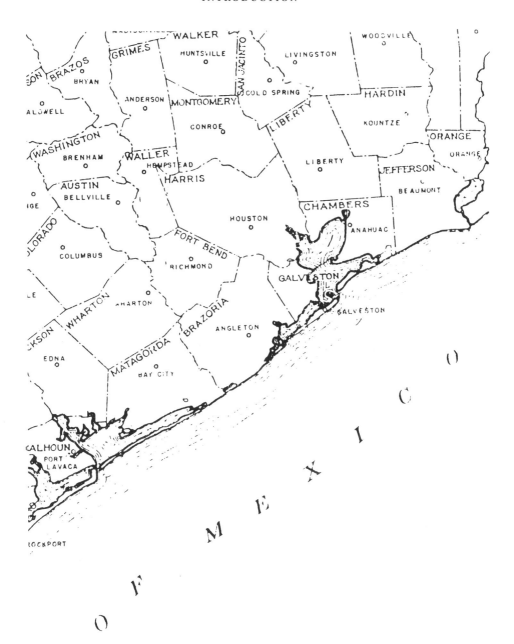

Portion of a map of Texas showing Upper Texas Gulf Coast counties and county seats. Courtesy Archives and Records Division of the Texas General Land Office, Austin.

pany in Houston, which produced oil drilling equipment for the region's oil companies. Hughes Tool capitalized on the oil boom and during the first half of the twentieth century stood out as the largest producer of oil drilling bits in the world. Although shipbuilding did not become a significant industry until the late 1930s and early 1940s, it nevertheless helped round out the industrial transformation of the region. The demand for ships during World War II created new work opportunities for black workers, and as in the other four industries, posed new issues for black unionization.[3]

By 1940, Houston, the economic hub of the Upper Texas Gulf Coast, ranked as the largest city in the state, the second largest in the South behind New Orleans, and the twenty-first largest in the nation. It also held the distinction of employing more black Americans in manufacturing jobs than its southern rival cities of Memphis, New Orleans, and Atlanta. From 1910 to 1940, its population nearly quintupled, a record of growth exceeded only by Los Angeles in this era.[4]

Industrialization, migration, discrimination, and unionization shaped the New South experience of most black workers undergoing the complicated transition from rural life to the world of industrial employment. Occupational hierarchies and racially divided workplaces reflected the day-to-day experiences of these workers. Generally, white workers viewed themselves as privileged and more deserving of better-paying jobs. However, black workers thought of themselves as important members of the working class and entitled to the same opportunities as whites. This study examines the race and class struggles of black unionists in the longshore, oil, railroad, steel (specialized production), and shipbuilding industries. While black unionists aspired to full equality, white unions offered them gradual participation, sporadic inclusion, and minimal interracial cooperation.

Faced with widespread discrimination, racist white unions, and an ambivalent government, black unionists along the Upper Texas Gulf Coast drew upon an array of resources and strategies to build vibrant, progressive, and versatile labor communities to resist oppression. In some cases, blacks worked as strikebreakers, organized union auxiliaries, or chartered their own union locals. In other instances, they formed loose alliances with members of the black middle class, attended conferences and conventions, and utilized black newspapers to bolster their efforts.

What we know about black unionism in Texas is generally limited to the works of Ruth Allen and F. Ray Marshall. Ruth Allen's *Chapters in the History of Organized Labor in Texas* for many years served as the conventional point of departure on the history of black unionism in Texas. According to Allen, the black worker had "a total incapacity to think, act or speak in terms of the century and the order in which as a freedman he must live." Allen's focus on white workers prevented her from fully examining and articulating the experiences of black workers.[5] For the past twenty-five years, F. Ray Marshall's discussion of trade unions in Texas has served as the main source of information on Texas' labor movement. According to Marshall, industrialization initiated the growth of labor unions in Texas. The white-led labor organizations that followed this industrial growth failed to adequately accommodate black workers. The American Federation of Labor (AFL), for example, stretched its organizing efforts into the South and by the turn of the twentieth century concentrated on workers with specialized crafts and trades. AFL craft unions, however, resisted black worker access to skilled occupations and rejected notions of black membership.[6] Marshall acknowledged the pervasiveness of discrimination against black workers but failed to demonstrate how black unionists responded to these circumstances.[7]

This study differs from Allen and Marshall by focusing on the responses of black unionists to race and class domination and demonstrates that black unionists were anything but complacent workers when it came to their desire to be unionized. It first provides a background chapter that examines the economic, social, political, and ideological world of black workers from the late 1800s through the early part of the 1940s. Industrial expansion provided opportunities for wage jobs in urban complexes. Racial constraints, however, brought on by a culture of Jim Crow, were transplanted from the interior rural areas of Texas and bordering states into the industrial centers.[8] White-led labor unions imposed their version of racial oppression and in unionized settings relegated black workers to low-wage jobs, denied them membership in many unions, and restricted their occupational mobility. Public and labor policy generally deferred to the wishes of white workers and typically did very little to assist black unionists in their efforts to overcome a racist labor movement. Despite these circumstances, blacks developed a consciousness of resistance, tested the boundaries of racial constraints, and assembled a complex mix of visions and ideologies as tools of protest.[9]

This study places Texas' Upper Gulf Coast at the center of the southern labor history narrative. Recently, labor scholars have reexamined the relationship between black and white workers in the post–Civil War South. These academicians have built on the work of past generations of labor scholars whose writings reflected white worker domination and black worker subordination with little discussion about the strategies and practices the local black working class used to resist oppression.[10] The new southern labor historians, however, pose new questions about race, class, and unionism in the South. Eric Arnesen, Neil Foley, Michael Goldfield, Keith Griffler, William H. Harris, Michael Honey, Robin Kelley, Rich Halpern, Tera Hunter, Daniel Letwin, Merl Reed, David Roediger, Joe William Trotter, Jr., and Robert Zieger all have expanded the discourse on black unionism and included in their analyses are many of the strategies and practices black workers used to resist domination.[11]

William H. Harris refused to exonerate white unionists, employers, or the government when he asserted that "the history of black workers is the history of discrimination." Harris elaborated on the pervasiveness of discrimination that black workers endured. He placed at the heart of his study a discussion on the rise of the black-led Brotherhood of Sleeping Car Porters (BSCP) and the precedent it established when it organized in 1925 and received an AFL charter in 1937. Harris set the stage for further research, including Trotter's regional and original study on the black community in the West Virginia coal mining industry. Trotter found that black unionists and community folk took part in a "complicated transition" to an industrial setting. Although Trotter's black migrants enjoyed better wages, housing, education, and social services than in the rural areas, they nonetheless encountered the usual forms of discrimination and exclusion.[12]

Kelley, Arnesen, and Letwin chronicled the activities of black and white unionists in the South and their attempts to gain a greater share of the American economy. Kelley demonstrated that Birmingham's black workers were as active as white workers in their struggle for economic power. Black workers in Birmingham established a culture of opposition to discrimination and fostered a functional relationship with communists. Their attempt to establish interracial cooperation was a formidable endeavor, as was the case with the biracial campaigns of Arnesen's New Orleans dockworkers and Letwin's Alabama coal miners. Kelley's brilliant work confirms my findings about black workers in Texas. Although they established an aloof relationship with communists, black unionists along the Upper Texas Gulf Coast sought economic leverage for the advancement of the race. Their push for economic power, in large part, spoke to their perception of themselves and their role in the labor movement.[13]

Tera W. Hunter's unique work on black household workers and washerwomen in the South following the Civil War expounded on the nu-

ances of the black workers' struggle to enjoy the benefits of a capitalist economic system. As black women entered the New South era, a period of extreme racial intolerance and economic oppression for black Americans, they
constructed their own responses, including unions, to obstacles that hindered
their social, political, and economic progress. "As black women struggled to
overcome conditions of abject poverty and servitude," Hunter writes, "employers and public authorities worked even harder to repress and contain them
through every means at their disposal." Common racial oppression among
black Texans also spurred a range of strategies for those who faced the day-to-
day task of confronting biased white workers and profit-minded employers.[14]

The narratives of southern labor historians have not yet been applied to
topics in Texas. This oversight may be due, in part, to Texas' geographical
configuration, which lends itself to three distinct identities—West Texas, the
Rio Grande Valley, and East Texas.[15] "The Great Southwest . . ." as Maury
Maverick, a popular Texas lawmaker during the 1930s wrote, "is the land of
my fathers. The Old South, on the other hand, seems to me to be the land of
my forefathers, a strange and distant illusion." Moreover, Texas, unlike other
southern states, operated as an independent republic before acquiring state-
hood and for years maintained a measure of ideological isolation from other
regions of the country. The complex historical background of Texas places it
in a unique position of being partially identified with the U.S. Southwest, the
U.S. South, and the Mexican-U.S. border region, and may contribute to its
ambiguous historiographical placement.[16]

This study seeks to fill a historiographical gap in the history of black unionism. Chapters two through six analyze the experiences of black unionists in
the longshore, railroad, oil, steel, and shipbuilding industries. The emergence
of black union activity coincided with the appearance and growth of these
industries along the Upper Texas Gulf Coast. The pervasiveness and influence of black unionism in Texas varied between industries and adds a vital
dimension to the storied experiences of black workers. While some suffered
from the agonizing constraints of Jim Crow, others gained modest benefits
from racial separation and occasional cooperation from whites. The impetus,
however, of black resistance to race and class oppression in the union movement, to a large extent, came from the black unionists themselves. With
unflinching determination black workers shaped their own expectations of
the labor movement and formed the crux of sustained opposition to discrimination in a racist labor movement. From the late 1800s to the early 1940s,
blacks organized their own labor organizations, prodded some white locals

for membership into theirs, worked as strikebreakers during labor strife, re-shaped labor policies, redefined their place within the working class, and de-manded equal treatment and fair representation.

The final chapter of this study analyzes the effect of World War II on black unionism along the Upper Texas Gulf Coast. The United States's entry into the war generated a need for effective wartime industrial production and marked a critical turning point in the relationship between the government and black workers. Black unionists capitalized on the "Double V" campaign, which called on the government to promote the principles of democracy over-seas while mandating racial fairness in defense plants on the homefront. The government's response to the "Double V" campaign came in the form of the Fair Employment Practices Commission (FEPC). The FEPC investigated complaints of unfair hiring practices among defense employers. Although black unionists along the Upper Texas Gulf Coast filed numerous complaints with the agency, the response to FEPC intercession into the region's labor affairs varied between industries.

The conclusion of this study presents a discussion of the historical impli-cations of the black unionists' experience along the Upper Texas Gulf Coast. It introduces a number of theoretical arguments about the role and meaning of black unionism in the struggle for racial equality in the post–World War II era and proposes methodological strategies for researchers to examine in greater detail the intersection between black unionism and labor, economic, and so-cial history.

BLACK UNIONISM IN THE INDUSTRIAL SOUTH

CHAPTER 1

"A SERIOUS MENACE TO THE WHITE UNION MEN"

The World of the Black Unionist

BLACK UNIONISM along the Upper Texas Gulf Coast emerged within the context of industrial expansion in the South following the Civil War. The South lagged behind the North in industrialization during the antebellum period. After the war, southern leaders, concerned about the South's over-reliance on cotton, and northern business people, anxious to capitalize on available resources in the region, encouraged industrial growth. Railroad expansion and technological developments made possible the production of new commodities, while the demand for southern manufactured goods spawned the growth of new industries. Black labor's struggle to gain access to industrial jobs and acceptance into labor unions in industrial centers was greatly influenced by a culture of discrimination and segregation provoked by Jim Crow laws. The shift from agrarian jobs to urban industrial employment brought to the surface issues in race relations, regional politics, and government labor policy. For black unionists the road to unionization was influenced by a range of economic, political, and social circumstances.[1]

An understanding of industrial expansion in Texas helps put the rise of black unionism in a broader context. The emergence of railroads, for example, played a vital role in the growth of the Texas economy. Railroads connected the nation's domestic markets, providing cheap, fast, and dependable means to transport and distribute goods. Railroad building in Texas began before the Civil War, halted during the crisis, and restarted in the immediate postbellum years. Texas farmers used the railroad to promote commercial farming, while other industries, including cotton, flour mills, timber, mining, and petroleum, also capitalized on its usefulness.[2] Public resources and land grants increased railroad construction. Railroad investors in Houston provided the leadership and resources to expand the Southern Pacific Railroad Company and establish Houston as an important connection between the Gulf and West Coast and to interior southern markets. Increased railroad construction in Texas during the late 1800s enhanced a market economy along the Upper Texas Gulf Coast and made possible the growth of up-start industries, creating a means for companies to market their products into distant regions.[3]

Railroads also provided a link between oil fields and markets for crude. Until the Spindletop gush in 1901, oil played a minor role in the Texas economy, although commercial oil production had expanded during the 1890s around Corsicana, Texas. The Spindletop eruption spewed nearly one-half million barrels of oil and ushered in a new era of oil refining. Petroleum refining expanded between 1901 and World War I in the Beaumont area following the construction of large refineries. The expansion of the petroleum industry along the Upper Texas Gulf Coast, combined with the growth of railroads, catapulted the region into national economic prominence.[4]

Waterway improvements also influenced economic changes in the region. Federal grants in 1872, 1874, and 1886 improved Houston's Buffalo Bayou and its link to Galveston Bay and the Gulf of Mexico. This improvement enhanced inland access to and from the Gulf and improved commercial prospects for the region. In 1899 the Rivers and Harbors Act cleared the way for construction of the Houston Ship Channel. The completion of this project in 1914 connected Houston with the Gulf of Mexico, allowing large vessels to come seventy miles inland to load and unload cargo.[5]

Evidence of economic expansion in several neighboring cities illustrated that the ship channel region had established itself as a major contributor to manufacturing and distribution in the region. While Galveston remained a major cotton port, the number of manufacturing plants in Houston increased from 78 at the turn of the twentieth century to 429 in 1930. By the late 1920s Houston had surged past all other ports to become the leading exporter of cotton in the nation. The construction of a large public grain elevator along the ship channel in 1926 gave grain exporters a new outlook on the potential success of their industry. It is not surprising that the region's shipping industry also grew as a result of an expanded economy. The demand for shipping led to a vast expansion of docks and loading facilities. These docks became crucial to the exportation of goods and commodities. The total tonnage handled at the Port of Houston increased from 1.3 million in 1919 to nearly 14 million in 1929, when the port ranked sixth largest among ports in the country that handled foreign commerce, before climbing to more than 27 million in 1941. The construction of the Pan American oil refinery in Texas City in

The 1901 Spindletop gusher ushered in a new era of industrialization along the Upper Texas Gulf Coast. Courtesy Spindletop/Gladys City Boomtown Museum, Beaumont, Texas.

Houston became a leading center for cotton distribution after the Civil War; photo ca. late 1880s. Courtesy Houston Metropolitan Research Center, Houston Public Library.

1934 and the Champion Paper and Fiber Company, a large paper-manufacturing plant, in Pasadena in 1937 also gave a boost to the region's economy.[6]

The Sabine Lake region and its principal cities also contributed to the Upper Texas Gulf Coast economy. The Sabine River served as the eastern boundary between Texas and Louisiana. The river's deep and navigable channel emptied into Sabine Lake and eventually into the Gulf of Mexico. The dredging of the Neches River in 1916 in Beaumont helped attract large refining complexes, railroads, and shippers. The Sabine area initially grew as a timber processing and railroad center, but the oil boom after 1901 attracted a wave of new employers.[7] Beaumont, a dusty lumber mill town at the turn of the century, became a major shipping port city that boasted a refining capacity that tripled between 1916 and 1941. By the end of the 1930s, refineries in Jefferson County supplied 10 percent of the national output of refined products. Rice production and shipments in Beaumont and Port Arthur also helped make the Sabine region a thriving commercial center. Although rice growers believed that oil expansion threatened land prices and diverted labor and capital, the transportation boom compensated for the increased oil competition, and the rice industry was helped more than it was hurt by an expanding oil economy. Railroads and ships allowed growers to reach distant markets, which encouraged increased production and more capital investments. The emergence of a booming petroleum industry and improved transportation facilities led to a proliferation of new industries throughout the Sabine region, making the Upper Texas Gulf Coast a locus of refining, manufacturing, and shipping in the state.[8]

Industrialization increased the number of manufacturing jobs available to black workers. In 1900 Texas recorded 57,000 blacks in nonagricultural work, 38,000 working as personal or domestic servants, while others hired on as unskilled laborers. Blacks comprised 4,300 railroad workers; 3,200 worked in trucking and delivery services; 2,500 worked in sawmills. By 1920 the number of nonagricultural black workers increased to 98,000. Despite this increase, blacks were limited to unskilled jobs in most industries. The near 295,000 black industrial laborers working in Texas during World War II represented 32 percent of the total black population in Texas. Over 50 percent of these laborers were employed in unskilled occupations.[9]

Industrialization spawned a noticeable population shift to industrial centers along the Upper Texas Gulf Coast from the end of the Civil War through the 1940s. Notwithstanding the repudiation of plantation life, which most blacks associated with slavery, and the efforts of white landowners to restrict the movement of black workers, industrialization was the single most important development that shaped the transition of black workers from rural and semirural employment to the urban industrial workforce in Texas.[10] As the number of industries grew and industrial development quickened, the demand for new labor attracted multitudes of black workers to a variety of industrial jobs.[11]

Industrial expansion along the Upper Texas Gulf Coast attracted residents from bordering states. Although the population decline of several Louisiana parishes can be attributed to the movement of those escaping a war-torn South following the Civil War, industrialization along the Upper Texas Gulf Coast can also account for some of the movement. From 1910 to 1920 the overall black population of Louisiana declined from 713,874 to 700,257, and several parishes recorded substantial decreases in their general population. The population of Jefferson Parish, for example, fell from 17,767 to 12,166 between 1870 and 1880. Calcasieu Parish had a near 48 percent decline in its residents.

Cameron Parish recorded close to an 8 percent decrease, while St. Charles Parish had approximately 24 percent of its residents leave the parish. Plaquemine Parish followed a similar trend and lost around 19 percent of its inhabitants. Between 1920 and 1930 Beauregard Parish had a nearly 30 percent drop in its population, while Vernon Parish recorded a modest 4 percent decline by the end of the decade.[12]

Another explanation for the population movement of blacks into Texas was the emergence of World War I. It is widely accepted that the First World War represented a watershed in black history. During the war years blacks migrated away from rural regions and were drawn to industrial centers that offered decent-paying jobs. The war required the enlistment and drafting of large numbers of white workers, which, coupled with the decline in European immigration, created a tight labor market, especially in lower-paying unskilled jobs, necessarily leading to an increase in the employment of black workers. Mobilization for the war presented southern blacks with an unprecedented opportunity to escape the control of racist whites in rural communities only to find that the racial attitudes of many whites toward most blacks were firmly transplanted into urban areas.[13]

The movement of black workers across state lines had a profound effect on the Upper Texas Gulf Coast. "When the exodus of our people began" during World War I, the *Houston Informer* reported in 1919, "their places had to be filled in the local plants and institutions that depended upon colored employees, and as a result the exodus was counteracted . . . by a great influx of colored people from the rural districts and the state of Louisiana . . . into foundries, factories, mines, docks, and freight yards."[14]

Family migration was a particularly difficult process, requiring cooperation and sacrifice. Typically, married men left their families behind for a time while they sought work in the industries. Black women generally stayed with their children until the family could move. In other instances, couples relied on kin and friends to care for young children while they ventured off in search of employment. When twelve-year-old Leona Black took her seat in the "colored" section of a Southern Pacific passenger train in June, 1921, she was on her way from New Orleans to meet her parents, who had come to Houston earlier that same year prospecting for work. Although Leona's parents lamented their separation from their only child, they felt compelled to leave her in Louisiana with her aunt and uncle, Cily and Mose Walker, until the couple secured stable jobs. Sarah Walker Black's job as a domestic and washerwoman in the all-white Magnolia Park section of Houston and I. K. Black's work in

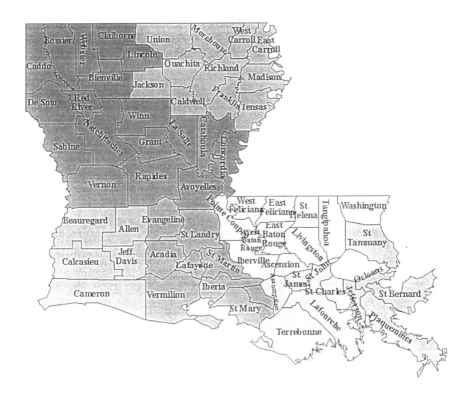

Louisiana parishes. Courtesy Division of Administration, State of Louisiana.

the oil industry and later the railroad provided the financial security they needed for their daughter's eventual departure from Louisiana.[15]

Industrial expansion also spawned extended-family migration. The search for jobs encouraged several of three-year-old Mack Middleton Merritt's family members to vacate Louisiana, keeping much of their family intact. As a young boy, Mack, his mother, grandmother, uncle, and younger sister left Thibodaux, Louisiana, in 1926 and headed to his aunt's house in the Fourth Ward section of Houston. Upon arrival, Josephine Merritt, Mack's mother, took on work as a domestic while his grandmother tended to the children and his father remained in Louisiana.[16]

Regional industrial expansion established a distinct pattern of population decline in several Texas counties between 1870 and 1940. Blacks and whites moved from small agricultural communities in the interior of the state to the

Born in 1887, I. K. Black eventually made his way to Houston in search of employment. Courtesy Leona Mercedes Black.

growing urban industrial complexes along the Gulf Coast. From 1870 to 1880 Hardin County lost 2 percent of its black population, while Polk County's overall population decreased 20 percent, and its black population declined nearly 40 percent. Twelve percent of Liberty County's white residents vacated during the same decade. From 1880 to 1890 Hardin County lost 2 percent of its black residents. Liberty County recorded a substantial 30 percent drop in its black population. Its white population fell just 2 percent during the same period. Tyler County reported 1,467 fewer white residents in 1910 than it did in 1900. Montgomery County lost 1,397 of its population between 1900 and 1910. During the same period, its white population decreased 18 percent. The black population of Montgomery County fell close to 11 percent from 1910 to 1920, while the white population of Polk County claimed a 60 percent decrease. The black population of Polk County during this decade suffered from a 17 percent reduction.[17]

The movement of the Texas population continued after World War I and lasted well into the 1930s. From 1920 to 1930, 1,085 blacks left Montgomery County. The overall population of Hardin County from 1920 to 1930 declined from 15,983 residents to 13,936. The county's white population decreased from 12,976 to 11,465, while the number of black residents dropped from 3,007 to 2,471. San Jacinto County reported declines in both its black and white population after the war. The county's white population dropped 7 percent from 1920 to 1930, and its black population also fell 8 percent. During the next decade, the white count of the county declined 6 percent, and the number of blacks decreased 7 percent.[18]

While the neighboring interior counties established a pattern of decline, Upper Texas Gulf Coast counties and cities experienced substantial increases in their population. The number of black residents in Harris County increased from 10,985 in 1880 to 103,745 in 1940 while the total population of the county grew from 27,985 to 528,961 during the same period. Jefferson County also experienced a black population surge when its black residents increased from 1,199 to 33,821. Chambers County black inhabitants more than doubled, while in Galveston the number tripled. At the turn of the twentieth century, 520,759 Texans lived in urban communities; 119,329 were black, and nearly 20 percent of the black urban population lived in Upper Texas Gulf cities. By 1940, Texas recorded an urban population of 2,911,389, of which 420,110 were black. Around 30 percent of Texas' urban black population resided in Upper Texas Gulf Coast cities. As the largest city in Harris County, Houston's black population increased from 6,479 to 86,302. While there was no record of the number of black residents in Beaumont in 1880, by 1940 the city had over 18,000 blacks. Port Arthur did not officially record a black resident until 1910. Nonetheless, its black population, according to the U.S. Census, increased by 1940. The black population in the city of Galveston was three times greater in 1940 than it was in 1880.[19]

Labor union leadership understood the dangers that a growing pool of unorganized black workers migrating to industrial centers posed to the labor movement, and white workers were keenly aware of the threat black workers presented to their job security. The first labor unions along the Upper Texas Gulf Coast relied on an elaborate system of Jim Crow laws that generated racially biased contracts, devised specific provisions to ensure job control for white workers, prohibited blacks from learning useful crafts, and denied non-whites equal access to unions.[20]

Initially, Uriah Stephens and Terrence V. Powderly, the two principal founders of the "Noble and Holy Order of the Knights of Labor," a secret organization composed of both craft and industrial unions established in 1869, made the organization palatable to black workers. At the peak of its power in 1886, the Knights boasted a black membership of 60,000 to 90,000 and became the most viable option for black workers who desired to join a national union.[21] The discriminatory practices of local chapters of the Knights of Labor, however, hindered unity between the races. The Knights dominated organized labor in Texas until the 1890s, when they faded from the union scene. The first local assembly in Texas was organized in 1882, and a statewide assembly was chartered in 1885. By 1886 Texas Knights recorded 213 locals. Only the district assemblies in New York, Boston, and Columbus, Ohio, exceeded this total. The group's commitment to industrial reform and working-class solidarity did little, however, to remedy local prejudices against black workers. Although black workers belonged to many Texas assemblies, held positions on the Knights' state executive board, attended their social functions, and served as delegates to their conferences, Texas Knights failed to establish equal work opportunities between the races and intimidated those who walked across picket lines.[22]

When blacks retaliated against the discriminatory practices of the Knights and used strikebreaking as a tool to entice employers to hire them in place of white strikers, it often polarized the races. When white longshoremen in Galveston, for example, went out on strike in 1885, the Mallory Steamship Company, fearing a loss in business opportunities, capitalized on available black labor and replaced white strikers with black employees. The company's refusal to rehire the white strikers compelled some two thousand disgruntled Knights to stage a disruptive citywide protest that ended when the strikers capitulated to several minor demands presented to them by black longshoremen. The white-led Galveston Screwmen's Benevolent Association (SBA) Local 4583, though itself an elite union that stood apart from the rest of the laboring community, white or black, learned a valuable lesson from the 1885 incident—later reaching out to black longshoremen when it helped charter several black unions and loaned its union flag to several other groups of black long-shoremen.[23]

Although Knights, black and white, collaborated on their differences and remedied a few of them, their inability to overcome a series of failed strikes and pervasive racial division in their union locals hindered most hopes for complete racial unity. These difficulties ultimately led to the demise of the Texas Knights and cleared the way for the American Federation of Labor (AFL) to emerge as the premier labor organization by the turn of the twentieth century.[24]

Blacks in the AFL experienced far more problems than they did with the Knights. White unionists in the AFL were reluctant to grant black workers equal work opportunities or union representation. Initially, the AFL, made up primarily of craft unions in the United States and Canada, wanted bias-free unions that served the interest of working-class people. The AFL president, Samuel Gompers, attempted to create an open union policy but claimed that he lacked the power to compel locals to comply.[25] Gompers predicted that the exclusion of blacks meant trouble unless the benefits of the organization were "extended to the colored man, in order that he may no longer be so utilized to antagonize our interests."[26]

The few black delegates allowed to attend the early AFL conventions and conferences in Texas used these opportunities to speak on behalf of numerous black workers who sought fair treatment in the labor movement. P. Abner, a schoolteacher from Groveton, Texas, and a member of the Federal Labor Union (FLU), an organization that formed a coalition of black workers who could not attain membership in normal trade unions but could be organized by the AFL into "federal locals," was the first black delegate to the Texas AFL. When Abner appeared at the AFL convention in Fort Worth in 1904, he made it clear that black workers understood and were willing to exercise their leverage to obtain full representation. As Abner put it, "the Negro is a growing question in the labor movement," and the black worker, he continued, "is here and must live. He must be taken in . . . a friendly way or he must be kicked out and fought." He assured the convention, however, that "the Negro when organized, is a loyal union man" and will "protect the white union man's cause."[27]

In 1913 members of the FLU in Port Arthur appealed for fair representation when they sent several of their own delegates to the AFL convention to complain to the federation about representation and to ask "that some steps be taken to stop discrimination of colored laborers."[28] The AFL, however, dismissed the concerns of the Port Arthur workers as "a purely local affair" and warned the convention that the emerging protest and activism of the black labor community throughout the state posed "a serious menace to the white union men."[29]

If black workers' struggle for fair union treatment posed a menace to white unionists in the AFL, then they created an equally serious problem for unionism in the railroad industry. Although the railroads gave black workers an alternative to lumber and agricultural work, employment did not lead to racial inclusion in railroad unions. The railroad unions, particularly the Big Four Brotherhoods—the Brotherhood of Locomotive Engineers, the Order of Railway Conductors, the Brotherhood of Locomotive Firemen and Enginemen, and the Brotherhood of Railway Trainmen—made little effort to include blacks, regardless of their skills or occupations.[30] The Brotherhood of Locomotive Engineers in Texas formed a legislative board in 1889 to help members of its union lobby the state legislature on behalf of its membership. The board was comprised of six delegates who represented six of the state's fourteen engineer divisions. The inability of the Engineers to adequately finance these annual trips to Austin led to the proposed establishment of a Railroad Employee's Cooperative Legislative Board in 1892. By 1895 several railroad unions, with financial help from the Cooperative Board, sent delegates to the state capitol to lobby for union interests. By the turn of the century, the Brotherhood of Railway Trainmen and the Order of Railway Conductors created their own legislative boards and worked in conjunction with the delegates from other unions to dictate union policy.[31]

Despite the lobbying efforts of Texas railroad unions and the creation of legislative boards, black workers enjoyed few of the benefits that resulted from their efforts. White railroad unionists still refused to extend fair treatment to black workers and insisted on maintaining control of the job market. When the Houston & Texas Central Railroad (H&TC) began hiring black laborers in a variety of skilled and unskilled occupations as early as 1890, white unionists demanded that company officials fire the workers despite employer insistence that "the colored man . . . rendered faithful and efficient service," and to displace him "would be unjust."[32]

Attempts to displace or undermine black unionists in the Texas oil industry by the turn of the twentieth century also reflected many of the circumstances that were present in the Knights of Labor, the AFL, and the railroad unions. Before the 1930s, oil workers along the Gulf Coast relied on the AFL to bargain with employers on their behalf. The failure of the AFL to satisfactorily negotiate labor agreements for oil workers throughout the country led to the formation of the Oil Field, Gas Well and Refinery Workers in 1918. The organization was represented by twenty-one locals from California, Louisiana, Oklahoma, and Texas. When black delegates from Beaumont and Port Arthur attended the first oil conventions, their presence indicated that black oil workers, as did most black workers along the Upper Texas Gulf Coast, intended to maintain a notable place in the labor movement despite the constraints that hindered their efforts to do so.[33]

White control over the political machinery of the state was one factor that interfered with the progress of black unionism. Early support for black unionism, therefore, relied largely on the political successes of black lawmakers. The well-educated George T. Ruby built a base of power among his Texas Gulf Coast supporters and was able to win election as a delegate to the state constitutional convention in 1868 and the Texas Senate in 1869. Ruby utilized and reinforced his power base during Reconstruction when he served as a member of the executive committee to the Colored National Labor Convention, largely a political organization, in Washington, D.C., in 1873. One of Ruby's concerns was to help organize black dockworkers in Galveston, inasmuch as black labor would give him a measure of clout among the black working class and make him a force to be reckoned with in state-level politics. The clout and influence that black politicians enjoyed depended on the political appointments they made in exchange for black patronage. Republicans often rewarded blacks with municipal jobs when they needed their support. Houston Mayor Thomas H. Scanlan, for example, appointed several blacks to his city council, designated James Snowball street commissioner, and hired several blacks to important positions in the police department.[34]

Norris Wright Cuney, a protégé of Ruby, and a respected politician and labor leader, also became an advocate for black labor. Cuney grew up privileged on a cotton plantation near Hempstead, Texas. Cuney was the product of Philip W. Cuney, a respected slaveholder in Texas, and Adeline Stuart, the head house slave. Following educational training at the Wylie Street School in Pittsburgh, Pennsylvania, he settled in Galveston around 1865, worked as a stevedore, operated a liquor and tobacco business, and studied law. Opportunities presented by Reconstruction allowed Cuney to put his interest in law to work when he served as sergeant-at-arms of the Twelfth Texas Legislature in 1871. In 1870 Cuney helped to rally black Texans to elect Governor Edmund J. Davis. From 1872 to 1896 he served as a Texas delegate to the national Republican convention and for several years was recognized as an important voice for Texas Republicans.[35] Cuney rose within the ranks of the Republican Party, and his

Norris Wright Cuney used his political, economic, and social influence to help black workers in Galveston. Courtesy Rosenberg Library, Galveston, Texas.

influence and clout helped empower black longshoremen, bring attention to racial discrimination in the labor movement, and demonstrate the need for middle-class blacks to assist black unionists in their struggles. Cuney defied white opposition to black unionization and established a precedent of organized protest among black workers when he organized the Galveston Colored Screwmen's Benevolent Association in 1883.[36] Cuney encouraged black longshoremen in Galveston to organize their own unions and work ships for less pay than whites. He focused on finding employment for as many black workers as he could.

The redemption of white Democrats in 1873 brought an end to Republican rule in Texas and slowed black participation in state politics. According to V. O. Key, the political situation in most southern states reflected a small ruling class of southern whites who successfully subordinated blacks and poor whites for their benefit. White redemption in Texas politics occurred through force and elections. Unlike the early Reconstruction period, black lawmakers were unable to form a significant bloc vote. Despite declining numbers in the statehouse, black legislators struggled to maintain a political voice in a hostile and Democratic-controlled legislature.[38]

The ideals of reactionary white legislators in the Democratic Party occupied state-level politics well into the twentieth century. Some white Democratic lawmakers maintained a rigidly racist stance on race relations well into the 1920s. "I do not believe in social equality oft [sic] the races," Texas legislator Maury Maverick, Sr., wrote to the national director of the American Civil Liberties Union in the late 1920s. "I have my prejudices which are mine. However, I should not deny a negro his civil liberties, and would go down the line to see that the Constitution is obeyed."[39]

The one-party system in Texas was driven both by race and economics and worked almost flawlessly until the 1930s. Conservative and liberal Democrats differed on the role of government in economic issues, but in practice shared similar approaches to race relations. Most white lawmakers during the thirties either avoided contentious racial issues or declared their convictions for white supremacy. On the other hand, political wrangling flared during the economic crisis of the thirties between supporters of the New Deal and lawmakers who were opposed to it.[40] The ambivalence of white lawmakers toward racial equality and the economic depression of the 1930s exacerbated racial prejudice against black workers. Despite the reform efforts of the New Deal, few lawmakers fought hard for programs aimed at aiding the black working class. Franklin D. Roosevelt refused to push such programs for fear of political retaliation by white southerners in Congress. Instead, he appointed blacks as New Deal administrators and allowed his wife, Eleanor Roosevelt, to act as his "ambassador to black America" and the "conscience" of his reform agenda. Despite the work of Mrs. Roosevelt, some of the much-hailed New Deal reforms actually harmed the poorest and most vulnerable segments of the black population. Federally funded New Deal jobs usually extended discriminatory treatment, as state governments deferred to white citizens in the administration of these programs.[41]

Black Texans suffered extreme privation during the Depression. Black cotton farmers became very concerned about the decline in the market value of their product and the acreage allotment provided to them under the provisions of the New Deal's Agricultural Adjustment Act (AAA). They feared losing more than one million dollars of income unless they received much-needed government subsidies to compensate for lost revenues. Although blacks believed they would be allowed to convert "feed stuff into pork, beef, lamb, or dairy and poultry products to offset reduced cotton production," they discovered that the AAA allowed them to devote only a few acres of alternative staples to qualify for relief. Cotton farmers shared their agony with unemployed blacks who competed against whites for jobs during the Depression. When black members of the Work Projects Administration (WPA) Workers Protective Union (AFL) passed a resolution in 1936 condemning George Bell's brutal assault of Robert Lucas, an unemployed black worker, they intended to bring attention to the pervasiveness of racial animosity and the intense competition that existed between the races over available jobs. It was generally known that New Deal agencies such as the WPA in the South deferred to the wishes of white workers. This often meant that whites received job preferences and better pay than black workers. Thus, when the Houston police arrested seventeen black relief workers who staged a sit-in strike in October, 1938, at the Harris County Relief headquarters to protest the unfair hiring and wage practices of the WPA, it drew little reaction from white workers or politicians.[42]

Some of the limitations of the New Deal can be traced to the domination of Congress by southern Democrats, while other constraints can be placed at the hands of state lawmakers and their supporters. The unity and power of these lawmakers compelled Roosevelt and other liberals to rethink legislation that conflicted with southern attitudes toward race. Often the price for any reform in race relations was the assurance that segregation would not be challenged. Throughout the 1930s, seniority gave congressmen from the one-party South control over important committees, and they used their considerable power to protect Jim Crow traditions.[43]

By the end of the 1930s, hard-line Texas conservatives who supported white supremacy and controlled Texas politics denounced an antilynching bill, and called for continued racial segregation. Governor W. Lee O'Daniel assisted reactionary groups in stirring up race hatred when he offered his rhetorical support for groups like the Christian Americans, a conservative political organization that advocated segregation between the races. Vance Muse, organizer of the group, encouraged antiblack sentiments and used race-baiting tactics as a common political strategy to resist changes to the Jim Crow system.[44]

Despite passage of the National Industrial Recovery Act (NIRA) in 1933, which served as the centerpiece of Franklin Roosevelt's New Deal labor agenda until the Supreme Court declared it unconstitutional in 1935, no real solutions for the plight of black workers in Texas existed. Despite the emergence of numerous government labor agencies during the World War I era, such as the National War Labor Board, the United States Commission on Industrial Relations, the United States Railroad Administration, and the Shipbuilding Labor Adjustment Board, black workers found little support from these agencies, and the National Labor Relations Board (NLRB), a government labor agency created by the Roosevelt administration to handle labor disputes during the Depression, was no exception.[45]

Senator Robert Wagner of New York led the way to obtain more federal protection for labor unions through the NLRB. The Wagner Act outlawed many labor practices traditionally used by employers to fight unionization. It compelled employers to recognize legitimate unions, fining employers who sponsored company-controlled unions and discriminated against unionists. The act also created the NLRB, which empowered labor unions in their dealings with employers but did little to eradicate racial inequities. Although the NLRB helped black workers organize a few unions, it failed to resolve fundamental issues of hiring, wage, occupational, and seniority discrimination. Senator Wagner, the chief architect of the NLRB, expressed sympathy for black workers but later admitted that he lacked the power to pass laws to challenge racial discrimination in the union movement. In exchange for votes from southern lawmakers, Roosevelt and Wagner avoided provisions prohibiting discrimination in labor legislation.[46]

The NLRB failed to establish policies to eradicate racial discrimination in labor unions, and black unionists throughout the Upper Texas Gulf Coast suffered from its failure to do so. When disgruntled black oil workers from the Magnolia refinery in Beaumont, for instance, held secret strategy meetings in their homes and in area churches to orchestrate a campaign for an NLRB-recognized union, it reflected their willingness to use subversive tactics to address their need for fair representation and to voice their concern about the treatment of black workers at the plant. The lack of union representation left black oil workers at Magnolia vulnerable to white workers and employers. Black workers at the plant, as Paul Anger, a black oil worker himself, remembered, were at "the mercy" of their white superiors. "If he didn't like you . . . you got the dirty" jobs and no overtime pay.[47]

Advocates for racial equality in the labor movement insisted that the Wagner bill be amended to outlaw racial discrimination such as the kind suffered by black workers at Magnolia. William Frances Dunne of the National Committee of the Trade Union Unity League, for example, demanded that the government put an end to "organized lynch and murder terror against the Negro masses of the South" by whites who prevented "their organization from obtaining political rights, and equality with white workers."[48] William E. Taylor, chairman of the Legislative Committee of the National Association for the Advancement of Colored People (NAACP), pleaded with Congress to address racial discrimination in the workplace. "Organized labor is hostile to colored people," Taylor lamented. "Practically every labor organization in the country denies Negroes the right of membership and those which admit colored people restrict their employment."[49] T. Arnold Hill of the National Urban League also objected to the NLRB permitting "labor organizations to exclude Negroes from membership in their bodies." Hill provided examples of racial discrimination and proposed amendments to the Wagner Act that would eliminate biased racial practices. Hill's appeal, however, went unanswered. Moreover, members of the Senate Education and Labor Committee steered clear of any commitment to these proposals. When the NLRB responded to the NAACP–Urban League recommendation, the agency asserted that neither racial exclusion from union membership nor segregation represented an evasion of equality.[50]

Not until the emergence of the Congress of Industrial Organizations (CIO), a labor federation that resulted from the new organizing opportunities presented by the NLRB, did blacks have a legitimate alternative to organize on an equal basis in a racist labor movement. Within the labor movement, the CIO, by the end of the 1930s, had become a powerful labor federation that established new boundaries for employer-worker relations and race relations. Through its centralized organizing campaigns and its public demonstrations it transformed unionism in the United States.

The CIO capitalized on a tradition of labor militancy in the South and conducted aggressive organizing campaigns throughout the region. The federation infiltrated the southern Piedmont region, which extended from southern Virginia to northern Alabama, and pursued what Robert H. Zieger contends was the South's largest contingent of industrial workers: some 200,000 cotton textile workers. The CIO promoted, for the most part, interracial unionism. One of the more profound examples of its quest to engender cooperation between the races occurred in the Texas meatpacking industry.

Fort Worth housed the largest southern outpost of meatpacking, and its 3,000 packinghouse workers at the Armour and Swift plants reconciled some of their differences during the 1930s and 1940s and coalesced with the CIO to protect their working-class interests.[51]

The Texas State Council for Industrial Organizations (TSCIO), the Texas chapter of the CIO, had, by the late 1930s, launched a similar drive for black longshoremen, oil workers, steelworkers, laundry workers, cooks, bakers, confectionery workers, barbers, brewery workers, auto mechanics, meat cutters, retail clerks, garment workers, tailors, musicians, moving picture operators, and stagehands. The first convention of the TSCIO occurred in Beaumont, Texas, on July 31, 1937. According to Murray E. Polakoff, the CIO sought to establish coalitions with black workers throughout the state and offered them an organizing alternative. As a matter of policy, the group mirrored the national CIO's support for racial equality.[52]

Armed with its Committee to Abolish Racial Discrimination, which promoted the idea of racial equality, the CIO emboldened black workers to challenge the motives of the AFL and other independent unions. A public meeting of black laundry workers in Houston was thrown into an uproar in 1939 when a woman in the audience rose to ask local and national organizers of the AFL if "colored workers join your organization will they in case of strike or trouble be protected by the unions?" Black laundry workers rarely attended AFL organizing meetings along the Gulf Coast and, as one woman claimed, could not "afford to lose their jobs fooling with unions" that failed to protect their interests.[53]

Opponents of the CIO made condemning speeches about the federation, distributed anti-CIO propaganda, and in some instances resorted to violence and intimidation to undermine the organization's campaign efforts. In the Texas lumber mills, CIO organizers reported meeting stiff opposition from their AFL competitors. Tensions between the AFL and CIO also surfaced when members of the AFL sprayed several Houston CIO tugboat operators with gunfire near the San Jacinto Battleground outside of Houston. When the tugboat operators went out on strike against the Shell Oil Company, which had attempted to form an independent union to challenge the CIO, the company had "gunmen hidden in the woods and brush along the sides of the channel . . . firing" ammunition. Texas CIO attorney W. J. Houston also caught the brunt of the AFL's wrath when he was badly beaten in a street fight in downtown Dallas. Local police apprehended several men with ties to the Ford Motor Company in Dallas, a plant that the CIO had been attempting to organize, and charged them with assault in Houston's beating. In yet another episode of confrontation, Roy Sessions, president of the CIO-controlled Oil Field Workers Union in Houston, fled a speaking engagement after AFL hecklers, who often expressed their opinions toward the CIO through violence, ridiculed him about his association with the organization. Because local police typically sided with the AFL and often engaged in raids and violence against the CIO, members of the Texas Rangers law enforcement team were present at the rally, perhaps at the request of Sessions, who feared serious violence would erupt. Indeed, when the gathering throng got out of control, Sessions was quickly ushered onto an awaiting airplane that saw his safe passage out of Houston.[54]

The tenacity of the CIO roiled loyal members of the AFL who took seriously the CIO's racial equality campaign and their alleged connections with communists. The AFL often associated the CIO with Leninism, or as some put it, "Lewisism," referring to the communist philosophy of Russia's dictator and its alleged influence on John L. Lewis and the United Mine Workers. Lewis, the CIO's president and chief organizer, met an onslaught of criticism from opposing unions and employers along the Upper Texas Gulf Coast, who claimed that Lewis and the communists, among other things, maintained subversive control of state politics.[55]

The emergence of communists along the Upper Texas Gulf Coast surprised many lawmakers and union organizers who regarded their appearance as an indication that the region was becoming a target for a communist takeover. When communists announced the formation of a Harris County Commission on "Negro work" in November, 1938, it drew a sharp reaction from Texas Congressman Joe H. Eagle, who contended that the aggressive organizing tactics of the communists had produced a membership of some eight hundred "Reds" in Harris County alone. "These communists," Eagle contended, "have drawn plans of every pipe running to the Baytown refinery." Mayor Oscar Holcombe of Houston clashed with members of the Teamsters Union (CIO) in 1939 when he insisted that they rid their organization of communists. Holcombe made his demand after members of the union, along with local leaders of the CIO, showed up to protest an anticommunist speech given by City Attorney Sewall Myer, who charged that "imported communist agitators and communist lawyers" were responsible for the tense labor climate along the Upper Texas Gulf Coast.[56]

Black communists attracted much attention when they flayed government officials, unions, and employers for their treatment of black workers. The presence of several "strong and robust" white bodyguards provided to protect internationally known black communist leader James W. Ford while he addressed a crowd of onlookers at a Houston church in October, 1940, demonstrated that the communist efforts to organize black workers was a serious endeavor and that blacks within the organization played a vital role in the process of fostering fair and equal treatment. Ford, a native of Alabama and a U.S. vice presidential candidate for the Communist Party during the 1930s, criticized labor unions, black political organizations, and the federal government for failing to reconcile the disparities that existed between the races within the labor movement. Following his closing remarks, Ford, having received word that an angry mob was beginning to gather outside the church, was abruptly escorted by the bodyguards to another location.[57]

Communist organizations and the CIO represented two of the growing number of alternatives for black unionists in their struggle for equal treatment. Black unionists also benefited from the resources and influence of the black middle class. The black bourgeoisie, following the Civil War, emerged in response to increased discrimination, a growing sense of race consciousness, continued black migration to urban industrial complexes, and an expanding black consumer class. The black middle class along the Upper Texas Gulf Coast became an influential voice of protest. Black editors, politicians, and other community leaders, for example, embraced the ideals of capitalism, a hard-working black laboring class, and a cohesive black community, and often presented themselves as an ally of and, in some instances, the leaders and spokespersons of black workers. Speaking and acting on behalf of the black working class, their views and actions did not always mesh with or satisfy those they claimed to represent. Black elites generally shared common financial interests but had differing views of black labor. Moreover, the limited authority they exercised over labor unions reinforced the importance of maintaining a strong and active relationship with organized labor. Consequently, black elites who advocated a strong and united black labor community faced two distinct obstacles. On the one hand, they ran the risk of alienating themselves from more conservative blacks. On the other hand, they struggled to build a lasting relationship with black unionists.

The wide range of responses that emerged among black elites indicated that not all black middle-class Texans shared the same opinions about opposition to racial inequities. But while their philosophies differed, their ultimate goal remained the same. They maintained a vision of a well-organized and unified black laboring class that could, when necessary, operate independently of white labor. Although the black middle class harbored suspicions toward most white unions, they realized the importance of the labor movement to working blacks. Typically, black elites encouraged black workers to rethink their union loyalties and place race advancement before class concerns.

The crux of black middle-class influence on black unionism, however, occurred during the twentieth century and more particularly after the First World War, when black elites built upon a tradition of protest established by their predecessors such as Norris Wright Cuney, George T. Ruby, Benjamin Franklin Williams, Matthew Gaines, Richard Allen, and Robert Lloyd Smith and looked inward to galvanize the black working class. They struggled to blend facets of ideological, institutional, and political perspectives into a unified core of resistance against race and class domination. The World War I era reflected a vast transformation for the black working class and for black unionism. Black working-class activism and labor protest seized upon the wartime rhetoric of democracy and a new orientation for racial equality. Instead of relying on organized labor to act on their behalf, black unionists began to use organizations such as the NAACP, the National Urban League, and the Universal Negro Improvement Association (UNIA), to convert wartime rhetoric into a fight to advance the cause of black unionism.[58]

Although black political and social organizations provided much of the leadership for black unionists, black workers, to a large degree, still depended on influential leaders in the community to spearhead protest. One of the more notable persons to address the concerns of black workers during the immediate post–World War I years was Clifton F. (C. F.) Richardson, Sr. Born in Marshall, Texas, Richardson attended Bishop College and graduated with a journalism degree. When Richardson formed the National Negro Business League, he provided a base for economic organization for the black community and created an alternative to the workplace for black workers who suffered from discrimination. Richardson's association with the NAACP, his ownership of weekly newspapers, and his community activism was a model of leadership for the black working class. He put his education and business expertise to work when he cofounded the *Houston Informer* newspaper in 1919, and later owned the *Houston Defender*. Although Richardson rarely mentioned Marcus Garvey's race pride campaigns of the early 1920s and despite the numerous chapters the UNIA had throughout the South, the influence of Garvey's movement was evident in his economic philosophy. Richardson was among the black leadership that, as the *Informer* reported,

C. F. Richardson, Sr. Courtesy Clarena Richardson.

represented "the growing consciousness of colored Americans" as he commanded "the ear of the enemies of the race." When Richardson addressed the black citizens of Port Arthur at the Sixth Street Baptist Church in June of 1919, he spoke of the "rapid strides" black longshoremen and refinery workers had made in their struggles to confront racial constraints. By December, 1922, Richardson and the *Informer* were printing weekly advertisements for the Colored Workingmen & Women's Association of Texas, an organization that met twice a month to promote black working-class progress. The association provided sick pay for its members and unemployment benefits for working families.[59]

During the 1930s, in contrast to the late nineteenth century and the first two decades of the twentieth century, black unionists rejected the strategies of the black middle class. Black workers began to look toward the organizing opportunities presented by the NLRB and the emergence of new labor federations than they did to black elites. By the thirties black unionists generally viewed the organizing efforts of the black middle class as self-serving formulas for personal and political gain. Moreover, by the 1930s the Upper Texas Gulf Coast comprised a large concentration of Texas' black workforce, and, unlike the late 1800s, when Cuney organized black longshoremen, black labor boasted significant numerical clout and consequently relied more on the efforts of the rank-and-file workforce to combat discrimination.[60]

Although black workers grew less dependent on the black bourgeoisie during the 1930s and 1940s, black elites remained a significant voice of protest for black labor. As president of the Texas Negro Business Association and an advocate of Booker T. Washington and the Tuskegee philosophy of self help, C. W. Rice, the self-appointed voice of Upper Texas Gulf Coast black labor, for instance, stirred controversy within the black community as he attempted to galvanize black workers and form his own independent union movement among the black working class. Rice expressed suspicion toward challenges to the racial and class status quo. His life experiences reflected a sharp contrast to those of the black working class he purportedly sought to protect.[61]

Born in 1897 in Haywood County, Tennessee, to Mary and Ezekial Rice, C. W. Rice began his formal education in the rural schools of Haywood County in 1905. In 1909 he entered the city school of Jackson, Tennessee, for one year. Following his primary education, Rice enrolled in the Lane College high school department while working as a domestic servant in the homes of some of the more prominent whites in the area. By 1914 Rice was in Texas lecturing on the subject of "why the black man should rally around the flag during World War I." But after touring several states in the deep South, Rice's opinion changed, and he renounced his position on black patriotism and began a personal quest to eradicate racism and discrimination.[62]

Rice started several businesses in Houston and used his financial and social clout to draw attention to the plight of the region's black workforce. He criticized Gulf Coast unions that denied black workers full benefits and encouraged black workers to cooperate with employers, abandon their union loyalties, and avoid "militant" blacks and any union that discriminated. Rice particu-

C. W. Rice. Courtesy Houston Metropolitan Research Center, Houston Public Library.

larly encouraged blacks to "organize in a solid bloc" and use racial solidarity as their most effective weapon against unfair treatment. Although Rice failed to organize black labor to his satisfaction, he relentlessly pursued his goal of a racially unified black labor community. To a certain extent, Rice reformulated an older view that held that blacks should ally with white capital and reject overtures from white labor. If white unions refused to recognize blacks as full members, then blacks were justified to work against the goals and objectives of the labor movement.[63]

Some black unionists, however, resisted Rice's efforts to organize black labor and were reluctant to join his movement. They especially resented his ownership of an employment referral service that many of them used to secure jobs. Those who relied on the agency often complained of being overcharged for the service, decried Rice's blacklisting of workers who spoke out against his hiring practices, and criticized the owner's business ties with white employers. In sum, these workers advocated labor unions and viewed Rice as an outside agitator and "renegade" with questionable motives. Rice stood in harm's way when he meddled in union affairs and pushed his labor agenda too far. The divisiveness between Rice and his critics often involved "pistols, knives, and mudslinging."[64]

Despite his shady reputation among some blacks, others lauded the editor for his efforts. McKinley Taylor, a Houston railway worker, commended and defended Rice's labor policy. He appealed to black workers to recognize the seriousness of Rice's efforts to "form a united front to promote . . . national progress" for black workers.[65] Taylor pleaded for black unionists to organize en masse and uniformly address racial discrimination. "By all evidence," Taylor charged, Rice was "struggling for our right position" in the labor movement. Taylor encouraged black workers to put aside their differences with certain members of the black middle class and end the needless "mudslinging and meaningless oratory" that had become so pervasive in the black labor community during the 1930s and 1940s.[66]

Black religious leaders played a vital role in the affairs of black unionists and they, like other influential leaders, worked to organize the black working class into a racially cohesive group. During the mid-1930s the Reverend Bertron M. Jackson of Houston founded the National Association of Industrial Labor for Colored People (NAIL). Jackson's organization intended to provide to the black working community an alternative to the labor movement. While Jackson's organization failed to garner much support, the vision of an intricate industrial and commercial trade network including the establishment of shoe and garment factories, saw mills for the construction of new homes, and the creation of lending institutions provided the potential for these newly formed businesses to employ black workers exclusively. Jackson's religious-based organization undoubtedly relied on "the divine power of God" but also depended on the indivisible allegiance of "sensible [sic] fathers and mothers, the Negro Press, and organized negro labor unions."[67]

The black middle class was vast and it reached into numerous business endeavors. Black business people typically found the time to tend to their respective enterprises but also devoted a fair share of their schedules assisting the working class. Richard R. (R. R.) Grovey, a popular local barber and civic leader from Houston, often complained about the lack of money infused into the black community and set out to redress it at the source. Helping black workers organize for better working conditions became one of Grovey's primary objectives. Following his success in organizing black barbers in the area, Grovey promised to do everything possible to unite black workers if they would simply cling to their labor union loyalties and avoid defecting to independent or company unions. Grovey, who occasionally wrote scathing editorials in the *Houston Informer* about black labor leaders who directed the black working class away from labor unions and federations toward independent and company unions, often invited "advocates of several schools of thought," to his labor forums and provided them an opportunity to "present and defend their views."[68]

Carter Wesley, a flamboyant editor and black businessman who permitted Grovey to air his position in his *Houston Informer,* was one of the most effective voices among the black middle class to support organized labor during the 1930s and 1940s. Born the third of three sons in 1892 in Houston to Mabel Wesley, a school teacher, and Harry Wesley, a laborer at the Southern Pacific Railroad, Wesley turned his *Houston Informer* newspaper into one of the more powerful tools for racial protest along the Upper Texas Gulf Coast. Personal experiences lay at the root of Wesley's commitment to racial justice. After graduating from Houston's public schools, Wesley attended the predominately black Fisk University and later served in World War I as one of the first black officers in a segregated U.S. military. Following a short legal practice in Oklahoma, Wesley returned to Houston in 1927 and invested his time and earnings to fight racism along the Upper Texas Gulf Coast. After a bitter falling-out with C. F. Richardson, Sr., his partner and cofounder of the *Houston Informer,* Wesley gained control of the newspaper and used it as a platform to expand the voices of opposition to the racist practices of labor unions. He preferred to fight the battle for racial equality throughout the Gulf Coast through boycotts, public criticism, and fund-raising. Although Wesley could boast of no prior experiences with the labor movement, he recognized that his resources offered black labor a base to help advance equality within the labor union movement. Wesley used his own judgment and experience to formulate and dictate his protest strategies. Thus, when Wesley fought for separate but equal

Carter Wesley. Courtesy Houston Metropolitan Research Center,
Houston Public Library.

labor unions for the races, he not only spoke to the issue of workplace equality but also to the numerical strength of black unionists, and, on more than one occasion, he made his opposition to integrated unions known.[69]

Wesley recognized a growing philosophical and sentimental shift away from company unions and toward labor unions that permeated the nation during the 1930s and early 1940s. He used the racial constraints of most white-led unions as a springboard to prod black workers to hold on to the segregated system. Wesley saw dual unionism as the most viable way to combat racial discrimination. He urged black workers to maintain the dual-union system, which, in the past, had helped to empower the black rank and file throughout the Gulf Coast.[70]

Wesley's push to preserve the dual-union system was met with resistance from many black workers who refused to place race loyalties ahead of union allegiance. Black workers at Hughes Tool, for example, remained reluctant to follow Wesley and believed that the only way to circumvent racial discrimination and to have adequate union representation was to organize on an integrated basis with labor organizations such as the CIO. The CIO, by virtue of its egalitarian policy promising to honor racial equality within the federation, had rejected the dual-union system and had worked to integrate its membership. The rise of organizations such as the CIO and the changing nature of the labor movement brought on by the Great Depression of the 1930s allowed black workers to steer clear of black elites such as Wesley and look more toward emerging labor federations as a partial remedy to the more racist labor organizations that had plagued their progress before the thirties.

Although Wesley welcomed the CIO's egalitarian claims to improve working conditions for blacks and often bragged about the support he and his newspaper received from most major labor organizations, he cared more about maintaining racially separate unions than facilitating biracial ones. Wesley's shrewd attempts to persuade black workers to cling to separate unions often turned out to be a personal campaign for worker loyalties. When Wesley spoke to black members of the Port Arthur chapter of the CIO at the Sixth Street Baptist Church in March, 1943, and suggested that the "future of the union depended upon their own ability to furnish leadership and to visualize the opportunities for the future," he undoubtedly was referring to his abilities to guide black workers through difficult days of struggle.[71]

Wesley discovered creative ways to infiltrate the ranks of the CIO even though the federation jeopardized his ambitions and created controversy when it aggressively recruited black members and placed them in integrated unions. On more than one occasion, near-riots erupted between advocates of the CIO and Carter Wesley's traveling entourage. In one instance, tempers grew short when Wesley and George O. Duncan, a black unionist who supported the CIO's integration policy, exchanged "considerable abusive language" at a labor forum in Houston in March, 1940. Each man charged that the other had gotten personal in their criticism of the other's labor position. "While no licks were passed," a frightened Wesley narrowly escaped the angry mob's wrath when he slipped away from the meeting.[72]

Wesley often blamed more conservative middle-class blacks such as Rice for much of the animosity that existed between black unionists and the black middle class. Rice's antiunion position made black workers distrustful of black elites and made organizing difficult for Wesley. Even though Wesley had advocated the separation of the races, he accused Rice of stirring up racial animosity with frivolous claims of eminent race riots in hopes that he could improve his less-than-admirable image among most black workers.[73] Wesley launched a barrage of insults toward Rice and accused the editor of "being the spokesman of employers and the bigger white people in the community" rather than a genuine voice for black labor. Public outcries against Rice's independent movement convinced Wesley that the *Negro Labor News* editor "did not now, and has not for years represented the thought of Negroes in the community." Wesley recognized black labor's strong commitment to organized labor, and he promoted the idea of utilizing distinct black union locals as a strategy to protest the discriminatory practices of white labor. Segregated unions strengthened the leverage of black workers. Although Wesley strongly urged black workers to maintain their association with organized labor, his segregationist ideas met with resistance from blacks who refused to accept racial separation as a retaliatory tool against white labor.[74]

The feuding between Wesley and Rice that began in the 1930s and extended well into the 1940s reflected the division among the black middle class. While Rice desired to break from the mainstream labor movement and Wesley advocated dual unions, organizations such as the NAACP embarked upon new courses of action that embraced the racial integration of labor unions. The NAACP emerged as an antisegregation body and a link between the black working and middle classes. The NAACP worked closely with prominent community figures, black labor leaders, and the black proletariat to curtail workplace inequalities. Founded in 1909 in New York City, the NAACP expanded its influence during the war years. The number of branches grew from less than a hundred before World War I to more than four hundred in cities and towns by 1921.[75]

NAACP national membership soared from around 10,000 in 1917 to nearly 80,000 in 1919. In 1918 four local branches of the NAACP in Texas joined the El Paso chapter, which was established in 1915 to expand the influence of the organization throughout the state. The NAACP recruited from within

the middle- and working-class ranks. The Texas chapters also pursued jani
tors, laborers, letter carriers, housekeepers, laundresses, and seamstresses, and,
as Steven Reich argues, the black working class likely constituted the core of
their membership. The establishment of the Beaumont branch of the NAACP
was initiated by Dr. C. B. Charlton in 1917. After receiving correspondence
from several Beaumont residents and following an organizing tour throughout Texas by Mary B. Talbert, president of the National Association of Colored Women's Clubs, the NAACP approved a charter for the Beaumont
chapter in 1918. At Galveston, black unionists from ILA union Local 807
organized a NAACP branch of their own. When the Houston NAACP staged
a public "ILA Day" in October, 1937, at the Bethel Baptist Church to honor
the community work of black ILA unions, it reflected not only the NAACP
support for longshoremen, but also black organizational support for black
unionists.[76]

The Houston chapter of the NAACP emerged as a crucial branch for black
workers along the Upper Texas Gulf Coast. Following the sudden death of
C. F. Richardson Sr., in 1939, the outspoken LuLu Belle White assumed the
role of interim president. White had become an activist with the organization
in the struggle to eradicate the white Democratic primaries in Texas. White's
concern for racial equality stemmed from her early days in Elmo, Texas, a
town known for racial tension and a hotbed for Ku Klux Klan activity. The
tenth of twelve children, White was born to Easter Madison, a domestic worker,
and Henry Madison, a landowner in Elmo. Following her primary education, White attended Butler College for one year before transferring to Prairie
View College, where she received a bachelor's degree in English in 1928. Shortly
after graduation she moved to Houston, where she met and married Julius
White, a prominent businessman and long-time member of the NAACP. Aside
from LuLu B. White's publicized feuds with Carter Wesley over separate-but-
equal opportunities between the races and activism regarding the integration
of the University of Texas, she helped propel the NAACP to a major civil
rights organization in Houston, one that coalesced with black workers in the
region. In 1943 she became its executive secretary and played a critical role in
the struggle against Jim Crow during the 1940s. She worked as a liaison between black unionists and the Fair Employment Practice Commission (FEPC)
during World War II. Serving as a gadfly for black unionists during political
campaigns, she often posed the following questions to candidates: "Do you
support organized labor in the state? Do you support the FEPC?"[77]

If black workers relied on black elites throughout the early decades of the

LuLu B. White. Courtesy Prairie View A&M University.

twentieth century, by the 1930s they had minimized their association with them. Black unionism did not depend solely on the approval of the black middle class. Many unions grew and black union activism expanded in spite of the intercession of black elites. Although the relationship between the black working class and the black middle class was floundering by the end of the

1930s, black unionists capitalized on the protest efforts of the middle class as the United States entered World War II.

During the war, black unionists and black leaders expanded their protests against unfair treatment and fully exercised the options available to them. The black press played a particularly important role in the struggle for equality during the war. The "Double V" campaign of black Americans against discrimination on the homefront and against the Axis powers overseas appealed to most black unionists. Typically, the black community voiced support for America's involvement in the global conflict and insisted that the federal government had an obligation to redress racial discrimination in defense industries.[78]

Although black labor leaders such as C. W. Rice and Carter Wesley failed to resolve their philosophical differences over labor issues, the two newspaper editors put aside their bickering when it came to the war effort. Each helped launch an all-out campaign for democracy overseas and in the region's workplaces during World War II. The animosity between the two men subsided as each persuaded their constituency to support the U.S. war effort against the Axis powers while simultaneously working to improve conditions in the workplace for blacks. Each hoped to achieve two outcomes: To bolster black patriotism and obtain racial equality in defense industries. Rice took the lead in moving black workers toward the goal of equality. He published several editorials addressing black labor's "two front war." Rice cautioned politicians not to "do Hitler's work for him by stirring up race hate and disunity."[79] Wesley responded to Rice's call for unity and organized "a monster patriotic rally," at Emancipation Park in the predominantly black section of Houston's Third Ward community. Wesley encouraged several prominent black community leaders to affirm their support for the war and attend the rally. This act of mass unity among blacks presented an interesting phenomenon. Blacks did not hesitate to show their patriotism. The black labor community recognized early on that patriotism was one way to obtain concessions from a typically ambivalent government.[80]

The past failures of numerous government labor agencies to adequately remedy labor race problems made patriotism and the creation of the FEPC a welcomed alternative to combat workplace inequities during the early part of the 1940s. Despite resistance from employers and white workers, who rejected its authority and worked together to undermine its work, the FEPC played into the strategies of black unionists and many of their community leaders. The agency began preliminary investigations of Gulf Coast industries in 1942.

It became a powerful symbol of progress for black workers who had long struggled to gain commitments from the federal government to forcefully grapple with racial discrimination in American industries.[81]

In the overall context, the world of the black unionists along the Upper Texas Gulf Coast consisted of a culture of discrimination in a rapidly changing industrial, political, and social environment that the FEPC or any one strategy could not overcome. The responses to these conditions were wide-ranging. Black unionists sought to eradicate injustices while working to build alliances within the union movement. They recast the class-race nexus and despite daunting odds struggled to build and sustain full and equal participation. To a large extent, they relied on their rank and file with occasional help from middle-class blacks, other outsiders, and ultimately the federal government. What follows is an appraisal of the struggles of black unionists in five of the most vital industries along the Upper Texas Gulf Coast from the latter part of the nineteenth century through the first half of the twentieth.

CHAPTER 2

"FIFTY-FIFTY"

Black Longshoremen and the Racial Paradox

THE INITIAL RISE of black unionism along the Upper Texas Gulf Coast occurred among longshoremen and was closely tied to the production and distribution of cotton, timber, and other staples that made the region a focal point of the southern economy following the Civil War. Commerce along the waterfronts throughout the American South required a pool of workers to perform the difficult and sometimes dangerous task of loading and unloading much of the same type of cargo. From Baltimore to Pensacola to Mobile to New Orleans and Galveston, longshore work characterized waterfront labor and unionism. The influence of black longshoremen contradicted conventional beliefs that blacks were at the mercy of white workers and employers. Nothing could be further from the truth. As historians Sterling Spero and Abram Harris contended, black longshoremen probably played a more important role than they did in any other labor union. Despite the clout of black workers, waterfront work reflected racial fragmentation, and many ports became the sites of racial conflict. The story of black longshoremen along the Upper Texas Gulf Coast suggests that blacks realized that their economic advancement rested upon their ability to exercise their numerical clout against employers and biased white unionists.[1]

The docks and wharves along the Gulf Coast came alive after the bloody Civil War as job opportunities attracted numerous workers into the area. In many Gulf Coast ports black workers comprised a majority of the labor force. The emergence of black unionism in the longshore industry along the Upper Texas Gulf Coast followed a wider pattern that can be traced to attempts by southern white dockworkers to organize their own unions, improve their wages, and curtail the unfair labor practices of shippers. The New Orleans Screwmen's Benevolent Association, established in 1850, for example, was one of the oldest waterfront unions in the South and one of the first to organize dockworkers in the region. Its all-white membership consisted primarily of an Irish and German immigrant workforce. New Orleans dockworkers established a sense of unity when they staged successful strikes against employers and negotiated admirable wages.[2]

The tight packing of cargo with power cotton compresses and screwjacks had become an efficient way for dockworkers to handle cargo. These specialized tools allowed longshoremen to pack and stow bulky bales of cargo more efficiently in the holds of ships, which helped increase the profit potential for shippers. The packing method also afforded screwmen a substantial bargaining position against employers, gave them a monopoly over the screwjacking trade, and gave them a significant measure of control over the waterfront workforce. Although black workers had appeared on the New Orleans docks before the Civil War, a vast influx of black laborers seeking employment showed up to work after the war.[3]

Unlike Texas Gulf Coast longshoremen, New Orleans dockworkers, Eric Arnesen argues, established an early pattern of biracial cooperation. At least from 1880 to the early 1920s, New Orleans stood out as an example of biracial unionism that witnessed an equal division of work between the races, equitable wages, and joint contract negotiating teams. Moreover, the Cotton Men's Executive Council bound together most dockworkers into one federation that aspired to worker solidarity. Despite periodic setbacks to interracial alliance—as during the Depression of the 1890s when white longshoremen and screwmen, anxious to maintain a measure of leverage over the industry, refused to work with any blacks or for any employer who hired them—biracial unionism flourished.[4]

Interracial alliances and biracial unionism were less apparent during the early unionizing years along the Upper Texas Gulf Coast. As industrial growth in the region encouraged migration from rural Texas and from many parts of Louisiana, black and white workers found their way to Texas docks, where they devised strategies to protect their interests in an expanding labor market. The long-standing divisive relationship between black and white dockworkers in Texas originated in the immediate postbellum period with the evolution of the Galveston Screwmen's Benevolent Association (SBA). In 1866 twenty-three white screwmen drafted a constitution that resembled the bylaws of the early New Orleans screwmen constitutions. The thirty-four "original members" (those who signed up before the second meeting) who formed the SBA established qualifications for membership, set initiation fees, determined monthly dues, and included no black workers in their organization.[5]

Black longshoremen's tolerance of the racist attitudes and exclusionary practices of white dockworkers was short-lived. Unable to obtain access to

Black longshoremen unloading cargo at Galveston, ca. 1900.
Courtesy Rosenberg Library, Galveston, Texas.

the Galveston screwmen's union, black longshoremen fostered a strategy that would serve as a basis for expanded protest and further resistance against biased white unions. As strikebreakers, they accepted jobs from employers, and by October, 1879, steamers around the Galveston port, cognizant of potential losses in business brought on by labor strife, undermined white strikers and began sending "colored gangs on board to do the work" typically reserved for whites.[6]

Strikebreaking became an effective way for black dockworkers to resist unfair treatment by white unionists. When Norris Wright Cuney, a respected black labor leader and politician from Galveston, organized the Colored Screwmen's Benevolent Association (CSBA) in 1883, he ignored white strikers and encouraged blacks to accept jobs offered to them by employers and, if necessary, to organize their own unions and work ships for less pay than whites. Cuney wanted to find as much employment for as many black dockworkers as he could and break white longshoremen's virtual monopoly on the Galveston

Employers often relied on black workers during labor strife with white dockworkers; photo ca. 1920. Courtesy Rosenberg Library, Galveston, Texas.

docks. When Cuney recruited workers from New Orleans to augment the black longshoremen already available along the Upper Texas Gulf Coast, he significantly increased the number of black workers available to employers, and placed white workers at a serious disadvantage during labor strife.[7]

The labor strife between black and white dockworkers in Galveston often tempted employers to use strikebreaking as a tool to exercise their authority over their workforce and reject undesirable worker demands. When the Texas Trades Assembly, a statewide labor organization that many white longshoremen unions belonged to, interceded on behalf of the white strikers in Galveston, it demonstrated that assertive black dockworkers, who refused to accept mistreatment, had seized the attention of white unionists. Aware of employer schemes to undermine their strikes by hiring unorganized black workers, white delegates from the Texas Trades Assembly reevaluated their attitudes about black unionism. It was not long before they lifted certain racial restrictions. By 1884 black dockworkers began to establish segregated union locals, gain a share of contracted work, represent themselves at Assembly meetings, and apply for representation with the Trades Assembly. Despite these concessions, the Mallory Steamship Company continued to use unorganized black dockworkers who typically worked for less pay than white and black unionists.[8]

Pay inequities often surfaced as a point of contention for black dockworkers who gained added confidence when the Trade Assembly modified its racial labor policy. Although white delegates from the Texas Trades Assembly capitulated to some of the equal pay demands made by the CSBA, profit-minded employers often disregarded these bilateral agreements and muddled attempts by workers to reconcile wage disparities. When the Mallory Company imposed a $.10 pay reduction on its white workforce during the economic depression of the 1890s, it simultaneously cut the hourly rate for black workers by $.20.[9] The company's threat to replace protesters with nonunion workers sent black unionists into a frenzy. When the Mallory steamship *Colorado* sailed into the Galveston port in late August, 1898, "it was met by several hundred Negro longshoremen carrying stones," and wooden billets. They formed a "complete cordon guarding every avenue of approach." Their demand was simple—job security and fair wages.[10]

The violent uprising was instigated by George and Harvey Patrick, two brothers who had organized Galveston's Federal Labor Union (FLU) 7174, one of the many black labor organizations that formed a larger national coalition of black unions unable to attain membership with most white-led federations. "We don't want scabs to do the work at union wages, but we want union men and union wages," George Patrick declared. "Living requires something to subsist on," Harvey Patrick insisted in an emotional speech to the crowd of black longshoremen. "The Mallory line steamer is here offering reduced wages upon which we cannot live" and allows "scab labor" to "come here for three or four months to gobble our work."[11]

Although white unionists occasionally agreed to equal pay between the races, they rarely insisted that employers honor the wage demands of black unionists. They refused to help them in their struggles with employers and remained idle while Galveston city officials, who reacted with disdain to the labor protest, attempted to muscle the Patricks and their followers into submission. Galveston police tightened restrictions on Union 7174 and refused them access to the city's docks. Mayor Ashley Wilson Fly added further insult when he warned the throng of their "unlawful assembly" and of his intention to offer protection to "all who wanted to go to work at the . . . wages" offered by the Mallory Company. Fly, who was born during the heyday of slavery in

Mayor Ashley Wilson Fly sided with employers during labor strife; photo ca. 1894.
Courtesy Rosenberg Library, Galveston, Texas.

Yalobusha County, Mississippi, had lived in Galveston County a little over twenty years where he taught anatomy and surgery at Texas Medical College and Hospital. He practiced medicine at Galveston City Hospital before becoming mayor in 1893. Fly detested corruption and an unruly working class. His proposition to offer jobs to nonunion workers incited the Patricks and their supporters, who rushed Fly and his police contingency. Unable to establish control, the Mayor and his law enforcement contingency drew their weapons and began firing. The fatalities resulting from the barrage of gunfire, however, made the demonstrators more "sullen and defiant," and over the next several weeks the Patricks and their followers held union strategy meetings while local police vigilantly patrolled the docks.[12]

Black dockworkers from Union 7174 responded decisively to the growing constraints of city officials and to the Mallory Company's continued use of nonunion blacks. When members of 7174 discovered some hiding in nearby sheds and unloading ships one month after the first violent incident, another full-scale riot between police and angry workers erupted. Bricks and pistols filled the air as local police charged "the mob," while frightened scab workers sought refuge in the Gulf of Mexico.[13] When the body of a white screwman was discovered in the aftermath of the riot, it encouraged both black and white unionists to curtail the violence, expand their organizing efforts to eradicate labor strife, and pay closer attention to jurisdictional disputes involving nonunion workers "earning their living doing longshore work." The obvious remedy was to resolve the racial strife that existed among black and white unionists. Interracial cooperation and increased union organizing strengthened the ranks and naturally pressured employers to acquiesce to union demands. During the 1890s several labor organizations struggled to obtain this end. The Texas Labor Council adopted a constitution and sent representatives to state labor conventions for the initial purpose of improving race relations between black and white dockworkers.[14]

Attempts to eradicate racial discord had minimal success in most parts of the Upper Texas Gulf Coast. Racial strife in the Sabine district reflected many of the trends found in Galveston. Several of the unions in this area began as screwmen associations, and, as the Texas economy expanded, they evolved into longshoremen unions. Most of the members in the first unions came from New Orleans and later from Galveston. Despite attempts to resolve racial division, black and white workers, each eager to maintain control of the workplace, allowed employers to further divide the ranks along racial lines. The first longshore organizations in the Sabine area appeared in 1897. By 1898 longshore Local 51, organized by a group of black dockworkers, assumed much of the work. Despite the racial hostilities that existed in the region, black long-shoremen from Local 51 welcomed whites into their ranks and elected them to some of the most important offices in their local.[15]

White unionists, however, jumped at any opportunity they could to break away from the black-controlled union. Consequently, attempts at racial co-operation in Local 51 were short-lived. Racial strife led to a deterioration of the union and cleared the way for new union locals. When workers from Local 51 struck for pay increases, the black members, who were in the major-ity, suggested that white members round up additional groups of white long-shoremen to strike along with them. Despite the customary racial cooperation in Local 51, white workers from 51 refused to back black strikers, quit the union, and started a new one of their own in Port Arthur. The failure of white longshoremen to back the strike and the fear of being replaced by scabs forced blacks to settle for $.35 per hour instead of the $.40 an hour they had origi-nally demanded.[16] By 1903 Local 51 had disappeared and Local 440, which consisted of mostly black workers, worked most of the docks in the Sabine district. White longshoremen, on the other hand, controlled most of the work in Port Arthur, which had become an important port for Gulf Coast com-merce from 1903 until 1913.[17]

The early decades of the twentieth century witnessed an increase in the number of dockworkers and the birth and growth of many longshoremen unions throughout the country and along the Upper Texas Gulf Coast (see table 1). Much of the progress was due to the formation of the International Longshoremens Association (ILA). Organized in the Great Lakes region be-fore 1900, the ILA boasted a membership of fifty thousand workers by the turn of the century. Founded by Dan Keefe, an Irish tugboat captain, the ILA struggled to preserve the integrity of marine divers, steam pump operators, mill men, freight handlers, coal, grain, oil handlers, as well as general longshore work. Several groups of waterfront workers applied for charters with the ILA. In 1900 a group of Galveston longshoremen obtained one of the first ILA charters in the region, and in 1909 the Galveston Dock and Marine Council, consisting of several ILA locals, was formed. Officially chartered in 1910, the Galveston Dock and Marine Council struggled to protect waterfront workers from the "unfair and unjust" hiring tactics of employers, and worked to eradi-cate racial strife between black and white longshoremen.[18]

As efforts to organize longshoremen intensified, employer antagonism to-ward unionization increased. Employers particularly fought the growing power

Table 1. Total Longshoremen, Number and Proportion
of Blacks for the United States, and for Selected States, 1910–1920

	1910			1920		
	Total	*Blacks*	*% Black*	*Total*	*Blacks*	*% Black*
Total US	51,841	15,000	28.9	85,928	27,206	31.7
Total 8 States	16,390	12,074	73.6	22,394	7,519	78.2
Alabama	888	715	80.5	1,117	1,010	90.5
Florida	1,709	1,530	89.5	1,470	1,312	89.2
Georgia	1,762	1,683	95.5	1,799	16,809	2.8
Louisiana	2,654	1,587	59.9	4,320	2,862	65.2
Maryland	2,975	1,933	64.9	4,394	3,179	72.3
So. Carol.	560	513	91.6	762	733	96.2
*Texas	2,386	843	35.2	3,601	2,052	54.2

Source: U.S. Department of Commerce, Bureau of the Census, *Census of Occupations,
1910–1940* (Washington, D.C.: Government Printing Office, 1940).

of the ILA locals and protected their own financial ambitions with a campaign that fueled racial division between waterfront workers. Employers often "took advantage of the division" and placed "gangs on ships so that" black and white workers "would compete with each other." Employers also resorted to lockouts to combat unionization. In June, 1914, for instance, the J. H. W. Steele Company in Texas City locked out members of Local 636 and took in nonunion workers provided to them by the Mallory Line. In the same year, white Local 538 was locked out by the same company in Port Arthur. Although whites had gained control of most of the work in Port Arthur, employers still sought greater profits when they offered work opportunities to those who would replace white strikers and work at lower wages. Local 538 lost much of its bargaining leverage against their employer when zealous black unionists from Local 440 in nearby Beaumont ignored warnings from Local 538 to stay away from nonunion labor, took in black workers off the streets, and set out to meet the labor demands of the Steele Company.[19]

Recurring problems over racial cooperation and equitable division of work between the races attracted the attention of the ILA. As early as October, 1913, T. V. O'Connor, president of the ILA, had come to Port Arthur "to investigate complaints against the introduction of colored labor on the docks." Because the behavior of longshoremen in the Sabine district and Port Arthur threatened stability for the ILA, Locals 538 and 440 were urged to take part in the ILA's "fifty-fifty" work plan that many longshoremen unions in other parts of the Gulf Coast had already adopted. The preponderance of black long-shoremen in the Gulf Ports and the willingness of employers to use them at will led to a call for an equal division of work between the races. The ILA had debated the fifty-fifty plan as early as the turn of the twentieth century. Both blacks and whites on the Gulf Coast criticized the plan. Blacks felt that their numerical representation in the industry entitled them to more work. Divid-ing the work equally deprived many black longshoremen of employment. White longshoremen, on the other hand, felt that too little work came their way. They argued that the overwhelming number of black workers took work away from whites; they sought assurances from employers and the ILA that work would be distributed equally. Port Arthur's white workers refused to play a subordinate role to blacks in the longshore industry and stubbornly refused to adopt the proposal until the ILA issued an ultimatum to report for work under the plan or risk a Local 440 work monopoly.[20]

The fear of a black worker monopoly over waterfront work around the Houston Ship Channel compelled white longshoremen to cooperate with black dockworkers. The first longshoremen in Houston lacked waterfront experi-ence and were unorganized. For these reasons, black and white unionists from the Galveston docks initiated an organizing campaign in the city. The open-ing of the channel and the combined efforts of the Galveston workers in-creased longshore work in the city and spurred the growth of unions. Two early unions, Local 872 (black) and Local 896 (white), were formed in 1914. The two groups worked peacefully until the Mallory Line decided to under-mine the relationship. Agents for the company capitalized on the larger mem-bership and lower pay demands of Local 872 and locked Local 896 out of the docks.[21]

The attempt to divide Locals 872 and 896 ironically led to internal division among black workers from Local 872. The "Buffaloes," a group of black long-shoremen who broke from 872 and worked "anything that sailed up the Buffalo Bayou" or along the channel, believed that equal distribution of work under-employed blacks. They eagerly accepted the Mallory offer. The "Buffaloes" eventually received their own ILA charter, and within a few months their new Local 1409 extended its jurisdiction to cover intercoastal docks around Hous-ton while they also competed for deep-sea work.[22] It was not uncommon for aggressive black longshoremen to break from contractual agreements and garner work as they saw fit. The more moderate factions of Local 872 advo-cated the equal work concept and distanced themselves from the "Buffaloes."

They dared not tangle with the Buffaloes or interfere with their efforts to seek additional work. An angry group of white dockworkers from nearby Local 1273, however, voiced strong opposition. They presented their complaint to the Houston City Council and persuaded the lawmakers to adopt a resolution guaranteeing them no less than half of all work at the Houston port.[23]

While longshoremen worked to remedy their racial problems during the early decades of the twentieth century, antiunion sentiments of the post–World War I era engendered more concerns for Gulf Coast dockworkers. When longshoremen threatened to disrupt the flow of cargo at the Galveston port in 1920 after the Morgan and Mallory lines refused to grant a $.20 pay increase for sixteen thousand coastwise longshoremen, it fueled animosity between the workers and state lawmakers. Governor William P. Hobby intervened and placed several thousand troops on the island to protect nonunion dockworkers that the companies had employed to unload their ships. The subsequent passage of the Open Port Law, which outlawed interference with the free passage of commerce in the state, reflected the general attitude toward organized labor by state politicians.[24]

The resulting effects of the 1920 longshoremen strike weakened unionism among Gulf Coast dockworkers and forced ILA officials to exercise more stringent control over its union locals. The 1920s presented a particularly unique opportunity for black workers to experiment with their union loyalties and find ways to survive during crucial periods of labor unrest and economic setbacks. In 1924 the district convention of the ILA revoked the charter of Galveston Local 329 for working ships in the Gulf alongside nonunion labor. Fearing 329 might retaliate and continue its alliance with unorganized workers, the ILA rescinded its decision and reinstated the charter. When black longshoremen ignored the ILA's fifty-fifty plan and aligned with nonunion dockworkers, it angered white unionists, who blamed "the ignorance of the negroes . . . for a good deal of the trouble" that the ILA had "in keeping the Texas Ports organized."[25]

Despite the continued increase in the number of longshoremen in the south, racial division and animosity between the races persisted along the Upper Texas Gulf Coast throughout the 1930s (see table 2). White dockworkers often ridiculed "the smart nigger" who protested labor policy or operated outside of the boundaries of organized labor. As Gilbert Mers, one of the chief labor organizers of the 1930s, put it, some white longshoremen attempted to demoralize their black counterparts with condescending remarks: "Aw, Sam,

Table 2. Total Longshoremen, Number and Proportion
of Blacks for the United States, and for Selected States, 1930–1940

| | 1930 | | | 1940 | | |
	Total	*Blacks*	*% Black*	*Total*	*Blacks*	*% Black*
Total US	73,954	25,434	34.3	73,611	22,855	31.0
Total 8 States	20,790	16,775	80.6	22,298	17,223	77.3
Alabama	1,433	1,383	95.8	1,410	1,319	93.5
Florida	2,028	1,882	92.8	3,150	2,923	92.7
Georgia	1,608	1,554	96.6	1,527	1,479	96.8
Louisiana	5,322	2,334	68.6	3,546	2,150	60.6
Maryland	3,400	2,334	68.6	3,546	2,150	60.6
So. Carol.	unav.	unav.	unav.	803	783	97.5
*Texas	3,926	2,739	69.8	4,890	3,072	62.8

Source: U.S. Department of Commerce, Bureau of the Census, *Census of Occupations,
1910–1940* (Washington, D.C.: Government Printing Office, 1940).

you know things ain't never as bad as they seem. Didn't we build you toilet
facilities just last month? Cost us like hell too. By the way, tell the boys just to
use 'em for shittin' and not for restin. Go back and tell your boys to quit their
gripes and be happy."[26]

Black and white longshoremen could have learned much about interracial
cooperation from the actions of the ILA Ladies Auxiliaries. In October, 1931,
the wives, daughters, sisters, and mothers-in-law of black and white ILA locals from the Port of Houston formed auxiliaries to aid the union locals in the
area. The auxiliaries created a calm atmosphere as "there was less cussing and
more actual work." They initiated both fraternal and benevolent endeavors.
These women organized to "help enforce the union label" and to keep up
with the affairs of the Houston Labor and Trades Council. Moreover, they
solicited clothing, provisions, and medical assistance and established com-
missaries for the families of strikers. It was a welcome courtesy when "the
ladies of two auxiliaries, both white and colored, prepared midnight lunches
and hot coffee" for striking workers.[27]

One of the more admirable attempts to establish interracial cooperation
was the Ship Channel Progressive Community (SCPC). During the crucial
decade of the 1930s the SCPC became a leading voice for longshoremen at the
Port of Houston. The organization's weekly newspaper declared its political
agendas, posted union advertisements, announced the meetings of union

locals, and corresponded with longshoremen throughout the country. The Ship Channel Progressive Committee collected dues from each member and met every Thursday at its clubhouse to discuss pertinent longshoremen issues. The Committee called on "every colored and white man" to support the union movement and "take an intelligent, firm and progressive stand," to protect the interest of the working class.[28]

Black longshoremen who worked to eradicate racial barriers during the 1930s were often disappointed when their efforts to do so were thwarted by biased employers, uncooperative whites, and disgruntled blacks. Beaumont's black locals, for instance, "would not work ships until they organized a white local." Employers often penalized blacks by hiring more whites. According to R. C. Parker, a leading voice among dockworkers in Beaumont's black Local 325, employers reduced wages of black longshoremen to anything they wanted to when they knew they could hire whites in their place. In 1932 white longshoremen in Beaumont "went over to take some of the work from the colored Local 1306," and were met by blacks with guns who shot and wounded several of those who had come to take their jobs. They blamed "a bunch of hillbilly whites" who accepted jobs they did not deserve for much of the trouble between the two races.[29]

Racial separation suited some black longshoremen who avoided expending too much energy toward the seemingly unattainable goal of racial harmony along the waterfronts. Most docks continued to place their employees in racially separate work crews, with black workers on one end of the ship and white workers on the other. Segregated toilet facilities, showers, and water fountains were common.[30] One of the black organizations that prospered under these conditions was the Lone Star Colored Benevolent Association (LSCBA), founded in 1934, whose membership contained "some of the best waterfront workers on the Port of Houston," and who secured contracts with employers that resulted in shorter work hours, pay increases, and a sizeable treasury. The LSCBA's annual "ILA Day" program, usually held in the presence of standing-room-only audiences at local churches, brought in local singers and prominent citizens who presented song and testimony on behalf of the "benefits derived from organized efforts" of the group. During the dock wars of 1936 the LSCBA displayed unity and resolve when it filed suit against several steamship operators in the area. The workers claimed that an earlier contract negotiated on their behalf by the ILA was invalid since many of its workers were denied employment as a result of the agreement. Although they lost their case, their willingness to utilize the courts demonstrated that the LSCBA intended to use reasonable options to obtain equitable work opportunities.[31]

By the end of the 1930s the number of union locals along the Upper Texas Gulf Coast had grown considerably (see table 3). Indeed, the 1930s marked a crucial decade for the longshore industry. The coming of the CIO offered longshore unions an organizing alternative. But the federation was not eager to make the ILA a strong national organization. The core of the CIO-affiliated International Longshoremen's and Warehousemen's Union (ILWU) was formed along the West Coast. The "Big Strike" of 1934, which spanned the nation and lasted eighty-three days, ended several years of employer domination. It ushered in a new era of grassroot worker involvement among longshoremen unionists and demonstrated the unity, militancy, and the leftist political orientation of the unions' leadership and rank and file. By 1937 the Pacific Coast district of the ILA had voted to join forces with the CIO and end its affiliation with the AFL.[32]

The CIO and Gulf Coast longshoremen, however, responded much slower to years of flagrant abuses by employers than did West Coast dockworkers. Organizing the Gulf Coast meant facing unrivaled racial division. During the Galveston dock wars of 1936, for instance, few blacks joined white strikers in their effort to garner higher wages from employers. Ship owners, again, encouraged black unionists to disregard their union allegiances and take advantage of the extra work opportunities. This time, however, white longshoremen put up stronger resistance. In April, 1936, there were several days of sporadic violence between white longshoremen and local law enforcement who attempted to make safe passage for those willing to work.[33]

The inability of black and white longshoremen to form a unified labor contingency challenged the usefulness of the fifty-fifty plan that the ILA had attempted to rigorously enforce by the mid-1930s. To J. J. Rogers of Houston's white Local 1273 the "fifty-fifty" was virtually nonexistent in most Texas ports. Rogers spoke on behalf of many white longshoremen who resented the power of black unions and their occasional blatant disregard for the fifty-fifty plan when he hurled a litany of complaints at the 1936 ILA Gulf Coast convention. Rogers was particularly troubled that black unions, which boasted a larger number of members and unions, received more charters and a greater share of the work. Black dockworkers rallied together at the convention, however, and resisted attempts by the ILA to merge white Locals 310 and 317 in Galveston and combine the city's two black Locals, 329 and 851. Black delegates chided the maneuver as a scheme to underemploy a sizeable num-

Table 3. Longshoremen Unions, Black and White,
along the Upper Texas Gulf Coast, 1930s

	Black	White
Beaumont	Local 1306	
	Local 325	
Galveston	Local 329	Local 317
	Local 851	Local 310
Houston	Local 872	Local 1273
	Local 1271	Local 1231
	Local 1331	Local 1330
	Local 1409	Local 1351
	Local 1345	
Port Arthur	Local 1001	Local 538
	Local 440	Local 1029
	Local 1175	

ber of their workers if amalgamation took place and the fifty-fifty plan was carried out.[34]

Indeed, the refusal of black longshoremen to defer to the desires of their white counterparts reflected the clout they exercised in the industry. The Houston ILA locals had set aside some of their differences and conducted orderly joint labor contract meetings until they parted ways in 1939 over a work distribution dispute. When the black-dominated biracial Port of Houston Dock Marine Council rejected a proposal endorsing the fifty-fifty plan, a group of angry white longshoremen again took their grievance to members of the Houston city council and asked that black workers be ordered to relinquish half of all work entering the port. The symbolic resolutions passed by the city council admonishing black longshoremen and endorsing the fifty-fifty plan were largely ignored.[35]

Black longshoremen introduced resolutions of their own at labor conferences and conventions. Freeman Everett, a long-time black longshoreman, labor activist, and recognized spokesman for black dockworkers throughout the state, consistently voiced his concerns about racial strife in the industry. Everett, who always eased white unionists' fears by reassuring them of black worker loyalty to the labor movement, circulated a resolution among a delegation of black dockworkers at the Thirty-second Annual South Atlantic & Gulf Coast ILA convention supporting the U.S. war effort in Europe. Because World War II deluged many Upper Texas Gulf Coast ports with tanks, guns, ammunition, food, and fuel, longshoremen in the region faced the monumental task of overseeing the distribution of these wartime goods and supplies. Thus, loyalty was essential to the day-to-day operations of the industry. "America is the bulwark of free people and democratic government," Everett exclaimed, and black longshoremen and all "working people" needed to assist the government despite "those Americans on the home front who are un-American and undemocratic."[36]

Although undemocratic practices such as segregation and discrimination persisted during World War II, it did not compel black dockworkers to relinquish their power or share of the job market. Black longshoremen unions along the Upper Texas Gulf Coast required little help from outsiders, mainly the black middle class, but they offered their workers a measure of protection against biased white employers and white unionists. They shared an interest in shaping labor policy, regulating labor supply, and curtailing racial competition. Establishing formal and informal alliances with white workers proved useful in achieving these goals. As industry along the Upper Texas Gulf Coast grew, black unionism broadened its resistance to inequalities. Black unionists in the railroad industry used many of the tactics common among black longshoremen but extended the politics of separatism to combat race and class oppression, improve their standard of living, and bolster their union aspirations.

CHAPTER 3

"BUILD ... ONE OF OUR OWN"

Railroad Workers Broaden the Struggle

BLACK UNIONISTS capitalized on the growing southern railroad industry just as they had done in longshore work following the Civil War. The South, Gavin Wright wrote, shared fully in the national railroad-building frenzy between 1865 and 1875. Historian John Stover also observed that "by 1866 Southern rail recovery was so complete that nearly every state had new railroad projects in mind and in some cases, work had actually begun." These new railroad projects spawned the rise of interior and coastal cities. The entrepreneurial rush that followed necessarily required an expanded labor force. The Great Railroad Strike that erupted in 1877 reflected workers' fear of rapacious employers but also demonstrated a fundamental concern about the powerlessness of railroad labor. The 1894 Pullman Strike also exacerbated employment problems between labor and management and exposed racial division in the industry. Neither railroad employers or white strikers cared much about the equal participation of blacks, and they often imposed stipulations that interfered with employment opportunities for blacks. The eradication of slavery, as Wright argued, cleared the way for railroad employers to benefit from a workforce once held as personal property. Since the origins of American railroading, blacks have comprised a vital part of its labor force. By the late nineteenth and early twentieth centuries, blacks worked as track layers, repair or maintenance-of-way crew members, coach and car cleaners, firemen and brakemen, dining car waiters, porters, maids, and red caps, but they struggled to gain fair treatment.[1]

Black railroad workers along the Upper Texas Gulf Coast had as much reason to appeal for racial equality as any group of workers. The rebirth of the cotton industry and the increased distribution of timber products greatly influenced railroad expansion in the region. Government bonds enhanced railroad construction as new tracks connected the docks and wharves to the rest of the country, transforming the region into a booming railroad center for domestic trade.[2] Black railroad workers, however, did not enjoy an equal share of the benefits brought on by this rapid expansion. White railroad workers undertook efforts to remove, displace, or undermine their progress. Although blacks hired in as common laborers, they toiled in just about every segment of the industry and were often relegated to low job classifications and received less pay than whites for the same work. The Brotherhood of Locomotive Engineers, the Order of Railway Conductors, the Brotherhood of Locomotive Firemen and Enginemen, and the Brotherhood of Railroad Trainmen (BRT) limited their membership to white workers and sanctioned discrimination, as did various local railway shop unions, including the Railway Carmen (coach cleaners), Railway Clerks, Boilermakers, Blacksmiths, Machinists, Sheet Metal Workers, and Electrical Workers.[3]

Blacks who hired into skill occupations relied, ironically, on the employers, who helped establish many of the racially restrictive guidelines that hindered their mobility. When the Houston & Texas Central Railroad (H&TC) began hiring black workers in departments other than the service sector in the 1890s, white unionists from the Brotherhood of Railroad Trainmen responded with a work stoppage and demanded that officials discharge all the new hires. Despite their appeal, company management refused to comply. When white unionists from the same brotherhood called for the replacement of black switchmen with white workers in 1909, H&TC officials again rejected their demand and insisted that "the colored man . . . rendered faithful and efficient service," and to displace him "would be unjust."[4] White workers closely monitored the occupational mobility of blacks in order to protect their own jobs. When the Brotherhood of Locomotive Firemen published an August, 1917, magazine article complaining about "negro firemen" being "placed on locomotives as firemen," it reflected white workers' concern about blacks who were contractually classified as porters being given opportunities to upgrade their rank and pay.[5]

The freedom of railroad employers to use black workers and underpay them at the same time often influenced their hiring decisions. Disputes over wages became important issues between the races and for the country during World War I. The federal government mediated wage disputes arising from collective agreements after it outlawed yellow-dog (antiunion) and closed-shop (prounion) contracts and race-based labor policies. The United States Railroad Administration (USRA), along with other government agencies, coordinated wartime production, promised stringent control and centralized management of freight traffic, and reevaluated employee wages. Black organizations petitioned the USRA on behalf of their members and black railroad workers who suffered from the abuses of the railroad unions. The USRA issued General Order No. 27 in 1918, which, among other things, equalized wages between the races. The ruling mandated equal pay for black and white firemen, trainmen, and switchmen. In essence, the order reclassified workers, particularly those engaged in similar or identical work. Until the railroad administration clarified its position on train porters, the imprecise language of the general order created questions about the status of black train porters who handled brake work, mail, baggage, tickets, and performed many of the same tasks as white trainmen and firemen.[6] Maligned white unionists' concerns about the classification and seniority of black train porters led to Supplement Order No. 12 in 1918, which relieved the government from interfering with worker rank and allowed for employers and unions to remedy seniority disputes.[7]

The conflict over seniority, wages, and occupation, coupled with the refusal of the white brotherhoods to accept black workers, compelled aspiring black unionists to look inward to their rank and file and establish labor associations that would speak on their behalf and confront the racial constraints that had long plagued their progress. In the midst of the antilabor union atmosphere of the 1920s, the Brotherhood of Sleeping Car Porters (BSCP) emerged as a central force in the organization of Pullman car porters. The BSCP, by most accounts, became a recognized symbol of black working-class advancement. The Pullman Company offered quality rail accommodations to travelers throughout the country as early as 1867. George Pullman, founder and owner of the company, capitalized on a tradition of black labor in the service sector and began hiring numerous blacks as waiters and baggage handlers. By the turn of the century, the Pullman Company recorded twelve thousand black workers and was the largest employer of black laborers in the United States.[8]

Despite their overwhelming numerical composition, black porters still suffered from long workdays, low wages, limited promotion opportunities, abusive white managers and passengers, and were compelled to maintain a servile demeanor toward white patrons. When James Saunders, a train porter who found his way from Summit, Mississippi, to Texas in the early 1900s, hired on with the Pullman Railroad, he faced many of these haunting problems. When black porters were accused of providing poor customer service, Saunders insisted, they generally relied on white patrons to vouch for their job performance. They faced long workdays, little to no vacation time, and, in Saunders's case, worked "four nights and three days with an hour and a half sleep each night." In the dining cars, employers placed them "in the corner at a table somewhere." The Pullman Company segregated its coaches and required black employees to "charter a whole pullman car" if they desired to travel with family members and friends.[9]

Challenges to these conditions occurred as early as 1912 when porters in Oakland, California, formed a union to resist the oppressive practices of the company. The greatest impetus for change, however, occurred when A. Philip Randolph organized the BSCP. Born in 1889 to James and Elizabeth Randolph in Crescent City, Florida, A. Philip first spoke about organizing the porters when he addressed their athletic association in New York in 1925. The BSCP did not enjoy early successes in organizing black workers. The effort to do so was an uphill struggle. Employers regularly dismissed men who signed up for the BSCP from service and in some cases refused to hear their appeals for reinstatement. Once black workers overcame their fears of ruthless employers and Randolph established a solid base of support along the Gulf Coast, porter organizers mingled freely among trainmen until enough interest was generated to launch an all-out campaign to organize black porters in Texas. By the late 1930s the BSCP began electing chairmen of newly established district locals to handle worker complaints, which they forwarded to the BSCP headquarters in New York.[10]

By the end of the decade, the BSCP had chartered several chapters throughout the United States and Canada. While the Eastern, Detroit, Midwestern, and Pacific Zones of the BSCP recorded early and consistent growth in most major cities, the Southwestern Zone, with its principal cities of St. Louis, Memphis, New Orleans, Dallas, and Houston, recorded low membership during the early years. The union won a substantial victory in 1937 when it entered into an agreement with the Pullman Company that resulted in a wage increase.[11]

The emergence of the BSCP represented a new era in the organization of black railroad workers as it acknowledged the vital role of black women in the unionization of the black industrial workforce. When Randolph organized the BSCP and its locals, he foresaw the advantages of mobilizing their wives. The women, Randolph concluded, could be utilized for moral support, fundraising, and recruiting. A clairvoyant Randolph recognized that a community of cooperative wives improved his chances of organizing car porters effectively. Despite their skepticism about affiliating with labor unions during the intensely racist and antiunion climate of the 1920s, many women at the Pullman Company capitalized on the opportunity to enhance their own role in labor affairs and mass organization. Perhaps the most important contribution, however, of the BSCP Ladies' Auxiliary was the idea of gender cooperation within the black working class. "The Brotherhood," in the words of Rosina Tucker, "brought out qualities of strength and courage in the porters and their wives."[12]

The BSCP was not the only group of black railroaders to challenge the economic and racial hardships in the industry. The drive to rally black locomotive firemen and brakemen was as intense as the effort to galvanize Pullman porters. By the early twentieth century, blacks in the operating trades and yard service confronted hostile whites, particularly those belonging to the BRT and the Brotherhood of Locomotive Firemen and Enginemen. For decades rebellious white unionists from this segment of the industry undermined black workers and stifled their union ambitions with strikes, threats, and violence.[13]

The Texas and Louisiana branch of the Colored Trainmen of America (CTA) worked relentlessly to mobilize segments of the black railroad workforce. The CTA represented workers such as I. K. Black, who, like so many other blacks, had gravitated to the railroad industry from various parts of the country seeking employment. In Black's case he secured work with the Texas & Pacific Railroad in 1922 as a train brakemen although the company and the union refused to upgrade his pay or grant him the proper job title to reflect the work he performed. From its headquarters in Kingsville, Texas, the CTA served as a clearinghouse of information and a symbol of unity for black trainmen. Once the CTA organized its conventions, black members made extra efforts to attend them. Damon McCrary, for example, inquired about CTA conferences and made sure that he had time to make his arrangements; he hoped "to have a good delegation" of black workers with him when he attended. The CTA also entered numerous agreements with railroad employers and white unions with respect to wages, job titles, and work rules. An agreement between the Gulf Coast Lines and "Colored Brakemen," for example, went into effect in January, 1929. Unlike previous agreements that consistently designated black railroaders as "baggagemen," the 1929 contract created several new job classifications and pay scales for black trainmen. The new contract recognized blacks as passenger train brakemen, freight brakemen, work brakemen, local and mixed brakemen, engine foremen, and switchmen.[14]

Despite changes in job classifications and pay, black brakemen and firemen still struggled for union representation within the Brotherhood. The 1930s, however, marked a time of increased organizing activity. Black trainmen took advantage of new laws governing labor-management relations. The 1926 and 1934 Railway Labor Acts required employers to recognize railroad unions. The National Mediation Board that grew out of the legislation determined the legitimacy of elections and certified new unions. When the board investigated the payroll records of the Gulf Coast Lines following complaints made by black trainmen about the lack of adequate representation, it found that eight of eleven white yard conductors had authorized the BRT to be their sole bargaining agent while refusing to let black workers cast a vote.[15]

Blacks enjoyed little to no representation from the organization. The BRT, which claimed to represent all the workers on the line, ignored many of their grievances. Labor contracts between the BRT and railroad employers along the Gulf generally reflected specific language that catered to white workers and hindered the progress of blacks. When the Missouri Pacific Lines and the New Orleans–Texas–Mexico Railway Line came to a contractual agreement with the BRT in May, 1935, they included no mention of black workers but made clear that the contract only governed the "wages and working conditions of white flagmen and white brakemen."[16]

Contracts for black trainmen typically resulted from the formal meetings held between CTA leaders and railroad employers. When W. G. Choate, general manager for the Pacific Lines and the Gulf Coast Lines, met with Lloyd Allen, general chairman for the Colored Firemen Grievance Committee, and W. H. Jefferson, general chairman for the Gulf Coast CTA, at Choate's Houston office in October, 1937, he agreed to a $.40 per day pay increase for black workers in freight service, passenger service, and yard service.[17] As long as black trainmen remained outside of the BRT, however, they stood little chance of enjoying the full benefits of the industry or the union. The CTA did not exhaust too much energy appealing to employers or white unionists for representation and protection but instead took advantage of the organizing opportunities presented by the Railway Labor Act. The CTA contested the BRT's jurisdiction over black railroad workers. Its main point of contention centered on the inability of black trainmen to participate equally in union elections.[18] Despite its claims to protect railroad workers, the Mediation Board largely disregarded CTA complaints. When the CTA issued a preliminary statement complaining about inadequate representation, the Board demonstrated its deference to the old order of exclusion and reminded the organization that the Board "was created by and is a product of an agreement to which Colored Trainmen of America is not a party."[19]

As the Mediation Board, white unionists, and employers discouraged black advancement, black workers from the CTA redoubled their efforts to overcome workplace obstacles. I. O. Benberry, president of the CTA Lodge No. 10 in Louisville, Kentucky, spurred on black railroaders along the Gulf Coast when he submitted an editorial to the *Negro Labor News* in January, 1938, which called on them to unite forces. "How long," Benberry pleaded, "before we will see our condition on the railroads and get together?"[20] It did not take long for CTA members to heed Benberry's appeal. Less than two weeks after his article appeared, the CTA circulated a petition among its workers calling on the BRT and employers to abolish the practice of white junior brakemen "being hired today having any bumping rights" over black senior brakemen. The petition went on to assert that the CTA did not "believe in a man hiring this week and be allowed to exercise his seniority to displace a senior under no circumstance . . . now and never. We do not believe in 'vice-versing' seniority."[21]

Concerns about seniority were but one phase of the CTA's plight. The organizational strength among black trainmen and the establishment of an administrative hierarchy allowed them to also counteract railroad employers' ambivalence toward their demands for an equal share of the work. The installation of Gulf Coast CTA officers at the Bethel African Methodist Episcopal (AME) Church in Houston in July, 1938, suggested that black trainmen were serious about their organized efforts to confront workplace inequities.[22] On several occasions CTA officials requested that employers fill job vacancies with available black labor, but L. A. David, assistant general manager for the Orange North Western Railroad, refused to deviate from contractual agreements that required the sole use of white flagmen and brakemen.[23] A February, 1939, CTA resolution presented to white unionists and railroad employers called for the implementation of the "full-crew" agreement, which most understood to be a noncontractual understanding between railroad employers, white unionists, and black trainmen that ensured a set number "of colored brakemen of the Gulf Coast Lines on all trains and yard-engines."[24]

Nonbinding agreements merely placed trainmen at the mercy of their bosses and the BRT. Although they rarely worked as strikebreakers, black trainmen generated an atmosphere of racial unity. When Gulf Coast trainman Damon McCrary wrote a letter to fellow trainman F. C. Caldwell in Memphis, Tennessee, he assured his "dear old pal" that he had "the boys . . . in line" with the CTA. He went on to explain how his followers admired and tried to emulate the Railway Men's International Benevolent Industrial Association (RMIBIA). This organization was one of the more impressive black-led railroad associations and it served as a unifier of all classes of black railroaders who were denied membership in white-led unions. Founded in 1915 and led by dining car waiter Robert L. Mays, the RMIBIA boasted a membership of fifteen thousand by 1920. In Chicago the organization claimed seventeen chapters with nearly twelve hundred members in 1922. Because of the meaningful benefits achieved by the RMIBIA, McCrary stood in opposition to black railroad workers joining white-dominated unions and instead embraced Mays's vision of a massive union of black railroad workers including porters, dining car cooks and waiters, black brakemen, firemen, switchmen, yard engine men, shop workers, boilermakers, machinists, coach cleaners, laundry workers, and track laborers. A strong black union was enough to satisfy McCrary, who rejected white unions and encouraged his workers to "keep away from them and build . . . one of our own."[25]

McCrary did not speak for all blacks in the railroad industry. He was aware that some black labor leaders maintained different perspectives on unionization. McCrary admitted that A. Philip Randolph and his supporters had done a good job organizing the Pullman Porters with the AFL but reaffirmed his own commitment to a racially unified labor organization.[26]

The CTA intensified its efforts to protect its share of trainmen jobs. By 1941 the Gulf Coast CTA formulated a constitution that modeled that of the BRT. The race-specific language called for "unity, justice, and protection" of black trainmen. We organize, the document stated, "to unite the Colored Trainmen of America, to promote their general welfare, and advance their interest socially, morally, and intellectually . . . for the interest both of our members and their employers." The constitution established guidelines for annual conventions, funding, constructing new lodges, funeral arrangements for deceased members, grievance procedures, and representation.[27]

Their diligence in maintaining an independent union paid dividends and helped establish a more amicable relationship with employers. The organization cautioned its workers about affiliating with the AFL, the CIO, or any labor union "which the white race had anything to do with." Attempts to get black trainmen at the Southern Pacific Yards to join the CIO, the *Negro Labor News* reported, failed to garner much support since "only a few Negroes even attended any of the meetings." The Southern Pacific's Shop Craft Association, a company-sponsored union formed in 1920, enticed some blacks and attracted them away from the major labor federations as well as from the CTA.[28] Employer-based contracts satisfied the CTA, provided that management complied with the terms of the agreements. They refused to back down from those who did not. When the CTA requested a conference with H. F. Roll, the chief personnel officer for the Orange North Western Railroad, to discuss pay increases and the use of "two Colored Brakemen. . . as article 15(a)" of their agreement stipulated, they waited five months before Roll agreed to meet with them. The meeting placed company management on notice about the CTA's resolve to monitor the treatment of its members.[29]

The unity among black workers in the CTA spurred on black railroad workers in other areas of the industry. The Brotherhood of Dining Car Employees (BDCE) was organized by Rienzi B. Lemus during World War I. The nucleus of the BDCE was established in 1918 when black cooks and waiters from the Boston and Albany Railroad united their rank and file. Subsequently, black employees from the Pennsylvania Railroad formed the Dining Car Cooks and Waiters Association, which later merged with the cooks and waiters out of New York and Massachusetts. By the 1930s the BDCE had grown to become a large and influential black-led organization that operated beyond the control of the major white-led federations in many parts of the country. Thus, most of its dealings involved railroad employers instead of antagonistic white unionists. In Texas, however, unorganized black dining car cooks were relegated to an AFL auxiliary status. Throughout much of their early history, black dining car employees at the Southern Pacific in Texas appealed for greater union representation and better working conditions. When Clarence R. Johnson, the national general chairman of the Dining Car Employees Union arrived in Houston in January, 1938, to negotiate a contract for the black dining car employees auxiliary at Southern Pacific, his demands were largely ignored.[30]

Judson W. Robinson, a black dining car waiter and founder of Dining Car Employees Local 582, an auxiliary in Houston, spoke out against biased racial practices at the 1939 Texas State Federation of Labor convention and denounced Texas House Bill 487 that mandated racially separate passenger compartments, which prohibited blacks from working dining cars in the absence of a white supervisor. While Texas railroad employers obeyed the policy and avoided fines and penalties ranging up to $1,000, dining car employees stood in unyielding opposition to the law.[31] Robinson's outspokenness against House Bill 487 generated little support from railroad employers or from white unionists. The Missouri Pacific Lines, for example, showed no intention of disobeying laws that called for segregation. The company circulated a memo to office trainmasters advising conductors and brakemen that "colored passengers will transfer from the Madison–San Antonio coach at Harlingen to the Brownsville-

Houston coach, leaving the colored compartment in the Mission–San Antonio coach for colored . . . passengers only."[32]

Black railroad workers who were affiliated with the Brotherhood of Railway and Steamship Clerks (BRSC)—an organization that expanded its jurisdiction to include black freight handlers during the First World War and took on the Texas and New Orleans Railroad in a 1927 court case after the employer interfered with the right of their union to organize—pursued many of the same strategies to dismantle racial barriers within the BRSC that had hindered black porters, trainmen, and dining car workers. The racist AFL-affiliated BRSC extended few benefits and no real representation to black workers. The auxiliaries they belonged to were policed by officers of the white union and offered a "gentlemen's agreement" grievance procedure that union officials recognized at their discretion.[33]

The BRSC subjected black employees to a racist hierarchy. It wrote "white only" clauses into its constitution and restricted blacks to "second-class membership" in the organization. White workers received the more prestigious and higher-paying "Group One" jobs, such as record keeping, while the lower-paying "Group Three" jobs, such as freight-handling and common labor, went to blacks. Although Moses LeRoy, head of the black BRSC auxiliary 1534 in Houston, and his followers temporarily acquiesced to the limitations placed upon them by the BRSC, they viewed the creation of their union auxiliary as an initial step toward eradicating these discriminatory provisions. When they initiated their own efforts to obtain a national union charter with the AFL, they decided it would be best if they waited until BRSC ended its "lip service" and admitted blacks into the union on an equal basis.[34]

By the late 1930s and early 1940s the Upper Texas Gulf Coast had become a prime target area for black labor leaders to mobilize and organize black railroad workers. Randolph and his international vice president, Milton P. Webster, arrived in Houston in mid-October, 1938, along with over 500 hundred other delegates representing nearly 4 million workers from across the country, to attend the annual AFL convention and stage a determined, two-week fight to break down racial barriers within the federation. Randolph headed a delegation of black labor leaders, including Ishmael Florey, Paul Hortman of New Orleans, Ed Rhone of Mobile, Dock Hamilton of Galveston, and Freeman Everett of Houston. Webster made his way to the Trinity East AME Church to speak to black workers who had gathered to hear the labor organizer at an NAACP-sponsored labor forum. The convention offered a propitious opportunity to improve the BSCP's low membership in the area and redouble its efforts to attract more southern black train porters and other groups of black railroaders to their organization. By the time the 1938 convention began, Randolph had successfully secured a national charter for the BSCP and increased the membership of Texas Pullman porters from zero in 1933 to 161 by 1938, a figure, however, that lagged behind St. Louis and New Orleans, each of which recorded a larger membership than the entire state of Texas.[35]

The wide range of labor ideologies that emerged during the late 1930s complicated efforts to form a racially cohesive movement in the black railroad community. The BSCP and the BDCE latched on to the AFL, the BRSC worked to obtain representation within the federation, the CTA remained independent, and others refused to give up on company-sponsored unions.

C. W. Rice, a leading proponent of company-based organizations, used his *Negro Labor News* community paper as a tool to expose "the shame of railroad unionism." Rice charged the AFL, the CIO, and the railroad brotherhoods of being the biggest culprits of racial injustice. He was less concerned about the choice of unions black workers made and more worried about white-dominated unions being allowed to negotiate contracts on behalf of blacks who were denied membership. "If white labor organizations can get together," Rice lamented, "and make contracts for Negroes who are not permitted to belong to them, then the rights of all citizens are threatened."[36] As the general organizer and principal agent of a lawsuit brought against the Brotherhood of Railroad Carmen in March, 1938, he assumed center stage and challenged the jurisdiction of the brotherhood over black coach cleaners at the Texas & Pacific Railroad. Acting on behalf of the National Federation of Railway Workers (NFRW), a small, relatively weak, and fairly ineffectual organization formed around 1918 by its general president, L. W. Fairchild of Popular Bluff, Missouri, Rice charged that the Brotherhood of Railroad Carmen exceeded its powers when it claimed to represent nonunion black workers. The NFRW owed its limited successes, in large part, to the legal cases fought by Rice, Fairchild, and Charles Hamilton Houston, a member of the legal staff for the NAACP and counsel for the IARE. Rice's suit against the brotherhood led to a temporary restraining order blocking the Brotherhood's control over black carmen.[37]

The court decision did little to improve circumstances. When Robert F. Cole, a National Mediation Board–appointed mediator, "ignored" Rice's jurisdictional claims over black carmen and encouraged blacks workers to "go along with white organizations until they could learn more about the tech-

nique of the organized labor movement," he instigated an ideological confrontation that Rice was determined to win.[38] Rice redoubled his efforts and
organized an NFRW-affiliated regional delegation of black coach cleaners.
They met in Dallas in November, 1938, and in May of the following year
elected Ed Carter of Texarkana, Texas, Lincoln Washington of New Orleans,
and C. W. Rice to serve as their delegates to the International Association of
Railway Employees (IARE), an independent labor organization founded in
1934 by a handful of black train and engine service workers in Louisville,
Kentucky, at the 1939 national convention in Atlanta.[39]

The IARE helped many rank and filers improve their position within the
industry. One beneficiary was Herman W. Simpson of Houston, Texas. Born
in Trinity, Texas, in the early part of the twentieth century, Simpson followed
some of his family members into railroad work. In the summer of 1933 he
accepted a part-time position as a coal burner for railroads that passed between Houston and Palestine, Texas. By 1941 he had hired on with the
DeQuincy, Louisiana, division of the Missouri & Pacific Railroad where he
received his initial pay as a fireman. The establishment of the DeQuincy chapter
of the IARE in July, 1938, helped clear the way for black railroaders such as
Simpson to acquire modest but timely upgrades.[40]

Simpson and the IARE recognized the vital role that women employees
played in their struggles to overcome discrimination. They relied on the ladies' auxiliaries to serve as delegates to conferences, organize programs, invite
keynote speakers, make banquet arrangements, and put together other enter-
tainment festivities. When Mrs. W. C. Taylor of Memphis, Tennessee, president of the ladies' auxiliary, urged the wives and girlfriends of railroad men to
attend the Atlanta conference, she demonstrated the level of support, participation, and commitment these women provided.[41]

Rice adopted many of the IARE's strategies and used them to combat racial neglect. He discouraged blacks from joining railroad labor organizations
that constitutionally, contractually, or ritualistically excluded blacks from membership and placed them in auxiliaries under white jurisdiction. Rice demanded
that black workers request copies of railroad constitution bylaws and "read
and understand that no Negro could become a bonafide member" of any white-
led railroad union along the Texas Gulf Coast.[42]

Although the regional and national black railroad organizations offered
invaluable alternatives to the more racist white unions, they failed to satisfy
some blacks in the industry. It was not unusual for some black railroaders
across the Upper Texas Gulf Coast to affiliate with white-dominated unions

Delegates to the 1939 International Association of Railway Employees convention in Atlanta. Courtesy Houston Metropolitan Research Center, Houston Public Library.

and rebuff black ones. The precedent established by the AFL-controlled BSCP, the rhetorical promises for equality made by the CIO, and the difficulty of black labor organizations to obtain union charters weighed heavily in their decisions. Black coach cleaners at various rail shops were reluctant to join such black-led organizations. Their reluctance was due, in part, to their hopes of some day being fully accepted into the larger and more prominent federations and their distrust of middle-class blacks, who occupied key positions of leadership in many of these organizations. The black coach cleaners at the Houston Belt & Terminal, for instance, rejected the NFRW as its bargaining agent and solicited the Brotherhood of Railway Carmen of the AFL to be its representative, demonstrating their preference for the larger, more established labor federation.

Rice experienced his fair share of setbacks in his campaign to eliminate the AFL's control over black carmen. He found little support for his proposed amendments to the Wagner Act that included language to protect black workers by removing race-based restrictions in labor contracts. Moreover, when the

District of Columbia Court of Appeals upheld a decision by the National Mediation Board denying the NFRW a new election at the Texas & Pacific Railroad, and the Supreme Court refused to hear arguments on the case, it sanctioned the racist status quo that permeated the labor movement. Although the court recognized the right of employees to select their own bargaining agency, it concluded that Rice's suit to unionize black coach cleaners and to provide them with fair representation was motivated by race and amounted to reverse discrimination. The "authorization blanks" he distributed to them, which allegedly designated their membership to the NFRW, were no substitute for an official union membership roster. They carried little significance and workers who signed them felt no particular obligation to recognize the organization because it had no government charter, the court concluded.[43]

The fight for equality among black railroad workers did not begin or end with Rice's defeat in court. Despite the loss, the NFRW continued to use the legal system as a tool for resistance. Although most of its judicial successes came in states outside of Texas, Rice's earlier efforts served as a platform to build upon. When the black firemen and car riders employed at the Virginia Railway Company, for example, won a two-year court battle in July, 1941, to have their organization recognized by the company, representatives of the CTA were able to meet with their company management for the first time to discuss pay increases and working conditions.[44] Bester Steele won his lawsuit against the Louisville & Nashville R. R. Co. in 1944 over employment discrimination. Steele had been a firemen in Alabama in the Decatur-Montgomery division of the Louisville & Nashville Railroad since 1910 but lost his seniority rights when the company signed an agreement with the Brotherhood of Locomotive Firemen and Enginemen. Although this Supreme Court ruling avoided the question of whether a union, certified by the government as an exclusive bargaining agent, could legally discriminate, it proclaimed that unions had the right to exclude certain workers but forbade them from negotiating contracts on behalf of nonmembers. Charles Hamilton Houston recognized the importance of Steele's victory to black railroad workers in Texas. Houston helped litigate the Steele case and prodded blacks, who had gathered at the Cuney Homes near downtown Houston in the summer of 1945 to hear the attorney and to commiserate with Bester Steele himself, to utilize the judicial system or any other useful strategy as a tool to protest working conditions and unfair treatment.[45]

The systematic effort to displace black railroad workers such as Steele and to deny them equal work and hiring opportunities prevailed during the early

1940s. While the government was motivated by circumstances centering around World War II, black railroad workers were driven by a desire to obtain what they believed to be rightfully theirs: fair hiring standards, equal representation in labor unions, just compensation for duties performed, and protection of their seniority. The struggle to gain equality for black railroad workers along the Upper Texas Gulf Coast included a variety of protest strategies and engaged a wide range of prominent black labor leaders. The increased attention given to the plight of these workers reflected how important they were to the industry and to the region's economy. While the longshore industry was centered around coastal cities, the railroad expanded across the country and impacted a large cross section of the population. Black railroad workers along the Upper Gulf Coast became a part of that dynamic. They adjusted their protest strategies accordingly. Their struggles reflected many of the same trends in the oil industry where black unionists established themselves as a vital force to be reckoned with.

CHAPTER 4

OIL WORKERS AND THE FIGHT FOR MOBILITY

THE MODERN ERA of oil production in America, according to C. Vann Woodward, opened in January, 1901, with the discovery of oil at Spindletop near Beaumont. That year marked the beginning of oil-induced growth along the Upper Texas Gulf Coast. Oil production helped sustain the region's economic development. The discovery of oil, coupled with expanding longshore and railroad industries, added yet another dimension to the struggles of black unionists. In many ways, Spindletop, Woodward argued, deserved the title of "the world's greatest oil well." In its second year of production, the Spindletop Pool released 17,500,000 barrels. Before Spindletop, most oil exploration and production occurred in oil fields in western Pennsylvania, which provided much of the country's petroleum, but they rarely exceeded 10 barrels a day. The 70,000 to 110,000 barrels that gushed at Spindletop within the first nine days of its eruption provided the impetus for Eastern bankers and industrialists to invest sizable capital in the development of further production. On the eve of the discovery at Spindletop, the Standard Oil Company (New Jersey) dominated all phases of the oil industry in the country. In the decade after Spindletop, competition for market share in the industry increased dramatically, and the Texas oil economy, which shared in this advancement, quickly expanded and included the creation of several energetic, expansive new firms, the construction of large refineries, the improvement of transportation systems, new pools of exploration, the rise of spin-off industries, and the growth of numerous oil worker unions.[1]

The initial attempt among the working class to organize in the expanding Upper Texas Gulf Coast oil market occurred in the early part of the twentieth century, a time when oil employers established a pattern of cutting the wages of their workers. Oil workers at the Humble oil field near Houston staged a short, ten-day strike in 1905 after J. M. Guffy, owner of the operation, reduced the wages of his workers from $3.00 to $2.50. The work stoppage did help restore their original hourly pay. Faced with the possibility of future pay cuts, a segment of the Humble oil workforce requested an AFL organizer for the region. In December of the same year, the AFL chartered Local 11998 of the Guffy Oil & Gas Well Workers. Its marginal success in organizing several workers in the area was not enough to garner recognition from Guffy. It did, however, spur black workers to organize their own unions. In January, 1911, blacks affiliated with the Oil & Refinery Workers at Humble chartered Local 13124, which negotiated wages that were "highest for Negro workers on the Gulf Coast." The membership in many of these early unions waxed and waned for several years. Many disappeared almost as quickly as they were formed. "At times Local 53 in Port Arthur had more members than did Local 23," which was comprised of white workers. At other times the membership dropped off to the point where some had to cease operation.[2]

Despite rapid industrial expansion, oil workers were without much protection throughout the first two decades of the twentieth century. Black and white oil workers alike entered the labor movement facing the formidable odds placed before them by oil employers such as John D. Rockefeller and other oil tycoons, whose ruthless strikebreaking tactics in the 1913 Colorado coal miner strike reflected their disdain for labor unions. The early signs of oil unionism sparked a sharp reaction from most oil barons. Rockefeller, builder of the Standard Oil empire, had all but snuffed out many of the initial attempts at unionization in the businesses he owned. He initiated a vigorous campaign to eradicate the few weak unions that existed. Upon learning about the southern coal miners' strike in 1913, an infuriated Rockefeller declared that he would rather see the mines closed forever before recognizing any coal miner union. With the help of the Colorado state militia, Rockefeller momentarily stifled the organizing aspirations of his workers. Rockefeller's behavior outraged the public and ignited a furious attempt by oil workers throughout the country to capitalize on a wave of public sympathy and redouble their efforts to organize their rank and file.[3]

The capitalist assault on oil union organizing mirrored that of the coal industry. Oil workers, however, stiffened their resolve and held their own against the defiance of wealthy oil titans. In the summer of 1916, about 500 skilled workers at the Gulf Oil plant went out on a twelve-day strike over guidelines governing job security and working conditions. The intervention of a federal mediator helped prevent a full-scale walkout of the company's nearly 2,700 workers. Gulf's concession to a new set of shop rules was heralded as a significant victory for organized labor because it was the first time the employer had agreed to negotiate with union representatives. The agreement promised, among other things, wage increases, the continuation of the eight-hour work-day, time-and-a-half pay for overtime work, and the recognition of worker-elected shop grievance committees.[4]

As the nation flirted with World War I, oil unionists continued their efforts to gain leverage. With the help of the AFL and parochial labor organizations such as the Houston Trades Council, oil workers were able to organize a large union at Goose Creek, Texas, in the spring of 1916. The Goose Creek union, Local 15387, which later became Local 21, became a leader in Gulf Coast agitation among oil workers. The rising cost of living, poor working conditions, and employer domination served as a catalyst for change. When Gulf Coast oil employers refused to hear worker demands and saw no reason for them to confer "with strangers and outsiders," the workers responded with vigilance. In November, 1917, Local 15387 galvanized nearly 10,000 oil workers from seventeen oil fields and encouraged them to walk off their jobs in protest against employers who refused to recognize their unions, shorten the workday, or discuss pay increases.[5] The strike infuriated oil employers, who eventually agreed to a pay increase but not before a three-month standoff forced them to construct a large bull pen near the Humble plant to keep replacement workers from the reach of strikers.[6]

The Magnolia strike in Beaumont the following year demonstrated that oil unionists had gained a measure of respect from employers. When 250 boiler-makers at the Magnolia plant demanded a 20 percent increase in pay, the company's management offered a 7 percent raise for all workers. The less-than-satisfactory proposal fueled a two-week work stoppage by boilermakers, craftsmen, production workers, and a host of common laborers, who ignored a range of counteroffers and only returned to work when the Federal Mediation and Conciliation Service, a government agency created to curtail labor strife during the war, persuaded them to do so.[7]

The first ever convention of the International Association of Oil Field, Gas Well & Refinery Workers of America, held in El Paso in November, 1918, marked the beginning of a new era for oil workers. For sixteen days twenty-five delegates representing several oil fields from throughout the country met in a chilly and unheated labor hall and drafted the organization's first constitution, elected its first officers, and outlined the major principles of the union. Delegates were instructed to educate themselves and their fellow workers in the history of the labor movement and to cherish their union. The first resolution passed at the convention called for the federal government to nationalize the railroad, communication, utilities, and shipping industries. Failure to do so, the convention believed, meant a return to employer domination and retaliation, particularly from Standard Oil.[8]

Government intercession during the war years and the threat of scab labor led to an impressive show of worker solidarity and increased efforts by white unionists to organize black oil workers. It was not uncommon to see "men from all sections of the state coming to South Texas, attracted by wages offered oil field workers, . . . willing to work open shop," the *Gulf Coast Oil News* reported. The decision by white Local 21 to help organize black Local 85 at Goose Creek in 1919 stemmed perhaps from the Humble refinery's building of a large bull pen during the strike of 1917. This action motivated white Local 22 in Houston to aid in the start-up of black Local 77 and compelled white unionists at Local 94 in Houston to organize black oil workers into Local 106 in 1920.[9]

Black oil workers showed no meaningful intentions of using strikebreaking or separate unions as a retaliatory tool against white workers. They maintained a sense of worker unity and sought to protect the economic interests of both races. Black oil workers at the Magnolia refinery in Beaumont reflected these sentiments as they addressed classic union issues such as wages and union recognition while making their voices heard about other racial concerns. When black workers from black Local 39 at the Magnolia refinery supported white unionists during the two-week strike in 1918, they intended to show their commitment to the labor movement. As Albert Le Bert, leader of Local 39, put it: "When the Magnolia men went out, the Negroes were right behind them—all 1600, white and black, marching up the main street of Beaumont. The negro is just as good a man as the white—the main difference is that he gets $1.50 to $2 a day less."[10] Despite the support that black workers demonstrated toward white unionists, white workers rarely reciprocated. Although whites helped to organize black unions, they did so to circumvent the use of strikebreaking during labor strife. The animosity felt by many white workers toward black workers entering the oil industry was reflected in a 1921 article in the Magnolia refinery monthly news magazine. "Mules, niggers, wheelbarrows, and a few white men . . . form one of the largest and most essential departments of our refinery."[11]

Efforts to organize black oil workers during the 1920s often collided with these types of racial slurs. C. F. Richardson, Sr., was among the growing number of middle-class blacks who refused to retreat from such hostilities. He encouraged protest among black oil workers and warned whites, whom he regarded as the gravest enemies of black unionists, to carefully deliberate their treatment of black workers. His Colored Workingmen & Women's Association of Texas, in part, counteracted the obstacles placed before black oil workers. The organization's bimonthly meetings addressed many of their grievances. His meeting at Port Arthur's Sixth Street Baptist Church in June, 1919, prodded black refinery workers from the area to continue their struggle for equal treatment and fair representation.[12]

The antiunion sentiments of employers and the open-shop movement of the 1920s led to a dramatic decline in new labor unions while the prospects for company unions intensified. The oil unions' modest gains before 1920, however, had enough effect on employers to foster a new approach to dealing with employees. The Humble refinery, for example, recognized certain rights of workers when it created its first company union in 1920 and set up an Employee Representation Plan, modeled after Rockefeller's company plan, which he implemented after the public and government began to question and criticize his business practices. An equal representation of management and employees in joint contract conferences later evolved into company unionism and was generally viewed by many labor unionists as a strategy for employers to circumvent labor discontent and usurp power from their workers.[13]

In some cases, company unions expanded during the early 1930s but began to dwindle when they came under fire during the Great Depression as the National Industrial Recovery Act (NIRA) gave rise to a new era of labor organizing. In 1933 and the early part of 1934, the Oil Workers International Union (OWIU) proceeded rapidly in the organizing of petroleum workers. Oil workers themselves had had no effective national organization since the formation of the International Association of Oil Field, Gas Well & Refinery Workers of America during World War I. Most oil union locals operated with little representation or planning. It was not until the emergence of the National Industrial Recovery Act during the early years of the 1930s and the Oil Workers International Union (OWIU-CIO) during the late 1930s that Gulf Coast oil workers boasted stable union locals. The initial successes of the OWIU-CIO came during the World War II era. By the end of the war, the CIO had emerged as the single most important organization for refinery workers in the country and along the Texas Gulf Coast.[14]

White Local 228 in Port Neches is a good example of the impetus of this new era of oil unionization. Union activity among oil workers in Port Neches was severely limited until passage of the NIRA. Local 228 was originally chartered in September, 1933, with nearly 150 members. The organizers of Local

228 recruited heavily in the Port Neches area and held their first meeting at the Knights of Columbus Hall until a permanent union hall opened. Despite financial problems, unstable union membership, and unsubstantiated rumors of ties to a communist-led CIO, Local 228, some five years from its original charter, secured an agreement with its employer, the Pure Oil refinery.[15] Similarly, white Local 243 in Beaumont enjoyed the benefits of the NIRA and the CIO. Local 243 received its charter in October, 1933. This union consisted of mostly white refinery workers and a few black common laborers from the Magnolia plant. The jurisdiction of Local 243 was unclear. For many years it divided territory with 228 as the two unions occasionally covered each other's labor shortages during peak work periods. Local 243 worked for many years without a contract and did not receive one until a strike by its members forced Magnolia officials to produce a contract proposal.[16]

The NIRA and the CIO also created new opportunities for black oil workers to organize their workforce and to voice concerns about the labor practices of employers and white unionists. Fifteen years after black Local 39 was organized in Beaumont, little change had occurred in the discriminatory hiring and wage practices at the Magnolia refinery. By 1933, Local 39 had become Local 229 and assumed the role of the primary union for black oil workers in Beaumont. Its union leadership attempted to capitalize on the advantages of NIRA. Daniel C. Bromon, the outspoken leader of the union, appealed to the National Labor Board in December, 1934, about conditions at the refinery. The thrust of his complaint centered on the nearly five hundred black oil workers who were underpaid despite a minimum wage standard established by the NIRA wages code. Regardless of the occupation, "it's common labor if a colored man does it," Bromon argued. Few blacks ever obtained minimum pay even though they worked as painters, riggers, and cleaned out the coke of stills in unbearable heat.[17]

Biased supervisors at the Magnolia refinery exacerbated black worker resentment. "If he didn't like you, you got the dirty jobs and were more prone to lay-offs," one black oil worker insisted. Cleveland Nisby, a boilermaker helper, resented foremen who assigned blacks to the most dismal work. "You were completely at the mercy of your immediate supervisor." Black workers often shoveled oil-slicked floors on fume-filled tankers and were forced to work beyond eight hours a day without receiving overtime pay.[18] When it came to agitating for union recognition, black Local 229 represented one of the more active groups along the Gulf Coast during the thirties. By 1937 an all-out effort to organize black oil workers at the Magnolia refinery was un-

*Local 229 of the Oil Workers International Union was the first all-black union
at the Beaumont Magnolia Refinery. Members of the local struggled to
maintain their racially separate organization; photo ca. 1943.
Courtesy Oil Chemical and Atomic Workers Local 4-423
Beaumont, Texas.*

derway. Local 229 avoided company management and members of the company-controlled Employees Independent Union and held secret meetings in private homes, churches, and, at times, the NAACP headquarters, when they needed to rally black workers to discuss their concerns. Union organizing was nearly as difficult and dangerous as refinery work itself. "To become active in organized labor at that time," Nisby recalled, "meant that your life was threatened" by those who opposed black unionization.[19]

The 1930s provided an opportunity for blacks to expose the unfair hiring practices of Gulf Coast refineries. When Alex Joseph went to Washington to testify before the National Labor Board in 1934, he complained on behalf of black workers from Local 254—the first permanent black oil workers union to be formed in Port Arthur during the 1930s—about wage discrimination at Port Arthur refineries. "The only job classification for Negroes," Joseph lamented, "was common labor no matter what skilled work they did." Moreover, a black "poured concrete for $.38 an hour, but if a white man did it, he got $.20 to $.30 more." Black workers from 254 got a boost for their efforts when the CIO won a hard-fought battle to represent them in 1943. The road to the successful election was not an easy one for the CIO or its supporters since "every form of intimidation and trickery was used against them," by local police and company management.[20]

The changing nature of the labor movement during the 1930s offered white workers an opportunity to improve working relations with blacks. It was evident that some labor organizations had made concessions for the benefit of the labor movement. In April, 1938, Locals 229 and 243 filed a joint petition for union recognition with the NLRB. The two unions alleged that company representatives and members of its company union dominated and interfered with the formation and administration of labor organization at the plant. White Local 227 in Houston abandoned its long-standing practice of separating the races and admitted black members from the defunct black Local 244. It is not clear if Local 227 acted out of sympathy for unorganized black oil workers or from a desire to circumvent competition from nonunion labor. What is clear is that Local 227 became a significant force during the peak organizing years of the 1930s. Like many oil unions in the region, Local 227 resisted overtures from employers to form a company union, while it struggled to acquire recognition of its own union and others. Local 227 laid the basis for the formation of Local 367 in Pasadena. Unionists from Pasadena's Shell refinery had often complained about the great distance between the home office of Local 227 and the poor working conditions at the plant. Members from 367 responded to these concerns and helped organize a separate but equally integrated union.[21]

The amalgamation of black and white workers into integrated unions paid some dividends. A November, 1937, strike of nine hundred black and white oil workers from Local 367 at the Shell refinery provides yet another example of the support demonstrated by black oil workers toward the labor movement. The strike was called when the company delayed negotiations for a new contract. Several months had passed since workers operated under a legitimate agreement. Despite Shell's claims of an imminent agreement, workers forced management to close the plant by staging a walkout.[22]

Cooperation between the races at Shell reflected a growing trend in Gulf Coast refineries during the 1930s and early 1940s. Although white workers were reluctant to concede to racial equality and the advancement of nonwhite workers, the two groups seldom undermined each other's strike efforts. When black workers from Port Arthur Local 254 staged a work stoppage at the Texas Company refinery in the summer of 1945, they were assured by officials of nearby white locals that no white workers would fill their jobs. Instead, white unionists expressed hope that the Texas Company would not "embarrass itself by asking white union men to replace negro union men."[23]

Notwithstanding racial cooperation for unionization, union locals followed a pattern of racial stratification and discrimination. Upward mobility for black oil workers met with strong resistance from their white counterparts. "There's no question about it," John Crossland, a white unionist from the Shell Refinery Local 367 in Pasadena insisted. "The Negro was at a disadvantage. A lot of white membership . . . didn't want them to have a line of progression." The amalgamation of the races into biracial unions reduced the autonomy that blacks enjoyed in separate organizations. White workers from Local 367 strategically avoided dual unions and set up one biracial union to primarily serve the labor interests of white workers.[24] Despite its egalitarian claims, the CIO had done little to help blacks from Local 254 obtain jobs above the rank of janitor. Although the union started out strong in the early thirties with a membership of nearly two hundred workers, it quickly dwindled when blacks became discouraged about the racial hiring practices at the Gulf refinery. Blacks at the Gulf refinery were at the crossroads of their organizing careers and their union decisions carried far-reaching economic and employment implications. By 1936 the local reported only two paid members—although the number of nonactive members reached, by some accounts, over one thousand—and was in dire need of "new life" and for someone to send "some live men in" to reinvigorate the workers.[25]

While the CIO boasted about expanded unionization, it could not claim racial equality in Gulf Coast refineries. C. W. Rice, a known advocate of independent and company unions and opponent of the CIO, scolded supporters of the CIO-controlled OWIU and repudiated black oil workers who affiliated with the organization. He refused to credit the CIO with creating new job opportunities for black workers and instead lauded oil employers for making work available for blacks. His newspaper became a public relations tool for oil employers. Rice warned black oil workers about allying with white unions even though his own experiences reflected strong ties to the white community. Although Rice failed to mobilize black workers to his satisfaction, he refused to give in to labor unions. Rice faced an expanding labor movement that boasted large memberships during the 1930s and that set out to include groups typically excluded from other labor federations. The CIO that had been "shouting from the housetops about its race equality policy," Rice said, had failed to live up to its creed. When white unionists from the OWIU failed to speak on behalf of black participants at the 1938 OWIU convention held in the ballroom of a Jim Crow hotel that required blacks to use freight elevators instead of the guest elevators, it cleared the way for more of Rice's criticism and "caused much comment among the Negroes" about the CIO's commitment to fairness.[26]

Rice was just one of a few people who tried to curtail the CIO's organizing efforts in the oil refineries, but to no avail. The CIO oil organizing campaigns withstood the repudiation of its detractors, including local politicians, employers, and law enforcement. When Ewart Twine, a black CIO organizer, received his first paycheck from the Humble refinery in the fall of 1942, he was met by three deputy sheriffs at a nearby tavern who angrily challenged him about the large CIO buttons he was sporting on his hat. Despite the three bullets that sailed passed Twine, he refused to discard his union paraphernalia. It was not uncommon for Humble management to use local police to target labor organizers. Twine's efforts were in direct defiance of the plant's company union objectives. Humble resisted labor union organization and on occasion circulated bulletins to frighten white workers into believing that a vote for the CIO was tantamount to a "vote for absolute equality between the white and colored races on every job" in the Baytown refinery.[27]

Racial equality was not the main concern for employers and law enforcement in Port Arthur. Both rebuffed the CIO and in some instances stooped to threats and intimidation. Police chief H. F. Baker vowed to protect Port Arthur's Gulf refinery from the CIO. A native of Louisiana, Baker moved to Port Arthur in 1910. After many years spent in law enforcement and several years working at the Gulf refinery, he became a wealthy man as owner of Baker Independent Oil Producing Company. Baker's reign of terror as the city's chief of police placed the labor community under tremendous pressure. When CIO organizer F. H. Mitchell attempted to meet with Alex Joseph of Local 254 to discuss union activities, he was attacked and beaten by the chief and two of his officers. Baker made it known that there would be no "g— d— CIO in Port Arthur." Baker, a "notorious Negro-beater," inflicted so much fear among the black working class that only Alex Joseph dared testify about Mitchell's beating. On the eve of a 1943 NLRB-sponsored election, Baker and his men cruised the black sections of town, hurling threats at blacks who intended to vote and posting notices of a mandatory meeting between Baker and the black workers from the plant.[28]

The emergence of the NLRB gave new life to oil workers who had suffered from the inadequacies of the NIRA. Following several years of bickering with employers at the Magnolia refinery, white and black workers finally obtained union recognition through an NLRB-sponsored election in November, 1943, that gave its members a government-sanctioned charter and the first labor contract agreement in the company's history.[29]

The Magnolia contract included a 15 percent cost of living wage increase

*Police Chief H. F. Baker hounded CIO organizers and inflicted terror in the
black working-class communities. Courtesy Port Arthur History Center,
Port Arthur Public Library.*

and job security provisions. It created promotional charts for all lines of work
in each department and put an end to the arbitrary power of plant foremen
and management. It also established a grievance procedure, which included
negotiations between a union committee and a company committee as well
as remedies for overtime issues and safety and health standards.[30] The Magnolia contract was a bittersweet victory for black workers. Plant management
counteracted the apparent cooperation between the races and inexplicably
removed all black workers from semiskilled positions and concentrated them
into one department. Blacks who had worked as pipe fitters or boilermakers
found themselves digging ditches. Although they rarely received appropriate
pay or official job titles for performing these tasks, the demotion of the entire
black workforce to common labor jobs reflected a desperate attempt to undermine biracial unionism and the CIO.[31]

The impetus of the OWIU-CIO organizing campaign was evident in the
emergence of a sizeable number of biracial unions (see table 4). By the 1940s,
Local 229 and Local 254 were the only exclusively black oil unions along the

Upper Texas Gulf Coast. Both locals struggled to maintain their racially exclusive organizations as biracial unionism gained strength. Oil workers carried the momentum of their organizing successes well into the 1940s and refused to retreat from the gains they made. During the Great Strike of 1945, a time when oil workers throughout the country protested wage cuts as employers geared up for reduced production in a postwar economy, Locals 229 and 243 each went forward with their own agenda. As Cleveland Nisby put it, Local 229 "set out to bring about some real change" for black oil workers. Nisby and others demanded that the Magnolia Refinery reassign black workers to the jobs they lost from the 1943 Magnolia contract signing, open up positions for black truck drivers and riggers, and allocate equal pay for equal work between the races. It is not surprising that the Workmen's Committee, which was established to represent the grievances of every union member at the Magnolia plant, gave no attention to the complaints of these black unionists. As the labor movement gained strength and black workers became more aggressive about unionization, white workers intensified their efforts to maintain control of the job market.[32]

Fortunately for black oil unionists, the coming of World War II brought thousands of new workers to the industry who were young and more inclined to agitate against employers in the midst of widespread wartime employment discrimination. Minorities comprised about 2,200 workers or 6 percent of the Texas refinery workforce during this time. Nearly 90 percent of all black

Table 4. Oil Worker Unions, Biracial and Black,
along the Upper Texas Gulf Coast, 1930s

	Biracial	*Black*
Baytown	Local 333	
Beaumont	Local 243	Local 229
Goose Creek	Local 21	
	Local 85	
Guffy	Local 33	
Houston	Local 227	
	Local 94	
Pasadena	Local 367	
Port Arthur		Local 254
Port Neches	Local 228	
Texas City	Local 436	

and Mexican oil workers in Texas worked along the Upper Texas Gulf Coast.[33] The Humble refinery in Baytown recorded approximately 5,300 workers of which 484 were black. The company also employed about 100 Mexicans. The Gulf refinery in Port Arthur employed 3,000 workers and reported a black workforce of 800. In Beaumont's Magnolia refinery, blacks comprised about 500 of the company's 2,300 workers. The Sinclair refinery, located in Pasadena, employed around 1,500 workers. Their workforce included 250 blacks and 100 Mexicans. The Shell Oil Company maintained a large plant in Deer Park and employed around 1,800 laborers, including 140 blacks and approximately 30 Mexicans.[34]

Minorities, however, held few white-collar, professional, and managerial positions throughout much of the 1940s. Most oil companies used nonwhites primarily to meet their demand for unskilled labor. Approximately 77 percent of nonwhite workers held common laborer jobs that required them to perform much of the heavy physical work. A few black craftsmen worked as bricklayers, masons, and plasterers. Generally, labor contracts and social customs blatantly segregated blacks and Mexicans and prohibited them from progressing in the petroleum industry. Minorities rarely obtained employment in the pipeline and production areas, and employers usually paid lower wages to blacks and Mexicans than whites with comparable classification.[35]

The oil industry denied blacks and Mexicans occupational mobility and subjected minorities to segregated workplaces. Despite the increase of blacks and Mexicans in the industry, the two races failed to eradicate racial inequities. "For years," the *Houston Informer* reported, "Negroes had no place in the oil industry except as teamsters and other roustabout people." Black workers accepted physical separation but rejected wage discrimination. Mexicans, on the other hand, opposed segregation altogether and called for full integration.

Mexicans, as did blacks, entered the World War II era with an unprecedented opportunity to alter their traditional position as low-wage earners and to change a tradition of occupational discrimination. The few gains that blacks enjoyed in the oil industry during World War II generally resulted from the persistent agitation of the Mexican political and labor community. Mexican activists and Mexican oil workers engendered a few workplace improvements as they took advantage of an aggressive Mexican consulate and forceful leadership that channeled its energies and resources toward local and federal government, which resulted in a few modest gains for both black and Mexican workers.[36]

Black workers began early in the twentieth century to establish themselves as a vital component in the oil unions along the Upper Texas Gulf Coast. To a large extent, social norms encouraged subordination. Blacks workers were not as concerned about segregation as they were about unfair treatment. They worked to fulfill their longing for workplace equality and mobility. The oil boom along the Upper Texas Gulf Coast cleared the way for the growth of black unionism in the industry as well as increased activity in secondary industries. Black workers at the Hughes Tool Company in Houston not only benefitted from the jobs that the oil boom created for them, but they also took advantage of the assertive actions of black workers in related industries and embarked upon their own journey toward union representation and equal treatment.

CHAPTER 5

"FREE OF COMPANY DOMINATION"

Steelworkers Look Inward

THE OIL BOOM along the Upper Texas Gulf Coast cleared the way for the growth of black unionism in secondary industries and specialized manufacturing plants. The Hughes Tool Company in Houston capitalized on the expansion of the oil economy and, during the first half of the twentieth century, became the premier producer of oil drilling equipment for the region's oil companies. Hughes Tool also manufactured oil tools, which included much of the equipment capable of extracting crude oil from the earth, drill pipes, tool joints, rotary rock bits, valves, and blowout preventers. Black workers, as in other Upper Texas Gulf Coast industries, gravitated to Hughes Tool and initiated a drive to gain equal access to jobs and union representation. The history of black unionists at Hughes provides an example of the vitality and versatility of black workers in the labor movement. While some supported company-sponsored unions, others followed bona fide labor unions. The choices they made about representation were influenced by the racial policies at the plant, their relationship with white unionists, and the agitation fostered by black elites. White unionists at Hughes Tool could not ignore the resolve of black workers to organize their workforce. The push by black steelworkers to exercise their right of representation, despite the wage and occupational constraints placed before them, reflected their desire to resist workplace domination and control by white workers and company management. Autonomy played an important part in the organizing strategies of black workers, and, as they grappled for equal standing in the plant, they leveraged their union vote for representation.[1]

The Hughes Tool Company was founded by Howard Hughes, Sr., an oil drilling contractor who purchased the rights to a revolutionary drilling bit from Granville A. Humanson for $150 in 1909 and quickly turned his company into the primary national and international manufacturer and supplier

Black workers at Hughes Tool were relegated to yard work during the early years of the plant's operation; photo ca. 1917. Courtesy Houston Metropolitan Research Center, Houston Public Library.

of bits and equipment for the petroleum industry. The Hughes Company enjoyed continuous growth during the first four decades of the twentieth century. The Hughes Tool workforce increased from fifteen in 1913 to nearly sixty-five by 1920. As the number of employees grew, labor concerns surfaced, and the company responded with an attempt to organize its workers.[2]

Hughes Tool organized its first company union in 1918 in the midst of an era dominated by company unions. Employers throughout the nation attempted to undercut labor unions by forming their own organizations and placing them under tight managerial control. Welfare capitalism became a popular type of employer concession in their dealings with workers during the 1920s. Hughes Tool's initial attempt to galvanize its workers involved the creation of an employee welfare program. It followed the antiunion policy of the American Iron and Steel Institute (AISI). In 1919 the company adopted the AISI's American Plan of Employment as a model for the company's worker benefit program. The company implemented the American plan and assumed total control of wages and working conditions. Hughes established the Employee Welfare Organization (EWO), which gave rise to the Employee Representation Plan (ERP), and offered welfare benefits such as health care, life insurance, and burial services to its employees. The American Plan provided a range of benefits for steelworkers and allowed employers to counteract the organizing drives of labor unions. Howard Hughes, Jr., who took over the plant following his father's death in 1924, created a "separate but equal" welfare organization or company union in 1926. Jim Crow labor policies at Hughes Tool prevented black workers from enjoying equal benefits.[3]

Hughes Tool's management and its white workers collaborated to main-

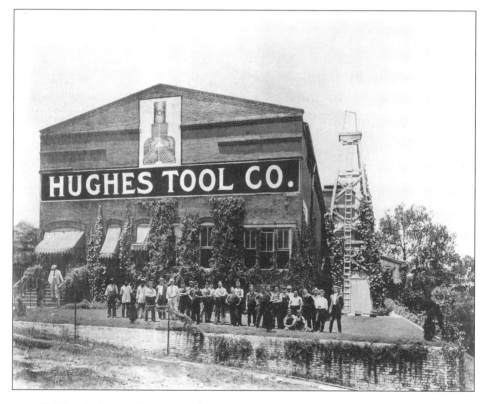

Black and white workers at Hughes Tool participated in the plant's company union during the 1920s; photo ca. 1921. Courtesy Houston Metropolitan Research Center, Houston Public Library.

During the 1930s and 1940s, one of the jobs reserved for blacks was charging furnaces in the Heat Treat Department. Courtesy Houston Metropolitan Research Center, Houston Public Library.

tain racial and economic control at the plant. They devised a job classification system to accommodate white workers and also created the Hughes Tool Colored Club (HTCC) to appease blacks. Despite the establishment of the HTCC, the company restricted the occupational mobility of its black workers, who were relegated to brooms, wheelbarrows, furnace work, and other common-labor jobs while whites occupied machine jobs, superior labor grades, and maintained better pay and rank.[4]

Fearing the encroachment of outside unions into the affairs of the company's labor policies, Hughes Tool Company President R. C. Kuldell worked to uphold the antilabor union views of the company and initiated efforts to have the HTCC play a more active role in the company's contract talks. By the late 1920s and early 1930s Kuldell had encouraged his officers to correspond with the leaders of the HTCC and to solicit their advice on how to improve conditions for black workers. More importantly, Kuldell wanted to resist attempts by labor unions to organize black workers. Because blacks made up almost 25 percent of Hughes's workforce, the company's management carefully examined the effect that a black labor union would have on its operations.[5]

Kuldell solicited the help of Richard Guess, a black conservative who rarely criticized the company's Jim Crow policy. Guess became the ideal person to head the HTCC, because management found him reliable and trustworthy. The company recognized Guess as one of the leading spokesmen for black workers. Guess often spoke on behalf of the black workforce at high-level company meetings, and he relied on the support of coworkers to defend him in his dealings with company management. According to the sometimes-biased *Negro Labor News,* black workers rallied around Guess and were "determined to stick together and bargain collectively with employers" and pay their club dues instead of sending them "to some big office to be paid to high union officials."[6]

Meetings between Guess, Kuldell, and members of the HTCC produced a variety of discussions that included a proposal to increase financial aid, legal counsel, and continued management supervision of black workers. The workers kept tabs on the much-heralded burial fund, which provided pay for funeral services of deceased members. The HTCC produced annual financial reports and from 1936 to 1937 paid out over $12,000 in loans, sick claims, charity, and burials. The HTCC's financial records could be called into question since the $12,000 that the *Negro Labor News* reported in July, 1937, inexplicably increased to $30,000 by September of the same year.[7] The agreement between the HTCC and the company allowed management to retain control over racial policy, work productivity, and seniority rights. During times of work reduction, the company reserved the right to retain certain workers while relieving others, regardless of years of experience. Despite the numerous concessions between the HTCC and the company, blacks still worked for less pay than whites and had to endure a two-year waiting period from the date of their employment before they became eligible for the company's life insurance plan. Whites on the other hand were required to wait six months.[8]

The agreement between the HTCC and Hughes management did little to improve the day-to-day working conditions for black workers, who eventually turned against Guess and the HTCC. Freeman Everett, a general organizer of black workers along the Upper Texas Gulf Coast, stirred up much of the commotion when he ridiculed the HTCC for its collaboration with company management. Everett rejected the HTCC's claim of being an independent union that was free of company control. Because outside organizers such as Everett carried much clout and influence, HTCC members lashed back when attempts were made to discredit their organization. Fred T. Williams, a member of the HTCC, responded at length to Everett's claim. "In regards to your statement," Williams addressed Everett, "we wish to challenge you to prove your statement. Our organization," Williams continued, "is free of company domination. Our minutes, bank records, and work agreement are ample proof that we are not dominated by the union."[9]

Williams's claim that the HTCC was free from company control was inconsistent with the plant's 1937 labor agreement with its workers. Although the contract agreed not to discriminate against members and nonmembers of particular labor organizations, it was clear that the company recognized the EWO and the HTCC, two organizations that the company formed, as the "sole bargaining agency for the white employees of the plant" and "colored employees of the plant." Despite its willingness to listen to other organizations, the plant used the agreement between the EWO and the HTCC as the model for the entire workforce. "We believe the experience of the past three years," the contract stated, "indicates that this plan will work to the satisfaction of the great majority of the employees and the company." Thus, the company continued to prod for substantial input in contracts and insisted on maintaining control over wages, overtime pay, rates of production, holidays, vacations, grievances, hiring, company functions, and seniority. The company, for example, still controlled "all hiring and discharging" through its personnel department and reserved the "right to select from each hundred men thus to be laid off . . . irrespective of seniority" during periods of employment cutbacks.[10]

Supporters of the company union worked to undermine the growing competition that labor unions posed. Following addresses by George O. Duncan, the HTCC's publicity director, and its president, Richard Guess, in September, 1938, who spoke to a group of loyal members about their choices of representation, the HTCC held a mock election. The "100 per cent against affiliating with the CIO" vote they bragged about afterward served as a confidence booster, although it did not include the vote or input of members who had already defected to other unions.[11]

High-ranking whites who warred against labor unions sought out blacks such as Guess to participate in important political functions and presented them as the conscience of black unionism along the Gulf Coast. Guess, for example, was "the only Negro union official attending the hearing on the confirmation of . . . labor commissioner" in Texas in 1939. Although he was scheduled to speak to the state's labor committee, Guess was advised that "the committee would not have time for further oral testimonies and that his telegraphic messages and letter from his union," which he had sent prior to his arrival, were placed on record and satisfied the labor commission as an endorsement from black unionists.[12]

The economic crisis of the 1930s, coupled with the changing nature of the labor movement, compelled black workers at Hughes Tool to direct their attention away from the HTCC and Guess and look toward the organizing opportunities presented by the NLRB and the CIO. The CIO posed serious challenges to the HTCC and fueled much of the in-fighting that surfaced among black workers. By the late 1930s a segment of the black workforce welcomed the CIO to recruit within their ranks. Allison "Bud" Alton hired in at Hughes Tool in 1936 as a tool helper, and he immediately joined the HTCC. Within a few years, however, Alton became attracted to the CIO and its talk of racial equality. "The only way we could have a real union," Alton claimed, "apart from the company union was to organize into with the CIO." Even though the NLRB helped workers to organize into new unions, the agency did little to help blacks fight racial inequities. Black workers, Alton contended, continued to strive to improve unequal working conditions. "We had fighters trying to improve the status of black people. There were no real learned people at the plant," but most of them understood the awkward tension between union loyalty and race pride.[13]

When the Steel Workers Organizing Committee (SWOC) filed an NLRB complaint against the HTCC in the fall of 1939, it exposed the organization as a company union, which by the late 1930s had been outlawed by the federal government. Created in June, 1936, by John L. Lewis and led by Philip Murray, the SWOC worked tenaciously to organize steelworkers throughout the country. The SWOC organizing drives focused new attention on race relations between white and black workers and the necessity of racial participation during labor's critical years. The SWOC realized that the stability of steelworker unions relied largely on their ability to include black workers on an equal basis. Inclusion, however, did not always improve the occupational mobility of blacks. Instead, it simply provided protection for black workers against employer-imposed unions. The creation of the SWOC marked a decisive step in the ascendency of the CIO as a prominent force in the rise of southern black unionism in the steel industry despite the fact that many black steelworkers remained trapped in low-wage jobs and Jim Crow and racism cluttered most union shops.[14] In Birmingham, Alabama, for instance, the SWOC, under the leadership of William Mitch, encouraged interracial unionism in its steel locals although white racism and prejudice formed a big obstacle for SWOC organizers. As one white steelworker lamented, "I'm not going to join your damn nigger organization." By 1937 the SWOC had sent organizers to Houston to organize the workforce at Hughes Tool as well as many other oil-tool producing companies. Despite criticism from white unionists, the SWOC established an integrated union for black and white workers and quickly formed a biracial contract committee to redress labor policy and racial discrimination at the plant. This, of course, disturbed the opponents of the CIO, who viewed the establishment of the biracial Local 1742 as the "worst type of dictatorship" to penetrate the union ranks.[15]

The much-anticipated NLRB ruling rejected the HTCC's claims of being an independent union having no ties to management. The NLRB ordered Hughes Tool Company to discontinue its relationship and contract talks with the HTCC. The labor board declared that the compulsory deduction of dues taken from the wages of workers who belonged to the company union facilitated an unfair advantage for Hughes Tool. The company, the board assented, had "dominated and interfered with the administration of the EWO . . . and the HTC Club" when it furnished meeting rooms, extended printing privileges, and "contributed financial and other support" to its union activities.[16]

The NLRB ruling disappointed members of the company union, and some members refused to accept the decision. The HTCC, with the support of C. W. Rice, who maintained that the HTCC offered blacks the best opportunity to exercise a measure of influence in shaping labor policy, defied the NLRB and continued holding company-sponsored elections. The company refused to recognize any organization except the HTCC as the sole bargaining agent for black workers during contract negotiations. Rice continued his propaganda war against the CIO and ridiculed the federation for "trying to scare colored Hughes Tool workers into joining the CIO" with fake contracts and bogus promises.[17]

Both advocates and opponents of the HTCC hurled charges of unfairness and unethical activities in the dispute over representation. Each side accused the other of betrayal. As the stakes for control of Hughes's black workforce intensified, black editors surfaced in the feuding, and they used their newspapers as tools to voice their support and objections to the affairs at the plant. Carter Wesley claimed personal victory in a February, 1940, article when he bragged about the NLRB's ruling. The NLRB decision, Wesley boasted, had finally exposed how Rice had "been deceiving the people" into believing that the HTCC was a legitimate labor union. Richard Guess, however, charged Carter Wesley with being the biggest "sell out" of black unionists, misrepresenting facts about the HTCC in his newspaper editorials. "I do not doubt the ability of Mr. Carter Wesley as a newspaper man or journalist but I do doubt if he knows as much about labor problems," Guess said of Wesley. Guess insisted that many blacks at Hughes opted to join the HTCC because they held little faith in racist labor unions that, as Fred Williams, a Guess supporter, contended, had "practically no influence in Texas politics."[18]

At times, the squabbling over union representation at Hughes Tool escalated into verbal assaults and violence. The factionalism demonstrated the widening gap between those who supported the HTCC and those who advocated labor unions. Insults and abusive language consumed a Third Ward Civic Club labor forum in Houston, for example, when Guess accused Wesley of misrepresenting information regarding the organizing of black workers at Hughes. "You might know law and how to run a paper," Guess scolded, "but you certainly don't understand labor and union conditions as they affect Hughes Tool workers." George O. Duncan, a Hughes Tool worker, also started a tuss with the editor when he "looked directly at Wesley[,] . . . shook his finger," and assured him that black workers at Hughes refused "to be led up the blind alley by a man who has a reputation of cheating the cheaters, robbing the robbers, swindling the swindlers and back biting the backbiters." Duncan's disparaging remarks nearly instigated a fist-fight between the two men. No punches were thrown, but the newspaper editor walked away from the meeting when Hughes Tool workers attempted to circle him. Wesley nearly incited yet another riot at an HTCC meeting when he flaunted a letter that the CIO had been circulating among Hughes Tool workers denouncing the HTCC. The flyers made reference to an NLRB ruling that concluded that Hughes Tool management had colluded with the HTCC to halt outside unionization.[19]

The HTCC made several attempts to undermine the CIO's propaganda drives with its own public disclaimers about the legitimacy of its union. It often slanted its propaganda to gain public support and attempted to gain control of the black workforce by maneuvering supporters of the CIO back into positions of power within the HTCC. In order to avoid disobeying the

NLRB's declaration outlawing company-controlled unions, members of the HTCC still presented their organization as a union in which the company had little if any input or authority. When the HTCC boasted of their "right to an independent union" and that "the HTC Club is truly independent," they neglected to explain the extent of the controlling influence Hughes Tool management had in the creation of the union or on contract agreements.[20]

The in-fighting over union representation elevated the stature of the CIO but did not help to significantly alter the racial practices of the company. The 1941 contract between Hughes Tool and its workers, aside from a few insignificant changes, generally reflected past agreements. Disparities between the wages and rank of black and white workers remained intact. By 1941 Hughes Tool employed approximately 3,787 hourly workers. Eight-hundred-and-six blacks worked at the plant by then. Although blacks worked in all major production departments, they held only 26 of the company's 270 skilled jobs. Hughes divided its six production units—machine shop, pattern shop, foundry, heat treat, shipping, and storeroom—into different pay brackets based on specific occupations. Employers designated higher-paying skilled jobs for whites and relegated nonskilled, dirty, and menial work to blacks. The company drew a clear distinction between "white men's jobs" and "Negro jobs," and no worker of either race crossed the line. Hughes restricted blacks to three levels within each unit. The lowest job classification and pay for whites generally equalled the highest for blacks. The minimum beginner's wage for white workers was $.45 per hour and for black workers it started at $.40 per hour.[21]

During the early stages of the CIO's organizing activities at Hughes Tool, the federation offered rhetorical challenges to the discriminatory conditions that existed at Hughes Tool. The CIO took a firm position in accordance with its nondiscriminatory policy and, for some time, would not organize rebellious and racist white workers who refused to work under conditions that made black workers their equals. Deferring to the demands of black workers in a racially divided workplace often engendered negative reactions from white unionists. Every time the CIO had an election, Maurice Easterwood recalled, "other unions would file for representation and there were a lot of hard feelings when you lost an election," and none, Easterwood claimed, made it without the support of black workers. "As whites divided their votes, African Americans, seeking relief from discrimination, as much as possible, sought to unite theirs."[22]

Table 5. Hughes Tool Company Departments, Segregated Pay Grades
and Pay Scales, Effective March 1, 1941

Dept.	No. of White Pay Grades	Pay Scales for Whites	No. of Black Pay Grades	Pay Scales for Blacks
Machine shop	6	$.65–1.28	3	$.48–.62
Pattern shop	4	$.80–1.30	1	$.54
Foundry	4	$.80–1.00	3	$.48–.60
Heat Treat	1	$1.08	2	·$.54–.60
Shipping Dept.	3	$.74–.87	3	$.48–.62
Storeroom	N.A.	N.A.	3	$.48–.62

Source: Botson, "Organized Labor at the Hughes Tool Company," p. 53; Botson,
"Jim Crow Wearing Steel-Toed Shoes," p. 105.

The eventual elimination of the HTCC had the potential to unite black unionists at the plant, but the situation grew more tense when several hundred black and white unionists, many from the all-but-defunct HTCC and EWO, rejected the CIO and refused to join its integrated local. After demonstrating they held no affiliation with management, the workers eventually filed for an NLRB-sponsored union election. After out-voting the SWOC-CIO 1,601 to 950, the NLRB awarded two new racially separate unions in August, 1941, as the sole bargaining agents at the plant.[23] Jim Crow customs and the defection of both black and white workers to the Independent Metal Workers Union (IMWU) created a major obstacle for the SWOC-CIO. Its insistence on having an integrated union challenged the tradition of racial segregation and stirred up more animosity, particularly among white unionists and the black middle class who advocated maintaining dual unions. Rice supported the idea of having racially separate union locals within the IMWU. Although he typically called for blacks to organize their rank-and-file workers apart from labor unions, he accepted the IMWU as the closest thing to a company union he could hope for.[24]

Notwithstanding the efforts to bolster its racial agenda, the SWOC was compelled to compromise its organizing plan and silence its critics, while at the same time protecting its black membership. When the SWOC chartered black Local 2457 to serve as the brother local to the white-led Local 1742 during the fall of 1941, it demonstrated that the CIO had reevaluated its racial equality plan and renewed its efforts to regain a favorable position among Hughes's workforce. Both black and white unionists from the SWOC voted to segregate the union in order to curtail a wholesale departure of workers to the IMWU.[25]

The newly formed IMWU, which in essence was the rebirth of the HTCC and the EWO, refused to allow old wounds to heal when it charged the CIO with intimidating and interfering with the rights of employees to vote for the labor organization of their own choosing. It charged the CIO with failing to improve working conditions for blacks and warned their members about its failed racial equality scheme. White unionists from the IMWU were equally remiss in their commitment to black workers after they demanded separate contract talks with the company, refused to include black Local No. 2 in its official charter, and blocked it from obtaining one of its own. Nonetheless, black unionists from the newly formed IMWU wasted little time promoting its cause and rallying its rank-and-file workers. Guess, former president of the HTCC and a new member of the IMWU, charged that the typical "CIO organizer or otherwise trouble maker, continued to mislead IMWU workers . . . by making them believe they have no seniority rights" or any input in the company's labor policy. In April, 1942, Local No. 2 held a mass meeting and intended to set the record straight when they presented what they considered to be "the real facts" about the IMWU's agenda. Albert Baker, a member of the grievance committee, addressed the throng and boasted about the amicable relationship they had with company management. Baker's assertion that "the IMWU Local does not go in for propaganda, . . . and false statements" was a direct reference to the CIO's continued active pursuit of the Hughes Tool workforce. "This union is pledged to do all business in an honest and upright manner," Baker insisted.[26]

The exclusionary practices of the IMWU, and not its dual-union policy, posed the biggest problem for the organization. Although the SWOC, which became the United Steel Workers of America (USWA), decided to split its membership into two locals, the organization allowed its workers to have equal representation and participation in union activities. Both races held seats on grievance committees. The black local, although not formally chartered, also participated in all decisions affecting jobs, wages, hours of work, and working conditions. In sum, the USWA's segregated unions provided greater opportunities for blacks than did the rigid constraints placed upon them by the IMWU. The CIO remained vigilant as it struggled to regain bargaining rights at the plant. The USWA conducted an intense recruiting drive among new hires and pursued vulnerable IMWU workers. By the summer of 1942, the USWA claimed it had acquired nearly 56 percent of the Hughes workforce.[27] All the commotion around union representation was not enough for the union to include several hundred women, who had attempted to take advantage of increased wartime employment when they applied for jobs, in the equation. It was "much to do about nothing," the *Informer* reported. All the excitement about women being hired at the plant sparked anticipation that women employees might be used to bolster union membership. Instead, the company admitted that they only intended to hire the women as maids to clean lavatories.[28]

The USWA's majority claim coupled with a soon-to-expire IMWU contract ignited rumors about yet another election. Workers at the plant learned as early as July, 1942, that the CIO intended to apply for a new election. As word of the impending election began to leak, leaders from the IMWU stonewalled when the CIO, convinced that workers from the IMWU were defecting, asked for a head count of its members and a "check off" of union dues. When the IMWU refused to divulge any membership figures, several workers from the CIO, including E. M. Martin, Henry Robinson, A. Van Winn, and Johnny LaBoue pleaded with Hugh Potter, who had been sent by the NLRB to investigate the complaints at the plant, for release of membership rolls. A few days after the documents were released to the NLRB office in Fort Worth, workers from the CIO sat through a pep talk given by J. E. Clayton, a school principal from Houston and government organizer of farm workers. Clayton cautioned workers from the CIO to be wary of imposter labor unions such as the IMWU and "line up with a bonafide national union."[29]

Following several months of wrangling, the Hughes election finally took place. After three days of voting in December, 1942, the NLRB declared a narrow victory for the USWA and granted the organization exclusive bargaining rights. Suspicious workers from the IMWU—who claimed that the 142 votes that separated the two organizations was, by their standards, an embarrassing victory for the CIO—accused the federation of resorting to ruthless tactics when they hired Richard R. Grovey, a popular black Houston barber and part-time labor organizer to visit the homes of black IMWU workers and urge their family members to persuade their husbands and fathers to join up with the CIO.[30] The election outcome was a victory for the IMWU. Considering the national reputation of the CIO and its financial advantages, the close election, the IMWU insisted, indicated that the USWA had run a poor organizing campaign. Although the vote count was not calculated by race, Local No. 2 charged that the CIO owed its victory to the white workers because the federation had only garnered 1 black vote for every 11 black workers.[31]

Despite losing the election, Local No. 2 held a "victory celebration" at the Catholic Hall in Houston and discussed their intentions of pursing more members with the sole purpose of one day defeating the CIO and regaining bargaining rights for the Hughes Tool workforce. Black members of the CIO held their own victory party a few days later at the same location. The CIO banquet presented a unique opportunity for the members of the two unions to resolve some of their differences when Joe Henderson and James Cooper, two members of Local No. 2, accepted an invitation to attend the CIO function. Attempts at reconciliation soured, however, when the banquet ran out of food just as the men arrived.[32]

Despite modest attempts to patch up their strained relationship with the CIO, black loyalists from the IMWU Local No. 2 refused to accept CIO jurisdiction and instead clung to their independent union allegiances. Their obstinance exacerbated competition for control over Hughes Tool workers and brought on more disputes between the CIO and IMWU supporters. The IMWU feared that surrendering to "white CIO" bosses hundreds of miles away would squander their autonomy. Members of the IMWU also disputed the CIO's claim of having an evenly divided biracial contract committee. The *Negro Labor News* reported that the committee actually consisted of twelve whites and seven blacks. The disproportionate number of white members to black members, the *Labor News* implied, gave white unionists an edge during contract negotiations.[33] One of the biggest misunderstandings between the two groups centered around bargaining rights and the freedom of workers to join any union of their choice. The IMWU had often accused the CIO of misleading workers into believing that once a union victory was declared and sole bargaining rights were established, workers were obligated to join the victorious union. The IMWU wanted to make it clear that workers were free to join any union they desired.[34]

CIO unionists became particularly disturbed when IMWU supporters refused to give in to defeat. When the Reverend L. V. Bolton, a black preacher from the Mount Corinth Baptist Church and employee of the Hughes Tool Company barged into the office of Rice in January, 1943, he demonstrated that some black unionists would not hesitate to resort to violence against those who supported the independent union. Wielding a "Texas Jack knife," Bolton vented his anger toward Rice after the editor, he claimed, had published several articles accusing the minister of issuing numerous "hot checks" to area merchants. Rice, however, remained convinced that the confrontation was instigated by "a labor union controversy" involving union representation. Rice had denounced the CIO's efforts to organize the company's black workforce while Bolton advocated the federation's labor campaign.[35] Although Rice had been cordial enough to print positive editorials about Bolton's church revivals and functions and often lauded the minister for his community contributions, guest appearances at banquets, and for being "one of the best and most widely known pastors in Houston," he nonetheless filed criminal assault charges against Bolton. Rice refused to let Bolton go "scotfree." To do so, Rice insisted, would amount to an "invitation to disregard and disrespect the sanctity of my private office and home."[36]

The 1943 contract agreement between CIO Locals 1742 and 2457 and the company, aside from including several blacks on the negotiating team, ended wage discrimination, eradicated contractual occupational segregation, and made no reference to race in its language. For the first time in the company's history, pay equities between the races were granted. Although the CIO enjoyed the benefit of negotiating the labor contract at the plant and conceded that workers were free to join either union, their troubles were far from over. The IMWU picked away at the CIO's jurisdiction by sending its own grievance committee members to meet with management and convinced the company to deduct union dues from its members' wages. When members of the USWA filed a petition with the War Labor Board, a government agency that awarded defense contracts, they intended to have the federal government intervene on their behalf and restrain the Hughes Tool Company from meeting with the IMWU.[37]

The membership and contractual inroads made by the CIO perhaps engendered feelings of paranoia among IMWU members. Having learned from the strong drive of the CIO on early campaigns, the IMWU resorted to desperate measures, the *Houston Informer* reported. The one-year contract of the USWA was nearing expiration and both organizations as well as the company redoubled their efforts to promote their own interests. The IMWU again claimed a majority membership and kept the pressure on the CIO. Plant management, which had for some time demonstrated its bias toward the CIO, got involved when it challenged an NLRB extension of the existing CIO contract. Although the CIO agreement had expired in April, 1944, the war created unique circumstances and wartime production for the federal government took precedent over the contractual ambitions of the company. The NLRB refused to hear arguments for a new election and instructed the company to meet only with the grievance committee from the CIO and to stop deducting dues from the paychecks of IMWU workers. The NLRB directive effectively depleted the coffers of the organization. When the CIO accused the IMWU union leaders of forging the names of CIO members, it ignited another flurry over the maintenance of its membership and raised suspicion about the company's unauthorized deduction of union dues. CIO workers were practically on the verge of an all-out revolt, the *Negro Labor News* reported, when their paychecks came up short. The missing pay presented an opportunity for the IMWU and company to embarrass their adversary.[38]

When a gathering of several hundred IMWU workers, who vowed to disobey the election results and regain their control of the plant, convened at a mass meeting in June, 1944, they voiced their discontent about "working without a contract" and denounced the CIO as a "do nothing and trouble making" organization that shortchanged its workers on their pay. "We read in the paper and listen to flowery speeches," Albert Baker, who was quite familiar with run-ins with the USWA, insisted, "about what the CIO is doing for Negroes up north and the no discriminatory policy which is headlined in the newspapers. I wish some of these people would come out to Hughes Tool and see what a mess the workers are in."[39]

While the IMWU flayed the USWA, the CIO responded with its own form of retaliation. The shooting that took place around the home of Albert Baker perhaps resulted from the swirling rumors about the company allowing Baker, a black IMWU member, to hold two jobs and work overtime while some CIO workers were refused overtime work and others remained laid off from their jobs. The extent to which CIO members would go to bring attention to the battle over representation at Hughes Tool was equally evident when the workers from the USWA locals defied the political wartime interests of the government and made their own labor demands a priority when they called a strike in June, 1944, to protest the missing pay and a litany of other concerns. It soon discovered, however, that the government was in no mood to have wartime production interrupted. Because the company played an important role during World War II in manufacturing aircraft struts, rock bits, tool joints, coil bits, valves, and other miscellaneous parts for the army and navy, the work stoppage created an uproar in Washington, D.C., and "it appeared certain that President Roosevelt would enter the dispute and maybe take over the company." The CIO called off its strike when most of its black members refused to walk out with the union. The threat of a government takeover jolted several members of the CIO, who had operated under the assumption that their work stoppage threatened the defense contract of the company and that the federal government would not seize control of the plant, thus clearing the way for the plant's management to negotiate a new contract before the termination of the existing one.[40]

The USWA found it difficult to repair its damaged reputation among its black members following the paycheck fiasco. The USWA distributed circulars throughout the plant and encouraged black and white workers to attend separate special meetings. When the workers discovered that the meetings were set up to discuss a possible strike, skepticism surfaced and a segment of the membership, still fuming from their loss of pay during the first walk-out, voiced their reluctance to get involved in yet another risky strike.[41]

The squabbling at Hughes presented enough concern for the War Department to turn over the plant's day-to-day operations to the army. A group of army officers arrived at the plant in early September, 1944, and notified company officials that they were taking over immediately. The seizure order was signed by the president, which gave the Secretary of War authority to move in. Army specialists from the Division of Air Technical Services were placed in command. Members of the IMWU seemed most distraught about the takeover and characterized the seizure as an un-American act. The seizure of the plant by the government, they felt, was "unwarranted, unjust, and unprovoked by any action on the part of the workers of the company and can serve no useful purpose." Government occupation at Hughes lessened the possibility of a new election and thus reduced the chances of a new bargaining agreement; this perhaps explains why CIO workers were "happy to have the government take over." Undoubtedly, the mass meeting for black steelworkers organized by CIO Local 2457 and its Ladies Auxiliary at Pleasant Hill Baptist Church October 1, 1944, was called to address the dire circumstances at Hughes. E. M. Martin, a long-time CIO organizer in Houston and president of the local, and Frank A. Hardesty, regional director for the steelworkers, delivered inspirational talks about the essential role that the CIO had played in organizing steel plants and in improving working conditions in the region. Hardesty avoided implicating the CIO in the government takeover but made a strong appeal for union loyalty during the crisis.[42]

Both organizations used the event to undermine the other's credibility and to promote their own organizing agenda. While the CIO welcomed the decision of the government to extend its contract and require workers to maintain their existing union memberships, they still feared the exodus of many of its workers who refused to forgive the federation for failing to recoup their lost wages. Despite the CIO's claim that the government had stepped in to increase wages and pay back wages, it became clear that they had arrived to carry out an executive presidential directive to extend an old contract and circumvent labor disputes and work stoppages.[43]

When the black CIO steelworkers gathered at yet another meeting at St. Nicholas Hall in late October, 1945, they had done so to breathe a sigh of relief over the army's withdrawal from the plant and to discuss the union's prospects for renewed negotiations with the company. The CIO had always contended that its union was entitled to the sole bargaining rights at the plant, with or without army occupation. Wesley, who often appeared at CIO meetings, defended the CIO's position during the trying days of the government takeover. He blamed Hughes management for telling "dangerous half-truths which makes the company almost guilty of telling a deliberate untruth." Wesley became disturbed when Hughes management refused to honor the government mandate that required them to deduct union dues from the paychecks of CIO workers and forward them to CIO headquarters. Instead, the company continued to credit the IMWU with these dues despite the fact that some workers never officially joined the organization. The company operated on the premise that they had no special obligation to obey the mandate, because, in its opinion, the IMWU rhetorically claimed the largest membership and deserved to be recognized as the bargaining agent at the plant. Wesley rebuked the IMWU—or, as he put it, the "goblin of fear"—for its demagogic attempt to control the direction of union representation through a campaign of misinformation, which frightened Hughes Tool workers into believing that the CIO promoted racial discord by making promises about racial equality it could not and did not intend to keep. Regardless of the CIO's motives, Wesley concluded, the federation operated as a "lawful organization," while the IMWU, he insisted, amounted to nothing more than a company-controlled union attempting to deceive unionists into joining an organization that went against the spirit of the American labor movement.[44]

The failure of the IMWU to convince the government to see things its way can be attributed in part to the anti–company union sentiment that had emerged during the 1930s. Thus, the battle for representation rights at the Hughes Tool Company reached a point of near obsession with most workers at the plant and was driven as much by labor ideology as it was by concerns over fair and just representation. The bickering, mudslinging, and name-calling among black unionists that permeated the plant not only took precedence over the United States's wartime objective of maintaining a harmonious homefront and effective wartime production through the duration of the war, but it also blinded some black workers to the opportunities presented by the war to remedy racial problems in the workplace. Black unionists in particular had an opportunity to capitalize on the egalitarian policy of the CIO and enjoy a measure of improved race relations at the plant. The industrial concerns during the Second World War, as demonstrated in this chapter, engendered a sharp reaction by the federal government to conditions at Hughes Tool. While the concern was driven less by racial strife and more by labor turmoil, it nonetheless revealed the significant role that black unionists played in shaping labor policy and the government's response to these policies.

CHAPTER 6

WAR, VIOLENCE, AND SHIPBUILDING

BY THE TIME World War II was in full swing and the United States became a serious arsenal for the allies, the industrial expansion along the Upper Texas Gulf Coast and the face of black unionism had undergone a profound transformation. Most of the major industries in the region played a significant role in the country's wartime economy. While the longshore and railroad industries provided the transportation of wartime goods, the petroleum industry supplied much-needed energy and fuel, and Hughes Tool manufactured oil and aircraft equipment, the shipbuilding business was catapulted into prominence as shipbuilders took advantage of defense contracts and began constructing ships at an unprecedented pace. Shipbuilding became an essential endeavor for the United States during the 1940s and was equally important to Upper Texas Gulf Coast unionism. Because the day-to-day activities in the region's shipbuilding complexes were so important, the U.S. government, as it had done at the Hughes Tool plant, kept close tabs on labor conditions. The role of the Fair Employment Practices Commission (FEPC), which will be discussed in greater detail in the next chapter, became a crucial agency for the government to monitor shipbuilding labor activities.[1]

In the last decades of the nineteenth century blacks served mainly as strikebreakers in most shipyards throughout the country. Only the Newport News Shipbuilding Company in Virginia, with its five thousand workers, of which two-thirds were black, claimed any significant concentration of black workers by the turn of the century. The 4,347 blacks working in the industry in 1910 constituted 6.5 percent of the total shipyard labor pool. The emergence of World War I and the demand for iron ships prompted the need for increased labor. Shipbuilders relied heavily on black workers to meet their production quotas. Despite an increase in black workers, most employers and shipbuilding unions fostered racial discrimination by setting wages to accommodate local customs. White workers were generally hired into skilled occupations and received higher pay while blacks were relegated to low-paying common-

Table 6. Shipbuilding Industry Total and Black Employment by Region, 1940

Region	Total	Black	% Black
New England	25,606	83	0.3
Middle Atlantic	65,293	3,113	4.8
Great Lakes	6,263	20	0.3
Pacific	21,175	124	0.6

Source: Extracted from U.S. Department of Commerce, Bureau of the Census, *Sixteenth Census of the Population: 1940*, vol. 3, The Labor Force, parts 2–5 (Washington, D.C.: Government Printing Office, 1940), table 18.

labor jobs with little or no union representation. The Shipbuilding Labor Adjustment Board, a government agency established during World War I to counteract labor strife, sanctioned wage discrimination between the races. Union policies during the World War I era reflected an industry that was effectively organized by the Metal Trades Department, which was dominated by the Boilermakers and the Machinists. Both groups barred blacks from membership, which stifled their opportunities to achieve fair and decent jobs and wages.[2]

The demand for shipyard labor increased dramatically throughout the nation during World War II, when the construction and repairing of ships and boats, although concentrated in few areas, played an important role in the war effort. The shipbuilding industry employed approximately 150,000 workers in 1940. By 1942 the number increased to 1.2 million, of which 66,000 were black. Black shipyard labor sprawled over the entire country. In all, blacks comprised less than 7 percent of the shipbuilding industry nationwide but their presence was felt in each region of the country (see tables 6 and 7). At Sun Ship in Chester, Pennsylvania, blacks comprised about 50 percent of the workforce and paraded an all-black yard crew under the supervision of a white foreman. Contracts negotiated with the New York Shipbuilding Corporation and the Federal Shipbuilding and Drydock Company formally prohibited racial discrimination. To combat discrimination, blacks in major West Coast cities, such as Los Angeles, San Francisco, and Portland, organized separate locals and formed other labor-focused organizations, which included the Shipyard Negro Organization for Victory in Portland, the Shipyard Workers Committee for Equal Participation in the Unions at Los Angeles, and the Bay Area Council Against Discrimination in San Francisco–Oakland. When Joseph James, San Francisco branch president of the NAACP formed the Shipyard

Table 7. Shipbuilding Industry Total and Black Employment
by South Atlantic and Gulf States, 1940

	Total	*Black*	*% Black*
South Atlantic and Gulf	33,668	6,430	19.1
Virginia	19,960	3,137	20.7
Georgia	90	19	21.1
South Carolina	3,276	414	12.6
North Carolina	295	22	7.5
Florida	2,561	303	11.8
Louisiana	1,997	384	19.2
Alabama	1,767	566	32.0
Mississippi	2,007	129	12.8
*Texas	2,715	456	16.8
Total U.S.	152,005	9,770	6.4

Source: Extracted from U.S. Department of Commerce, Bureau of the Census, *Sixteenth Census of the Population: 1940,* vol. 3, The Labor Force, parts 2–5 (Washington, D.C.: Government Printing Office, 1940), table 18.

Workers Committee, he intended to use the organization to eradicate the segregated auxiliary structure of the area's shipyards through a series of lawsuits.[3]

Blacks made up nearly 20 percent of all southern shipbuilding workers. In fact, the South recorded the largest percentage of black shipbuilders in the country by 1940, although some employers in the region were not as eager to hire nonwhites as others (see table 7). The Tampa Shipbuilding and Engineering Company hired a mere five hundred black workers in 1938 but saw this number dwindle by the end of the year. Black employment at the Charleston, South Carolina, Navy Yard increased during 1941 from 9.5 percent of total workers to nearly 18 percent. Blacks comprised only one hundred of the five thousand employees at New Orleans's Delta Shipbuilding Company in 1942. The largest yards, located in Newport News, Mobile, New Orleans, and Houston, each employed twenty thousand or more workers, both white and black, but held blacks to inferior jobs and less pay. Most employers refused to alter existing social and economic structures and dismissed black labor as useless by asserting prevailing myths that most suffered from illiteracy, inexperience, and poor health.[4]

Shipbuilding employers still relied on building and metal trade unions, as well as machinists, for handling the construction and repairing of ships. While many of the unions outside of the South admitted blacks, few accepted them on an equal basis. AFL locals and CIO locals in the South upheld southern customs and refused blacks training or upgrading opportunities. Until 1938, for example, blacks had worked in skilled jobs at the Tampa Shipbuilding Company. As defense jobs increased and contracts expanded, the company stratified its workforce and kept blacks out of skilled occupations. By 1939, only two blacks employed at the yard performed skilled tasks. The shipyards of Jacksonville and Mobile followed a similar pattern. Blacks who had worked in skilled areas were demoted to helpers and common laborers. The Delta yard in New Orleans kept blacks out of skilled occupations. White workers at the Alabama Dry Dock and Shipbuilding Company in Mobile were also un-willing to make concessions to their black coworkers' demands for an equal share of premium jobs.[5]

Most shipbuilding companies along the Upper Texas Gulf Coast held la-bor agreements with unions that discriminated against blacks and deferred to whites. The International Brotherhood of Boilermakers, Iron Ship Builders, and Helpers, Houston Metal Trades Council, and the United Brotherhood of Welders, Burners and Cutters denied blacks full membership opportunities while compelling them to pay the same union dues as whites and report to the nearest white local for direction. The International Union of Boilermak-ers in Houston refused to hire blacks in any skilled occupations, segregated their work environments, and placed them in the dirtiest and lowest-paying jobs. White employers and unionists held blacks to a different standard. In just about every department at the Houston Todd shipyard, they performed unskilled labor, rolled wheelbarrows, and picked up scrap iron. White work-ers from the Metal Trades Council at the company ignored black workers' requests for fair and equitable treatment and imposed a fee on blacks who requested pay increases or job upgrades.[6]

Competent black welders were refused access to the company's training school and had their military-earned work credentials rejected. Several black unionists from the Upper Texas Gulf Coast complained about these con-ditions through letters and affidavits sent to the FEPC. Solomon Garrett was one such worker. Garrett, who worked at the Todd Shipbuilding Com-pany in Houston, one of eleven shipping companies organized by the par-ent Todd Shipyards Company of New York, had his government-earned welding certification rejected by the company and was denied employment in its skilled divisions.[7] Albert Spiller's work history, which included thirty-five years of welding experience and completion of a government welding training course, was ignored when he applied for a welder's position in April, 1942. N. E. Waiters, likewise, held a certificate from the War Department. Waiters's mechanic's training did not aid him in obtaining a better-paying job at the Todd Yard. Instead, the company assigned him to the common-labor department.[8]

Intimidation and threats awaited blacks who violated workplace rituals. Richard Felder of the Tile Marble and Terranzzo Workers Helpers Union Local 108 complained about being harassed when he entered a ship to carry out orders from his foreman to do so. While being led away, Felder learned that blacks had been banned from conducting work on the ship and that the racial attitudes of white workers posed a threat to his safety.[9]

Black workers at the Todd Yard repudiated these types of scare tactics and discriminatory practices. They submitted their grievances about these issues to Felix Ward, a black worker who served as a liaison between black workers and the white unions and employers. Ward responded with a bold investigation of the company's refusal to hire qualified blacks in skilled positions. His requests for copies of employment records was flatly denied, and a few months later he found himself out of work when the company inexplicably terminated his employment. Todd management grew increasingly agitated at blacks who challenged their labor practices. Ward's abrupt firing illustrated the disregard whites had toward blacks and toward the principles of due process in the shipbuilding industry.[10]

Employer abuse and threats of violence and intimidation explain, in part, why shipbuilders and white unionists were reluctant to upgrade black workers in the industry. Numerous examples of racial hostilities developed in 1943 and created an uneasy atmosphere throughout the country. Violence erupted in Los Angeles, Detroit, New York, Philadelphia, Indianapolis, Baltimore, Newark, St. Louis, and Washington, D.C. Intense racial hostilities, particularly among workers in southern shipyards, escalated during World War II and threatened to disrupt wartime production. The once-recalcitrant Alabama Dry Dock in Mobile erupted into violence in May, 1943, after rumors circulated about twelve blacks being upgraded to welding jobs, in compliance with an FEPC directive. With little resistance from supervisors or uniformed guards, whites congregated in small groups and worked themselves into a fit of rage before they grabbed just about anything within reach to assault their black coworkers. The displaced anger exhibited by white unionists in the Mobile riot demonstrated the volatile meshing of the races in major, highly congested, defense production centers.[11]

The Upper Texas Gulf Coast suffered from many of these crises, and the resulting effect mirrored that of the Mobile melee. Race problems surfaced in Orange, Texas, a small town twenty-six miles east of Beaumont. Orange's Levingston Shipyard employed approximately two thousand white workers but no blacks. The company expressed no desire to hire nonwhite workers and wanted to avoid igniting "an unfavorable worker reaction" between the races. The Consolidated Shipbuilding Company, on the other hand, did employ blacks, but disgruntled whites at the company threatened violence against those who dared show up for work, forcing the company to keep the races separate at all times and on a few occasions send the black workers home early.[12]

The Beaumont race riot that erupted in June, 1943, culminated years of racial strife in the region and fell squarely within the race riot phenomenon. Conditions for black workers at Beaumont's Pennsylvania Shipyards reflected those of the entire shipbuilding industry. Wartime strains, competition for employment, and demographic changes necessarily required closer and, in many cases, undesired contact between the races. Two days of violence erupted in June of 1943 between black and white workers after the wife of a white Pennsylvania Shipyard worker claimed a black man raped her. After word circulated throughout the city, nearly three thousand whites at the yard halted work and marched to city hall, the police headquarters, and to the black sections of town in pursuit of revenge. The workers then looted stores, burned automobiles, pillaged restaurants, and beat blacks. According to Captain B. O. Craft of the Beaumont police department: "They came out of the ship-yards right up to the police station and flooded in. We tried to talk to them and reason with them, but they took charge. We even took a delegation through the county jail and showed them who we had there. A little after midnight we brought the lady down who had reported the assault. She looked at the Negroes we had but did not identify any of them. After awhile the mob finally broke up, but that was when our real trouble started."[13] The rape allegation ignited a powder keg of racial tension and left the FEPC with the difficult task of sorting through the social and economic fallout.[14]

When confronted with charges of promoting racial tension, neither union leaders nor employers accepted responsibility. Charles J. MacGowan, International President of the Boilermakers, Iron Shipbuilders and Helpers, wasted little time shifting the responsibility for working conditions and hiring prac-

Black shipyard workers in Beaumont, ca. 1943. Courtesy Tyrrell Historical Library, Beaumont, Texas.

tices in the region's industry to union locals. He defended the international office's labor policy, which in theory denounced discrimination. Shipbuilding employers also denied accountability. Ike Ashburn, Director of Industrial and Public Relations for the Houston Shipbuilding Company, refused to blame his company or any other employer since his employment office did not accept referrals for black workers who could compete for skilled jobs. Voluntary meetings among the FEPC, employers, and union officials exposed the racist labor practices that each group allowed to persist but failed to produce an adequate remedy for the racial hostilities permeating the industry. Notwithstanding the FEPC's persistence, Ashburn, with support from fellow shipbuilding employers, stood his ground and refused to modify the yard's practices.[15]

The fear of being publicly exposed for their part in sanctioning discriminatory practices convinced Todd officials to work toward their own plan for compliance or suffer through one of the FEPC's public hearings, which turned out to be, in most cases, an attempt by the agency to convey an image of government busy grappling with the stifling constraints of race prejudice. When workers and employers failed to produce an in-house proposal for compliance, the FEPC, with much hesitation from Clarence Mitchell, associate director of field operations, proceeded with a joint hearing. In the past, Mitchell had cited scheduling problems and concerns about credible evidence as an obstacle facing a successful hearing.[16]

The reluctance of the company union to submit a written plan for compliance moved the FEPC to draw up its own proposal. Scheduling problems became the most convenient excuse for the failure of the two groups to arrive at an acceptable plan. Union locals that failed to appear at compliance meetings usually did so to avoid FEPC reprimand, which amounted to nothing more than a written rhetorical directive calling for an end to racial discrimination. Houston Todd officials and its white unionists stubbornly refused to accept government mandates regarding racial equality. Thus, the FEPC ended its investigation having failed to garner much change.[17]

The FEPC's investigations of the shipbuilding industry, however, was far-reaching and stretched into other docks. One example of this was at the Brown Shipbuilding Company in Houston. Blacks in this yard confronted many of the same problems that surfaced at the Houston Todd yard. Herman Brown, a wealthy businessman from Houston, organized this contracting company, which later became Brown & Root. The Brown Shipbuilding Company contracted 100 percent of its work to the U.S. Navy, while other shipyards in the area contracted not only with the government but also with the private sector. During the war, the Brown Shipbuilding Company employed approximately 14,395 workers, 1,150 of whom were nonwhite.[18]

Several black workers alleged that the Brown Shipbuilding Company only offered them employment as janitors and common laborers and denied them fair access to better-paying jobs, even when their job duties entitled them to higher rank. Company layoffs gravely affected minority groups at Brown. Because most black workers held less seniority than whites, the company justified the disproportionate number of blacks released from the company. But when the company replaced laid-off black workers with new white employees, it raised suspicions at the FEPC.[19]

After the Brown Yard refused to relinquish its employment records, the FEPC pursued help from other government agencies. It called on the navy, which understood the FEPC's predicament, to help retrieve payroll records, which would reveal the company's pay, hiring, and layoff practices. Obtaining employment records represented but one phase of the FEPC's strategy to force compliance from the Brown Yard. The NLRB also stepped in and assisted in organizing a hearing. Historically, the NLRB did little to address issues of racial discrimination. Repeated failures, however, by the FEPC to adequately address the refusal of unions and management at Brown to include blacks on an equal basis or vote in union elections presented problems that justified NLRB intercession.[20]

As the FEPC struggled to gain a measure of respect from shipbuilding unions and employers, the NLRB became increasingly more important to their battles. FEPC officials realized that their aspirations for justice might be realized through the help of other more powerful government agencies rather than the sole efforts of a presidential committee. For quite some time, black workers had sought to have the NLRB recognize racial discrimination as a legitimate concern of union organizing. Unfortunately for blacks, it took the possible failure of wartime objectives and the dwindling appreciation for the FEPC to garner enough interest in racial issues for the agency to respond. Some black workers recognized this trend sooner than others and used it to their advantage, while others failed to effectively utilize the agency to their benefit.

An example of this was at the Todd Dry Docks in Galveston, a privately owned and operated ship repair yard. Like other yards along the Upper Texas Gulf Coast, the Galveston Yard failed to comply with FEPC mandates, and black workers failed to approach the NLRB for recourse. The Galveston Yard held contracts with the War Shipping Administration, the navy, and the army. By 1943, it hired more than four thousand workers, of which about one thousand were nonwhite. Of the total black workforce, none worked in skilled capacities.[21]

Information received by the FEPC revealed that the Galveston Dry Docks employed blacks solely as common laborers and helpers. Although the Galveston Yard made repeated assurances to correct the situation, it did little to improve conditions. Yard officials made many promises but took very little action to resolve the issues facing their black workers, insisting that the white "men would not stand for it." The Galveston Yard unions, like the employer, avoided their obligation to comply with the FEPC. Clarence Rehl, the union representative for the International Brotherhood of Boilermakers, contended that the members of the black auxiliaries at Galveston had as much right to be craftsmen as white workers. Rehl's claim, however, did not mirror reality.

In fact, most blacks at Galveston stood little chance of obtaining skilled positions or craftsmen's wages.[22]

The Galveston Yard blatantly overlooked black workers. Herman Hall of Galveston, for example, worked at the Galveston Yard in July, 1941. Although Hall received three months of training as a welder from a local training school, the Galveston Yard denied him an opportunity to utilize his skills but assured him that there were plenty of "good helper jobs" available. Hall's coworkers, Joel Millican and Ezekiel Muse, faced similar problems. Millican openly complained about inequalities in pay between white and black workers at the yard. Millican worked three large ships at one time. He bailed, painted, cemented, and buffed for $.73 per hour while his white leaderman received $1.30 an hour for the same work. Although the Yard upgraded Muse from a helper to foreman, his pay did not match that of the white foremen at the yard. When Muse hinted he would complain, the company threatened him with demotion and a reduction in pay. Alexander Pierce, a long-time black employee at the yard, knew of the company's reluctance to hire blacks. Still, he struggled to gain upgrades in several skilled areas until one official warned him that he was forbidden to perform certain jobs and if he continued his zealous attempts to upgrade he could "go somewhere else to work."[23]

Respected representatives of the black working class had difficulty persuading employers to alter their labor policies. George W. Singleton, president of black auxiliary Lodge A.45 of Boilermakers at the Galveston Yard, and liaison between black workers and the company, tried on several occasions to interact with union leaders and his employer about blacks being refused skilled jobs and membership into Galveston's Boilermakers Union Local 132. Singleton demanded an FEPC investigation and hearing, despite Galveston Yard president R. J. Vanderwende's objection to the charges brought against his company. The Galveston Yard refused a compliance plan but agreed to "make a speedy survey of, the pattern of vacancies, the skill of nonwhite workers in the plant, and the best location for a segregated upgrading procedure."[24]

The International Brotherhood of Boilermakers in Galveston yielded to FEPC pressure when its international vice president, J. P. McCollum, submitted a letter of compliance to the FEPC agreeing to end all forms of racial discrimination regarding wages, seniority, training, upgrading, vacations, grievances, and other matters pertaining to collective bargaining agreements. The letter was of little importance since most shipyard unions in the area exercised complete autonomy and the FEPC held no enforcement authority. Although written compliance helped the public image of yards throughout the

Upper Texas Gulf Coast, it did little to alter the fundamental circumstances of discrimination against black workers. A proposed plan to move blacks to the warehouse department while maintaining a segregated work environment merely appeased government officials and the yard's white workers.[25]

Despite cooperation from the NLRB, the collusion between Upper Texas Gulf Coast shipbuilding employers and white workers complicated matters for black unionists. The timely creation of the FEPC offered some recourse to the sorry state of the industry's race relations, but fell far short of black workers' expectations. The willingness, nonetheless, of the federal government to intervene on behalf of black workers reflected a sharp contrast with the government of old, which rarely, if ever, interceded in the racial affairs of any industry or union.

CHAPTER 7

BLACK UNIONISM AND THE FEPC

THE ACTIVE ROLE of the FEPC in the shipbuilding industry raises
several issues about the agency in other industries along the Upper Texas Gulf
Coast. During the industrial frenzy of World War II black unionists in the
longshore, railroad, oil, steel, and shipbuilding industries continued to use
many of the strategies they had adopted before the war as they established
their own relationship with the FEPC. Blacks throughout the country filed
over 90 percent of all FEPC complaints. The agency presented a new alternative for black unionists and reflected a bold attempt by the federal government to launch an offensive on behalf of black workers, racial minorities, Jews,
religious minorities, and noncitizens. Past government labor agencies had failed
to provide these groups with much help.[1] Franklin Roosevelt's Executive Order 9346 reconstituted Executive Order 8802 and expanded the jurisdiction
of the FEPC. It included the adjudication of complaints against employers
and unions engaged in the production of wartime material as well as departments and agents of the federal government. It also transferred the FEPC
from the War Manpower Commission and sanctioned it as an independent
agency under the Office of Emergency Management in May, 1943.

The FEPC was, for the most part, a relatively weak agency. It worked solely
from worker complaints and could not impose sanctions or file its own court
cases against those who violated its mandate. Although the agency did not
have the full authority to enforce the presidential order, it held public and
private hearings in an attempt to muscle compliance from defense contrac-
tors. Its dedicated but overworked biracial staff of administrators and field
investigators labored tirelessly as they investigated businesses, unions, military, and other government employers who refused to concede equal and fair
hiring practices. As Merl E. Reed noted, "the FEPC's work was unique. Never
before had an agency of the federal government cooperated in such a way
with minority groups" even though, Reed continued, "the Roosevelt administration . . . gave it lip service" and used it to "defuse black protest."[2]

Although historians typically associate pervasive racial discrimination with the South, FEPC records indicate that most parts of the country suffered from the crippling effects of racial prejudice in a variety of industries. Few studies, however, have examined the regional and field offices of the FEPC, which implemented federal and state-wide policies to combat discrimination. In eastern states black workers experienced employment problems and relied on these government agencies for remedy. One example of this was the FEPC and the Governor's Committee on Discrimination in Employment (GCDE), which operated simultaneously between 1941 and 1943 in New York state. Officially designated on March 29, 1941, a few months before the establishment of the FEPC, the GCDE, a biracial and culturally diverse agency, set important precedents for the FEPC and its regional offices. It educated white society about the perils of employment discrimination, spurred on black worker militancy, and helped to institutionalize civil rights. The FEPC also fought against discrimination in Pennsylvania's two major cities, Pittsburgh and Philadelphia. Combined, these two government agencies challenged unresponsive unions and employers in several eastern industries ranging from shipbuilding, government post offices, telephone companies, and bakeries.[3]

The major cities of West Coast states also experienced racial problems in employment that required FEPC intercession. Shipbuilding along the West Coast was one of the country's most prosperous businesses during World War II. Unions as well as corporations profited from the large increase in ship construction. The International Brotherhood of Boilermakers, Iron Ship Builders, and Helpers of America Local 72 in Portland, for example, became one of the largest, richest, and most glamorous unions in the country. Its racist hiring practices, however, excluded many blacks from enjoying the same prosperity. The question of black membership had annoyed the International Brotherhood for many years as black workers struggled to eradicate "white only" clauses from its rituals. The shipyards of California's West Coast also played a key role in FEPC investigations, where white boilermakers insisted that blacks pay union dues for the privilege of working, while employers and white unionists devised schemes to undermine their employment by firing blacks when ordered to do so by the unions. Black shipyard workers invested much of their faith in the ability of the FEPC to conduct public hearings to end these types of racist practices. The plight of black unionists in the San Francisco and Oakland area, as Albert Broussard has noted, prompted a wide range of complaints from black workers in the regions' shipyard unions as well as an array of other occupations.[4]

The South, perhaps, posed the greatest problem for the FEPC. Nearly a year after the issuance of 8802, the FEPC took on discrimination in the southern states when it held a public hearing in Birmingham, Alabama, June 18–20. Racial discrimination in many Birmingham unions followed familiar patterns. Blacks were generally denied defense training, restricted to unskilled and semiskilled jobs, or excluded altogether. During the hearings, one of the most vivid accounts of discrimination was the case of Mobile's Gulf Shipping Corporation, where thousands of black workers had labored during World War I, but now recorded a mere twenty-two black porters, according to FEPC calculations. Black workers from the shipyards in Tampa and Jacksonville, Florida, Savannah, Georgia, and New Orleans all turned to the FEPC and some were able to have their grievances aired at the Birmingham hearing, which became a proving ground for the resolve of the agency and those who opposed it. From the onset of the opening of the Birmingham FEPC field office, rumors swirled about the motives of the agency in the Deep South, and its advocates and opponents geared up for an intense confrontation.[5]

Numerous black unionists along the Upper Texas Gulf Coast became caught up in the fervor sweeping the South as they also used the FEPC to defy the discriminatory labor practices of white unionists and employers. Although they filed several complaints with the FEPC, the response to the agency's intercession into the region's labor affairs varied between industries. For some blacks, the FEPC appeared to be an agency that could redress their concerns, while for others it held little significance and represented nothing more than a symbolic government bureaucracy with no real enforcement power. White unionists and employers rejected attempts by the FEPC to intervene in their workplace affairs and both set out to undermine the agency as they reluctantly cooperated with its investigations. Black unionists in Texas initially submitted their complaints against employers and unions to the Office of Production Management in San Antonio, Texas, and to the FEPC office in Washington. The agency, however, focused much of its attention along the Upper Texas Gulf Coast, where the largest concentration of industries operated and the greatest number of blacks in Texas worked.[6]

The thrust of the early FEPC investigations was coordinated by Carlos Castañeda, a University of Texas at Austin history professor, and he put most of his energies into exposing discrimination in Texas refineries. The investigation of racial discrimination against the nearly 2,200 minority workers in the Texas oil industry illustrated complicated circumstances that involved black and Mexican oil workers and required FEPC intercession. Although Castañeda initially adopted a dual strategy that focused on the complaints of Mexicans and blacks, the fact that Mexicans often complained about citizenship and language barriers, at least in the oil refineries, illustrated that Mexicans and blacks did not always share the same workplace concerns.[7] Indeed, the labor of Mexicans, particularly in the southwestern states, had posed an indispensable necessity for the war effort and considerable attention from the FEPC. In its three-year struggle to address discrimination against Mexican and Chicano workers in the copper industry, the FEPC failed to champion the idea of racial equality in the scattered mining camps of Arizona and western New Mexico. In Los Angeles, where Chicanos constituted the largest minority group in 1941, the FEPC focused its attention in the aircraft and shipbuilding industries. Despite the heavy concentration of Mexicans and Chicanos, their concerns about discrimination, initially, were largely ignored by the FEPC.[8]

Mexicans in Texas experienced similar treatment, but activists such as Castañeda, along with the help of Mexican oil workers, officials from the Mexican Consulate at Houston, and the League of United Latin American Citizens (LULAC), set out to help eradicate years of racial discrimination against Mexicans as they eagerly prepared complaints against several Upper Texas Gulf Coast oil refineries on behalf of both Mexican and black workers.[9] Their fight against the Shell refinery and union Local 367 in Deer Park, in particular, focused attention on the significance of discrimination against minorities throughout the oil industry. Most of the trouble the FEPC faced in the refineries started when the Shell refinery promoted two Mexican workers from common laborers to a carman's helper and a truck driver and upgraded six black workers to helper status. John Crossland, a white member of Local 367, insisted that the upgrading of black and Mexican workers set off a firestorm of anger and resentment among white workers, who refused to toil alongside Mexicans or "work with niggers" or "have a nigger foreman." Their protest against the promotion of minorities was far-reaching, as two vice presidents at the plant resigned their jobs in support of the disgruntled white workers, who, on their own behalf, responded with two work stoppages, one of which included an all-day "stand-around strike."[10] The turmoil at Shell made the company's management reluctant to upgrade additional blacks or Mexicans without first consulting with Local 367. Their refusal to produce an adequate plan to promote minorities compelled the FEPC to call for a public hearing, at which time they gave Shell and Local 367 ninety days to eliminate all forms of discriminatory practices such as the segregation of time clocks, transportation facilities, pay windows, and drinking fountains.[11]

Most of Shell's representatives and white workers resented FEPC intrusion into workplace matters and they often searched for ways to defy the agency's directives and to protect their autonomy. They formed ad hoc committees to devise compliance strategies and made numerous requests to extend the ninety-day deadline before holding any hearings. Their tactics often gave the appearance that the company and white workers had good intentions of accommodating the workplace aspirations of minority laborers, but their strategy was primarily designed to avoid compliance with FEPC directives, appease white unionists, and circumvent future work stoppages.[12]

Following months of wrangling, white workers and company management from Shell begrudgingly accepted the hiring of blacks and Mexicans into occupations traditionally reserved for whites but insisted that work areas at plant facilities remain segregated. Shell's white workers were adamant about racial segregation. Black workers had long accepted separation but rejected wage discrimination. Mexicans, on the other hand, completely opposed segregation and denounced occupational discrimination. The modest gains toward equality at the Shell Refinery won Castañeda the praises of the FEPC. His efforts also earned him new duties as special assistant to the FEPC director on Latin American Affairs and director of a new regional FEPC office in San Antonio in 1944. Castañeda's departure cleared the way for Don W. Ellinger to be promoted to chief investigator for the Dallas regional office, which began looking into complaints from workers in other industries.[13]

Unlike Castañeda, who had exhausted much of his energy on the refining industry, primarily because of the concentration of Mexican labor, Ellinger, who guided FEPC investigations throughout the Upper Texas Gulf Coast, turned much of his attention toward the plight of black railroad workers, steelworkers, and longshoremen. Working for the FEPC presented a unique opportunity for Ellinger to fulfill a personal challenge of confronting racial discrimination. Ellinger's advocacy for racial equality and fairness stemmed from the lessons he learned from his father. As a cabinet manufacturer, the elder Ellinger had employed both black and white workers on an equal basis. The younger Ellinger displayed early signs of activism as a student at Washington University in St. Louis, Missouri. As an undergraduate he actively engaged in union organizing and worked to improve conditions for working-class people. The labor movement, according to Ellinger, offered the best method for social change, and he placed a high priority on obtaining racial justice and imposing his virtues on Gulf Coast industries. Despite his objection to U.S. involvement in World War II, Ellinger seized the opportunity to serve his country through the FEPC.[14]

Ellinger encountered his biggest challenge in the railroad industry, where whites at the Southern Pacific stubbornly fought to uphold their position in the industry and rejected racial equality. A. J. Pickett, general chairman of the Brotherhood of Railway Clerks in Houston, did not seem to understand all the fuss surrounding the FEPC complaints of black railroad workers, because his union allowed black auxiliaries, he contended, "to handle grievances and to protect the interests of their members." Blacks, on the other hand, complained that they were denied job announcements, despite the company's insistence that job openings "were advertised on bulletin boards at the customary locations," refused promotions, lost seniority rank, and stood little or no chance of obtaining better-paying jobs. When Pickett insisted that his union local did not make such laws for the Brotherhood and assigned blame to the Brotherhood's national office, it reflected a classic example of the buck-passing that had become common among employers and white unionists. The ambivalence of whites at the Southern Pacific was not unusual since many of these workers and representatives had learned of the FEPC's troubles during the oil investigations.[15]

Workplace discrepancies between the races at the Southern Pacific led to yet another call for an FEPC hearing but not before much trepidation, this time between the agency's regional office in Dallas and its national office in Washington D.C. During the railroad investigations, Ellinger encountered a skeptical and unrelenting Maceo Hubbard, a Savannah-born black staff member in the Washington, D.C., legal division of the FEPC and a Harvard graduate, who implied that Ellinger and his staff had done sloppy investigation work when he expressed concerns about what he believed to be insufficient information collected on the Southern Pacific case. "Someone," Hubbard blasted, "has got to get some evidence from somewhere if the case is to be handled at all." FEPC officials at the national headquarters maintained an especially cautious attitude toward labor-race issues in the South. Pressure from the national headquarters reflected the desire of the FEPC, and for that matter the federal government, to mount as much credible evidence against the Southern Pacific and in turn assert its wartime authority as it had done in its Birmingham hearings. Their greatest concern, however, was that the presence of the FEPC in the Deep South would alienate conservative lawmakers who had made noticeable political gains during the early 1940s or that it would cause all-out racial upheaval in the region. The government wanted to avoid wartime racial and labor strife at all costs.[16]

With this in mind, Ellinger sought to bolster the FEPC's leverage and improve its public image when he solicited the support of J. H. Bond, regional director of the War Manpower Commission (WMC), an agency responsible for overseeing wartime labor. It is unclear if Ellinger received permission from his FEPC superiors to involve the WMC in FEPC investigations but his decision to do so created an atmosphere of uneasiness among Southern Pacific management and white unionists. The WMC monitored the procurement of essential wartime labor and the racial discrimination at Southern Pacific impeded the full and rational utilization of its workforce. Any useful ploy that could foster progress toward compliance, Ellinger felt, would make for good "public relations" throughout the rest of the country and "would gain support in Texas where no other matters will and hasten compliance by other companies." Public support was greatly needed because the federal government, mainly the Roosevelt administration, had in the past bowed to a range of pressures, mainly from southern lawmakers, when it postponed the southern railroad FEPC hearings in January, 1943.[17]

The postponement drew an angry reaction from black Gulf Coast railroad workers, who played a large part in protesting the delay. When Prince E. Gallagher, Sr., president of Houston Auxiliary Local 582 of the Dining Car Employees, took it upon himself to "secure the signatures of many organizations and individuals" who opposed the FEPC's delay, he demonstrated the determination of black workers to voice their displeasure with the agency and the president's administration.[18]

By the time the formal hearing began several months later, the tensions among the FEPC, the Southern Pacific, and the unions had intensified beyond the point of reconciliation. Simon Stickgold, an FEPC legal representative, initiated an early confrontation at the hearing when he compared racial discrimination at the Southern Pacific to fascism overseas and questioned the company's refusal to promote "fair play" among its employees. "Here in our own midst," Stickgold lamented, "it has become necessary to hold this hearing because an American corporation and an American labor organization assert that negroes will not be permitted to work in certain essential railroad classifications." What has happened, Stickgold continued, "to the basic faiths of the founders of this great nation?" Stickgold's diatribe was less than impressive to company and union representatives who refused to change their attitudes on the company's race policy. "The constitution of the Brotherhood of Railroad Trainmen," Charles Murphy, representative from the Brotherhood of Trainmen, admitted, "expressly provides that the membership is limited to white males," and he questioned the authority of Stickgold and the FEPC to alter those standards.[19]

Unions and employers often retained good legal counsel. Murphy and the popular corporate attorney John Bullington, who worked for the powerful Houston-based law firm of Baker & Botts, provided a vigorous defense for the Southern Pacific. Unlike most law firms along the Upper Texas Gulf Coast, Baker & Botts became an important agent for change in the legal profession. It served as a model for corporate litigation in a state dominated by traditional partnerships. The use of sophisticated corporate litigation by unions and employers, in some instances, outmatched the legal representation of the FEPC. Bullington joined Murphy in defending the race policy of the Southern Pacific and insisted that the Southern Pacific and the union encouraged "peace and harmony among its employees and that neither was motivated by any prejudice against niggers or any desire to discriminate against them." Bullington's disparaging comment indicated the extent to which employers and unions would go to maintain their discriminatory policies.[20]

The FEPC ended its long battle with Bullington and its investigation of the Southern Pacific in 1945. Little could be done to compel the employer or union to comply with FEPC directives, which instructed both to end their practice of discrimination. The collusion between white railroad workers and Southern Pacific officials reflected the general behavior of most whites throughout the region.

The FEPC did not approach the racial problems at the Hughes Tool Company with the same zeal it did during the Shell Refinery and Southern Pacific investigation even though discrimination was pervasive throughout the plant and the company had admitted allocating jobs by race and refused to eliminate its discriminatory practices. The feuding and in-fighting over unionization among its black workers is one explanation for this. Their preoccupation with unionization during the 1930s and early 1940s made FEPC investigations a secondary concern for most black workers at the plant. Despite the 1943 CIO contract that rhetorically eliminated race-based occupations, blacks could not officially "perform jobs not assigned to them."[21]

A few black workers at Hughes did complain to the FEPC, however, about unfair hiring and wage practices. Harold Fatheree, a black trained electrician and twenty-four-year resident of Harris County, in an affidavit to the FEPC, insisted that Hughes Tool management and its contracted unions had ignored his requests for employment. "I made several attempts to fill an application at various projects . . . at the employment office," said Fatheree, "but was informed by those in authority that there was no available jobs for Negroes as skilled workers."[22]

Although the SWOC had made efforts to improve race relations among its members, Lee Pressman of the USWA voiced the typical anxiety about the discriminatory behavior of steel union affiliates. Pressman insisted that the discriminatory clauses in most steelworker contracts appeared because white workers wanted them there and employers conceded to their wishes. He assured the FEPC that his office would help to eliminate the problem. In doing so, Pressman agreed to file a petition with the War Labor Board to cancel discriminatory portions of labor contracts at Hughes. Hughes officials, however, encouraged the discriminatory arrangements, and Thomas Mobley, a plant manager, insisted that changes in procedures "such as putting Negroes on operators' jobs, would cause a great deal of trouble in the plant and possibly rioting."[23] Rioting did not occur and Hughes Tool refused to alter most of its racial practices. The FEPC concluded its investigations at Hughes Tool short of a hearing or any commitment for compliance from whites at the company. The agency conceded that there was little it could do to improve conditions for black workers because blacks demonstrated little interest in the agency. The lack of cooperation from whites was combined with the failure of blacks to recognize the FEPC as a legitimate option to remedy some of their labor problems. Instead, they steered clear of government intrusion and asserted their union aspirations as part of their struggle for an equal share of American prosperity.[24]

Upper Texas Gulf Coast black longshoremen responded to the FEPC in much the same way blacks at Hughes Tool did. During its investigations, the FEPC recorded just one case of alleged discrimination in the Texas longshore industry. Because black dockworkers had established a long history of successful labor activism and comprised a substantial percentage of the workforce, they, as did the steelworkers at Hughes, relied less on the FEPC. This does not suggest, however, that black longshoremen successfully eradicated all forms of racial inequities. Instead, their economic power and numerical strength allowed them to look after their own needs. The most pressing issue to surface for the FEPC and longshoremen involved a *Houston Chronicle* advertisement. When an ad seeking "200 White Men" appeared in the employment section of the newspaper it was reported to the FEPC.[25]

Longshoremen did not eagerly avail themselves to the FEPC, compelling the agency to appeal for help from the middle class. Ellinger, who handled this lone longshoremen complaint, sent a copy of the ad to LuLu B. White, president of Houston's NAACP, and asked if she could help determine its source. Because no union or employer accepted responsibility for the ad, it became difficult for White to ascertain its origins. Freeman Everett, representative for black ILA Local 872, later assured the FEPC that the request for white workers was merely an attempt to "help Local 1273 bring up its quota" of white workers.[26] As Everett put it, "Few understood the meaning of this advertisement the longshoremen set up. I admit it is hard to understand. The Colored longshoremen outnumbered the white by a large majority. The white local is supposed to furnish half the labor and that is why they designated white men."[27] Everett rejected the FEPC's request for a formal antidiscrimination statement from the unions and insisted that the longshoremen community was capable of resolving its own problems without help from the FEPC. Everett's explanation about the ad failed to satisfy a skeptical LuLu B. White, who held ongoing written communication with Ellinger and often availed herself and her organization to the FEPC and its efforts to remedy discrimination complaints. White rendered advice, helped with investigations, and arranged for the FEPC to hold strategy meetings at the local NAACP headquarters. White's active role in the discrepancy over the longshoremen advertisement seeking white workers helped prevent other discriminatory ads from appearing in local newspapers. Once the NAACP got involved, particularly LuLu B. White, unions throughout the region exercised a greater measure of caution not to push the racial issue too far. As far as the longshoremen issue was concerned, both white dockworkers from Local 1273 and black longshoremen from 872, the two groups apparently responsible for the ad, after learning that White had intervened, agreed to abolish the practice of printing ads that could be construed as discriminatory.[28]

Ellinger relied on the help of notable and influential members of the white and black middle classes throughout the FEPC's investigations. Despite uncooperative company representatives and white workers, the FEPC generated public support for its interrogations when it solicited help and "secured advice" and correspondence from the community. The ministerial community was just one segment of the influential middle class that the FEPC sought. Dr. Paul Quillian, a popular white minister from the First Methodist Church in Houston, and Reverend Bernard Hatch, a white pastor of the Milby Methodist Church, also in Houston, offered their input about racial discrimination and the best way to combat it. Although each man often appeared at FEPC meetings and collaborated with FEPC agents, neither boasted any real solutions for the racial discord in the region.[29]

Black business leaders also figured prominently for the FEPC, and the agency took advantage of their assistance. Carter Wesley heeded Ellinger's call for help and organized a small group of black leaders from the area whom he regarded as "particularly sound to discuss the matter" of FEPC investigations. Wesley and his contingency drew particular attention to the Shell Company. Although Castañeda had recorded some modest gains at the plant, Wesley still remained concerned about the company's refusal to take a firm position toward compliance with FEPC directives. Wesley also regarded the Southern Pacific hearings as being extremely important to the overall effort of black unionists to achieve fairness, and he cooperated with Ellinger by helping to search for workers willing to lodge complaints with the FEPC.[30]

Wesley did not have to work very hard to find complainants because many organizations and individuals had already taken the initiative to protest discrimination in defense industries. The Galveston NAACP complained to the Superintendent of Education of Texas. Its main concern was the lack of training and education black workers received. Such training could have qualified them to hold better-paying skilled jobs. In its letter to the Superintendent, which they also forwarded to Paul McNutt, then Chairman of the WMC, the NAACP appealed for help in eliminating discrimination of black workers in defense training programs, where the lion's share of federal funds was allocated to training programs for whites only.[31]

The FEPC also reached into neighborhood associations to expose unfair labor practices. Lawrence W. Cramer, executive secretary for the FEPC, requested that the Third Ward Civic Association furnish him with the names of persons employed at companies that discriminated. On more than one occasion, the FEPC contacted members of the organization, headed by R. R. Grovey, and kept them apprised of FEPC investigations.[32]

Appealing to the grassroot communities was one way for the FEPC to counteract the challenges they faced from employers, unions, and southern lawmakers who hindered funding and filibustered legislation that promised to establish a permanent agency. Much of the drive to eradicate the FEPC can be traced to Senator Theodore G. Bilbo of Mississippi who vowed that he would beat the "damnable, unAmerican and unconstitutional" FEPC to death. Bilbo had long resented the agency and believed that its creation resulted merely from the pressure brought to bear by black political leaders like A. Philip Randolph, who, as John Beecher indicated, had mugged the president with his march-on-Washington threat. Bilbo, who feared government encroachment into the hiring practices of small businesses, was unconvinced that the federal government could enforce compliance with 9346, and, most importantly, he wanted to protect the interests of the southern white voting constituency. Bilbo appealed to his congressional colleagues in a drawn-out filibuster to not yield to the enactment of any law that would prolong the existence of the agency. While Bilbo struggled in Congress, his message rang loud and clear in many southern states. Texas' lieutenant governor, John Lee Smith, who, as did most southern lawmakers, thoroughly despised the agency, dismissed the FEPC as merely a "device to get Negro's vote" rather than an effort to better the black worker economically. Texas state senator W. Lee O'Daniel advocated "abolishing the whole organization." He rejected the FEPC and characterized the agency as a component of government that "stirs up strife, and ferments hatred between people of different races and colors."[33]

The forced promotions of nonwhite workers seemed to be the greatest concern for most who opposed the FEPC in Texas, and they directed their complaints to Texas governor Coke Stevenson. One expressed to the governor that FEPC attempts to alter racial stratification were "undoubtedly the worst outrage and disgrace to be put over on the American people." Yet another warned the chief executive of the state that it was "time someone spoke up to stop the federal government from cramming the negro down our throat" through the FEPC. Stevenson pandered to those who felt that it was "high time . . . to make a determined stand to rescue" white Texans from "would be dictators and race agitators" in the FEPC and to preserve their "wonderful heritage" and protect racial segregation in the workplace. Protecting Texas' segregation laws and taking a stand against the FEPC was one sure way for Stevenson to satisfy his conservative constituency. Not surprisingly, he challenged the FEPC's jurisdiction and authority. In a letter to the FEPC, Stevenson accused the agency of engaging "in activities which countenance an open violation and defiance of some of the Texas laws providing for segregation of white and colored races."[34]

Despite strong opposition from right-wing lawmakers, the FEPC remained a symbol of racial change for many of its supporters. Advocates of the agency continued to justify a need for the organization. When the legislative council of the Texas chapter of the CIO met in Austin in January, 1945, at the Driskill Hotel, the organization, which included fourteen black delegates, voted unanimously to back efforts to retain a permanent FEPC. Moreover, when Frank Ward of oil union Local 254 in Port Arthur and black delegate to the council, spoke out in favor of a permanent FEPC and against antilabor organizations such as the Christian Americans and its conservative leadership, he "caused the conference to rock with applause." Sitting in the audience in support of Ward were several of his colleagues such as Will Hollier, John Syers, LeRoy Horton, Phillip J. Linden, also of Local 254, and O. C. Herbert and A. Van Winn from oil union Local 229 of Beaumont, who insisted on making their voices heard if "lily-white Democrats tried to pass back-to-yesterday legislation." In October, 1945, twenty-five black delegates from the TSCIO helped rally support for a permanent FEPC when they introduced resolutions during the organization's annual state-wide meeting held at the Rice Hotel in Houston. Black workers from a range of industries seized on the momentum established by the TSCIO Legislative Board and called upon black workers to take the lead in urging rank-and-file workers to operate in the best interest of the working class. One group that took the initiative to prod its workers to support the FEPC was the Gulf Coast longshoremen. At its 1945 convention in Galveston, several black long-shoremen from the South Atlantic & Gulf Coast District of the ILA signed a resolution endorsing a permanent FEPC and urged its officials to lobby state-house lawmakers about the need for the agency. Although they recognized Roosevelt's executive order that established the agency was "a mere wartime measure," they also saw it as an agency that could protect the job security of minority groups as the country entered the postwar period.[35]

Despite uncooperative white unionists and ambivalent employers, the FEPC received financial help and political support from a range of individuals and organizaions when it became clear that attempts to abolish the agency were well in place. LuLu B. White, for example, appealed to Texas' U.S. congressional delegation. "To deny the Negro their democratic right to equal employment," White complained, "is a denial of everything our country stands for. I appeal to you not as a Negro . . . but as a sincere patriotic American citizen," for the continuation of the FEPC. Local committees and labor organizations also raised up to thirty thousand dollars in support for a permanent state-wide agency. Contributions from prominent labor unions such as ILA Local 872, Houston Pullman Porters, Houston Barbers Union, and the Houston Negro Hospital also flowed in. The Houston Council for a permanent FEPC sponsored a "save the FEPC" rally at the Hester House Community Center in Houston's Fifth Ward neighborhood and allowed Ruth Koenig, a key figure in the Texas FEPC drive, to deliver a speech denouncing the forces lined up against the FEPC.[36]

The drive to save the FEPC presented radical expectations for racial change in a rigid Jim Crow region. While a segment of the population agitated for improved race relations in the workplace and continuation of the FEPC, others took antagonistic positions. A moderate segment also emerged and suggested gradual change as the best approach to the discrepancies in Gulf Coast industries. Houston's mayor, Oscar Holcombe, recognized this dichotomy and advised blacks to show less anxiety as they continued to fight for their rights. Speaking to the Negro Chamber of Commerce at the Antioch Baptist Church, Holcombe suggested that the "Negro has as much right to claim stock in Houston as any other citizen" and "the Negro race will see a great change in their affairs in the next fifteen years."[37]

Holcombe's comments, combined with the attacks on the FEPC and the failure of the agency to adequately respond to black occupational concerns, led to renewed anxieties and left some in the black labor community concerned and skeptical about its ability to remedy racial inequalities. The fact that blacks experienced difficulties obtaining fair employment during peak periods of wartime production left little hope that the problem of restricted employment opportunities for minority groups would change during the postwar period. Rice warned black workers to "not place the sole hope" of their salvation in "the Fair Employment Practice Law." He initially believed that the FEPC was committed to fair employment, because the agency employed "approximately 60% negroes and some black executives had white secretaries." The agency had failed, however, to fulfill his expectations of making life better for blacks in defense industries and by the war's end he dismissed the organization as "merely a gesture to avoid a nasty situation" of racial and civil strife. Rice warned black workers to prepare for hard times. "The labor and race problem," he lamented, "would be more complex," than it was before or during the conflict. Layoffs, reduced wages, and unsympathetic employers, he cautioned, promised to target black labor. The prospects of worsening conditions for blacks during the postwar years as forecasted by Rice helped change his mind about the need to continue a FEPC. Rice's call for a permanent FEPC was a sharp departure from his criticism of the agency when he declared it useless. As the war neared its end and the attacks against the agency intensified, Rice bemoaned its eminent demise. Rice viewed his efforts to save the FEPC as an exercise to fight southern lawmakers, "like the devil fights a saint," rather than a display of his confidence in the agency.[38] Rice's greatest concern, however, centered on black workers who disregarded the leadership of more conservative blacks and whites and played into the hands of what he characterized as "militant" black labor leaders, "labor racketeers, and professional agitators." These "demagogues," Rice insisted, pitted one race against the other and created a dangerous racial atmosphere at a time when support for the FEPC and black labor was most needed. He feared black workers would suffer most. He prodded black leaders and black workers to pursue economic and political power rather than violent solutions.[39] In a blistering Labor Day message in 1944, Rice charged that the responsibility to promote peace rested as much with the labor movement as it did with any other American institution, including the president and the FEPC.[40]

Although Rice and Wesley resumed their usual ideological debate over unionization, Wesley shared the same sentiments as Rice regarding the prospects of black employment during the postwar period. The establishment of a permanent FEPC, as far as Wesley was concerned, would help ease the "suffering growing pains" of black labor. "This seems a good time for laborers to consider widening their vision and broadening their platform," Wesley insisted, referring to the eminent end of the war and the seemingly bleak future for black unionists. "Every Negro laborer ought to be in favor of the bill to make the Fair Employment Practice Act [Committee] a part of our law so that it will continue after the war." Wesley still insisted, however, that one of the major problems for black unionists rested with divided black leadership. For some time, black leaders had splintered segments of the rank and file, who stood little chance of mounting successful resistance against white-dominated unions and biased employers unless their leaders overcame their differences and worked to unite black workers.[41] As Wesley put it, "Not all of the blame for the existence of the Negro . . . is the blame of the white unions. It is the direct blame of the Negro officials fearing they would lose their presidency. These little men are standing in the way of the best interest of the men they are supposed to represent."[42]

Wesley's observation about Upper Texas Gulf Coast black unionism spoke to the heart of one of the black worker's biggest dilemmas. Indeed, racist white unionists and employers hindered the progress of black unionism, but the decision to continue the struggle to assimilate or integrate into white-led unions, maintain separate-but-equal organizations, align with independent unions, rely on government intercession, or depend solely on the mainstream labor movement posed equally crucial challenges for black workers along the Upper Texas Gulf Coast. As the United States entered the postwar era these new challenges prevailed and the resolve of black unionists and black leaders would help form the foundation for postwar resistance against racial inequalities.

The emergence and work of the FEPC places the role of the federal government in proper context. The agency was but a part of the continual struggle of black unionist to stem pervasive discrimination and to enjoy the economic prosperity that others experienced on a day-to-day basis. By no means was the FEPC a panacea. The limitations of the agency were quite evident. Although it failed to secure the complete assimilation of black workers into industries and unions, its greatest contribution was to make the nation more discrimination-conscious and more responsive to calls for equality and fairness. The post-war period promised to offer an even greater challenge to the entire working class as the federal government retreated on labor's gains and the civil rights movement intensified throughout the country.

CONCLUSION

BLACK WORKERS stepped out of slavery and into an industrial economy that provided impetus for them to apply constant and consistent pressure for change. Their vision of equality, despite the varied approaches they used to acquire it, was focused and intense. The history of black unionists along the Upper Texas Gulf Coast from the latter part of the nineteenth century through the first half of the twentieth demonstrates the important role black workers played in the race and class struggles of the region. Black unionists labored in a vast and diverse industrial environment. Race and class stratification, industrialization, migration, and politics all influenced the rise of black unionism. Although the intensity and origins of black unionism varied from region to region, the experiences of black workers along the Upper Texas Gulf Coast reflected a wider trend in the country. Black workers in Chicago, Cleveland, Detroit, Milwaukee, Birmingham, Memphis, Atlanta, and New Orleans, for example, all made significant adjustments to an expanding industrial economy. Their experiences included race and class discrimination, which they fought tooth and nail to overcome.

Black unionists used numerous strategies to resist workplace biases and gain fair union representation. They put to use a combination of race and class consciousness and moved quickly to organize auxiliaries and union locals. Within these organizations they maintained a measure of racial cohesion while they challenged labor policies that hindered their advancement. They also established alliances with the black middle class, giving black unionists much-needed community support, which generally came in black-owned newspapers. The role of the black middle class and the black press was a part of a larger process of community involvement in the affairs of the black working class during the critical industrial transformation that occurred after the Civil War and lasted through World War II. Black unionists also appealed to government agencies for relief and remedy. Prior to the FEPC, few government agencies showed any interest in the travails of black unionists. Instead, most deferred to the customary racial practices, which allowed white workers to relegate blacks to second-class status.

In some ways the experiences of black unionists along the Upper Texas Gulf Coast differed from those of black unionists in other parts of the country. Although black unionists in most areas struggled against biased employers and white workers, the unprecedented industrial boom along the Texas Gulf Coast created unique circumstances. The region grew to dominate the southern economy in transportation, oil, and manufacturing. Few areas of the country could claim such a diverse economy that stretched across four counties. More importantly, while large numbers of blacks vacated the South for industrial jobs in the North, the Upper Texas Gulf Coast enjoyed an influx of workers to accommodate its industrial growth.

Black unionists along the Upper Texas Gulf Coast formed a dynamic community with diverse dialogue. Their travails lasted throughout the industrial boom of the 1940s. By 1945 it was clear that the multifaceted goals and visions of blacks influenced their day-to-day decisions involving race and class loyalties. Most sought equal pay and fair access to union representation. Indeed, black unionists became an important vehicle in advancing these concerns. As the United States moved into the post–World War II era and the modern civil rights movement, black unionists along the Upper Texas Gulf Coast took with them many of the lessons they learned from their experiences with labor and entered a new era of struggle with a sound base to sustain effective protest, despite the realities of racial divisions.

World War II is generally accepted as a turning point in American race relations, and the creation of the FEPC reflects an initial effort by the federal government to remedy workplace inequities against blacks. World War II and the FEPC redefined the role of government in redressing workplace discrimination. They also reshaped the manner in which blacks approached their struggle for equality. Since World War II, blacks have used the "Double V" motto to their advantage. The relationship between wartime necessities and patriotism became an effective form of resistance against racial discrimination on the homefront during both the Korean and Vietnam Wars. Moreover, the creation of the FEPC demonstrated that the government would respond to real threats of social protest. The fear of civil disobedience moved government officials to grapple with the concerns of black workers. Blacks learned from this experience and used them to combat racism in the decades to follow.

As blacks continued to struggle for occupational justice after the Second World War, the forces lined up against them resisted change. Government still proved unwilling or unable to resolve many of the injustices they faced in the workplace. Ultimately, white unionists reconsidered their relationship with blacks and made efforts to include black workers on a more equal basis. This change resulted, in part, from a shift in attitude and policy of the federal government toward organized labor during the postwar period. The passage of the Taft-Hartley Act in 1947 represented an open assault on the Wagner Act and on the labor movement. Conservative policymakers resented the enormous powers the Wagner Act granted labor unions during the Depression, and postwar conditions such as reduced industrial production and recurring labor difficulties intensified those resentments. The Taft-Hartley Act did not gravely affect big unions and federations although it loosened restrictions on employers and added several restrictions on unions. The act outlawed closed shops (workplaces in which no one could be hired without first joining a union), regulated and limited the scope of strikes and interunion cohesion, and allowed states to deny protection to striking workers and unions through right-to-work laws. The Taft-Hartley Act did not destroy the labor movement, as many workers and labor leaders had predicted. It did impair the status of weaker unions, particularly in loosely organized industries, and made organizing more difficult.[1]

The restrictive provisions of Taft-Hartley pleased conservatives, who viewed union power as a social evil. It angered most workers and labor leaders, who denounced it as a "slave labor bill" and served as a wake-up call for the labor movement. Several pro-labor forces rallied to condemn the policy, including liberal policymakers and prominent labor leaders such as William Green and Philip Murray. Harry S. Truman, a supporter of labor, needed little persuasion when he vetoed the measure.[2] A congressional override of the veto served as a symbol of the repudiation of New Deal politics and a denunciation of the labor movement.

It remained to be seen if Taft-Hartley would create an antiunion trend in the United States and move white workers to rethink their position toward racial equality. The shift in the government's attitude toward organized labor meant that white workers could no longer afford to ignore the concerns of the black worker. Instead, a cohesive core of worker solidarity was needed to withstand the forces aimed at undermining the labor movement. Unless labor solidified its ranks, it could not expect to overcome the wave of conservative and antiunion thought permeating national politics during the postwar years.

Despite the weakening of labor unions and the need for worker solidarity, white workers continued to resist racial equality. The passage of Taft-Hartley and the demise of the FEPC compelled the Upper Texas Gulf Coast black unionists to again reevaluate their strategies for equality, rethink their outlook on unionization, and reconsider their reliance on government. In the aftermath of FEPC failures, black unionists on the Upper Texas Gulf Coast faced the task of choosing a method of struggle that best served their needs. To ignore the power of collective resistance promised to lead to the perpetuation of racial discrimination in the workplace. As black workers moved into the postwar years, they faced challenges that government alone could not resolve. Instead, solidarity within the black labor circle, alongside government intercession and cooperation from white unionists, offered the best chances for fair treatment.

The end of World War II marked a major transitional point for organized labor in the industrial South. The CIO recognized the important role of black unionists and the vulnerable state that organized labor placed itself in without a solid base of black members. Backed by a $1 million budget and 250 organizers, its "holy crusade," which began in May, 1946, was a last major surge to gain union dominance in the South. It turned out to be, however, a battle for the federation's survival. Of the 340,000 southern workers the federation targeted for membership, "Operation Dixie" could only muster a disappointing 25,000. Multiple problems led to the CIO's failed drive, which included red-baiting and other union-busting strategies by conservatives, racism and racial customs, ineffective organizing strategies, and internal factions.[3]

Neither the CIO nor government agencies proved capable of completely satisfying the needs of the black labor community as the country moved into the decisive civil rights decades of the 1950s and 1960s. Many black unionists themselves went forward to voice their anguish through social protest. They understood the cost of relying solely on government agencies or labor federations to protect their rights. They took advantage of their common struggles, organized their communities, and put the power of mass resistance to the test.

The pressure of black protest resulted in the eradication of discrimination in public accommodations and public education. It also forced the government to once again redress racial discrimination in the workplace. The 1954 *Brown v. Board of Education* decision placed intense pressure on U.S. labor leaders. The AFL-CIO enthusiastically declared its support for the mandate at its first convention in December, 1955. Despite the overwhelming negative southern response to the ruling, southern union leaders, in the midst of a crumbling labor movement, understood the potential implications for labor. Equality in public schools translated to equality in the workplace, and for struggling organizations such as the AFL-CIO, it meant the possibility of salvaging the movement. Moreover, the creation of the Equal Employment

Opportunity Commission (EEOC), an outgrowth of the 1964 Civil Rights Act, served a function very similar to the FEPC. The investigation of workplace discrimination and effective enforcement procedures demonstrate the valuable lesson that the government learned from a weak FEPC. The EEOC, unlike the FEPC, reserved the right to penalize employers for discriminatory practices. Although government intercession changed the behavior of white workers and employers in the workplace, the extent to which it altered their attitude about racial equality cannot be measured.

As historians look back on the struggles of the American working class, let them take notice of the voices, narratives, and experiences of the black unionists. What was on the black worker's mind? How did they respond to labor, economic, and social constraints in other parts of the country? These questions and many others challenge students of labor history to examine these dynamics in much greater detail.

Notes

Introduction

1. Leona Mercedes Black, interview by Ernest Obadele-Starks, Houston, Texas, Dec. 13, 1997, in possession of author; *Galveston Daily News,* Nov. 12, 25, and Dec. 13, 1865; Robert E. Zeigler, "The Workingman in Houston, Texas, 1865–1914" (Ph.D. diss., Texas Tech University, 1972), pp. 1–25.

2. Black interview.

3. *Galveston Daily News,* Nov. 12, 25, and Dec. 13, 1865. Also, see Zeigler, "Workingman in Houston, Texas," pp. 1–25; Joseph A. Pratt, *The Growth of a Refining Region,* pp. 3–11; Joe Feagin, *Free Enterprise City: Houston in Political-Economic Perspective,* pp. 58–59; Walter L. Buenger and Joseph A. Pratt, *But Also Good Business: Texas Commerce Banks and the Financing of Houston and Texas, 1886–1986,* pp. 12–39; John Meyer, "Regional Economics: A Survey," *American Economic Review* 53 (Mar., 1963): 19–55; Harry Richardson, *Regional Growth Theory;* and Harvey Perloff, Edgar Dunn, Jr., Eric Lampard, and Richard Muth, *Regions, Resources, and Economic Growth.*

4. U.S. Department of Commerce, Bureau of the Census, *Population of the United States at the Sixteenth Census* (Washington, D.C.: Government Printing Office, 1940); Pratt, *Growth of a Refining Region,* pp. 3–8.

5. Ruth Allen, *Chapters in the History of Organized Labor in Texas,* pp. 169–70.

6. F. Ray Marshall, "Some Reflections on Labor History," *Southwestern Historical Quarterly* (hereafter cited as *SHQ*) 75 (Oct., 1971): 139–57.

7. Marshall, "Some Reflections on Labor History," pp. 139–57. Other incomplete histories on black labor in Texas include Grady Lee Mullenix, "A History of the Texas State Federation of Labor" (Ph.D. diss., University of Texas at Austin, 1955); James Maroney, "Organized Labor in Texas, 1900–1929" (Ph.D. diss., University of Houston, 1975); F. Ray Marshall, *Labor in the South;* Zeigler, "Workingman in Houston, Texas"; Charles Mac Gibson, "Organized Labor in Texas from 1890 to 1900" (M.A. thesis, Texas Tech University, 1973); Harold Shapiro, "The Workers of San Antonio, Texas, 1900–1940" (Ph.D. diss., University of Texas at Austin, 1952); and Murray E. Polakoff, "The Development of the Texas State CIO Council" (Ph.D. diss., Columbia University, 1955).

8. On the emergence of the Jim Crow culture see C. Vann Woodward, *Origins of the New South, 1877–1913,* pp. 205–35; C. Vann Woodward, *Strange Career of Jim Crow;* George B. Tindall, *The Emergence of the New South, 1913–1945;* and Neil McMillen, *Dark Journey: Black Mississippians in the Age of Jim Crow.*

9. See Allen, *Chapters in the History,* pp. 187–90; Marshall, "Some Reflections on Labor His-

tory," p. 144; and Robert Eli Teel, "Discrimination against Negro Workers in Texas: Extent and Effects" (M.A. thesis, University of Texas at Austin, 1947). For observations on the strategies of the black working class in the southern labor movement, see Eric Arnesen, "Following the Color Line of Labor: Black Workers and the Labor Movement before 1930," *Radical History Review* 55 (1993): 53–87; Eric Arnesen, ed., "It Aint Like They Do in New Orleans: Race Relations, Labor Markets, and Waterfront Labor Movements in the American South, 1880–1923," in *Racism and the Labour Market: Historical Studies,* ed. Marcel van der Linden and Jan Lucassen, pp. 57–100; and Eric Arnesen, "'What's on the Black Worker's Mind?': African American Workers and the Union Tradition," *Gulf Coast Historical Review* 10 (1994): 5–18.

10. The classic works on blacks in the labor movement include Charles H. Wesley, *Negro Labor in the United States 1850–1925: A Study in American Economic History;* Sterling D. Spero and Abram L. Harris, *The Black Worker: The Negro and the Labor Movement;* Lorenzo J. Greene and Carter G. Woodson, *The Negro Wage Earner;* and Horace R. Cayton and George S. Mitchell, *Black Workers and the New Unions.*

11. For analysis on the emergence and theoretical framework of southern labor history and the black working class, see Gary M. Fink and Merl E. Reed, eds., *Race, Class, and Communities in Southern Labor History;* Gary M. Fink and Merl E. Reed, eds., *Essays in Southern Labor History: Selected Papers, Southern Labor History Conference, 1976;* and Robert H. Zieger, ed., *Organized Labor in the Twentieth-Century South.* Recent works that address aspects of black unionism in the New South include Daniel Letwin, *The Challenge of Interracial Unionism: Alabama Coal Miners, 1878–1921;* Tera W. Hunter, *To Joy My Freedom: Southern Black Women Lives and Labor after the Civil War;* Michael K. Honey, *Southern Labor and Black Civil Rights: Organizing Memphis Workers;* Eric Arnesen, *Waterfront Workers of New Orleans: Race, Class, and Politics, 1863–1923;* Eric Arnesen, "The African-American Working Class in the Jim Crow Era," *International Labor and Working-Class History* 41 (spring, 1992): 58–75; Robin D. G. Kelley, *Hammer and Hoe: Alabama Communists during the Depression;* and Joe William Trotter, Jr., *Coal, Class, and Color: Blacks in Southern West Virginia, 1915–32.* Also, see Michael Goldfield, *The Color of Politics: Race and the Mainsprings of American Politics;* William H. Harris, *The Harder We Run: Black Workers since the Civil War;* Neil Foley, *The White Scourge: Mexicans, Blacks, and Poor Whites in Texas Cotton Culture;* and Emilio Zamora, *The World of the Mexican Worker in Texas.*

12. See Harris, *Harder We Run,* p. 3; Trotter, *Coal, Class, and Color,* pp. 2–5.

13. See Kelley, *Hammer and Hoe,* pp. 1–10; Arnesen, *Waterfront Workers of New Orleans,* pp. 119–59; Letwin, *Challenge of Interracial Unionism,* pp. 152–56.

14. Hunter, *To Joy My Freedom,* p. viii.

15. One exception to this is Foley's *White Scourge,* which examines the role of black cotton workers in the Southern Tenant Farmers' Union in Texas. See Foley, pp. 188–91.

16. Maury Maverick, *A Maverick American,* p. 224; Judith Kaaz Doyle, "Maury Maverick and Racial Politics in San Antonio, Texas, 1938–1941," *Journal of Southern History* 53 (May, 1987): 196. For more on the historical identity of Texas, see Walter L. Buenger and Robert A. Calvert, "The Shelf Life of Truth in Texas," in *Texas through Time: Evolving Interpretations,* ed. Walter L. Buenger and Robert A. Calvert; Light Townsend Cummins and

Alvin R. Bailey, eds., *A Guide to the History of Texas;* Frank E. Vandiver, *The Southwest: South or West?;* James Sutton Payne, "Texas Historiography in the Twentieth-Century: A Study of Eugene C. Barker, Charles W. Ramsdell, and Walter P. Webb" (Ph.D. diss., University of Denver, 1972).

CHAPTER 1

1. See Howard N. Rabinowitz, *The First New South: 1865–1920;* Gavin Wright, *Old South, New South: Revolutions in the Southern Economy since the Civil War;* Woodward, *Origins of the New South.*

2. John S. Spratt, *The Road to Spindletop: Economic Change in Texas, 1875–1901;* Christopher S. Davis, "Life at the Edge: Urban and Industrial Evolution of Texas, Frontier Wilderness—Frontier Space, 1836–1896," *SHQ* 89 (Apr., 1986): 443–54; Abigail Curlee Holbrook, "Cotton Marketing in Antebellum Texas," *SHQ* 73 (Apr., 1970): 456–78; L. Tuffy Ellis, "The Revolutionizing of the Texas Cotton Trade, 1866–1885," *SHQ* 73 (Apr., 1970): 478–508; Mary Laswell, *John Henry Kirby: Prince of the Pines;* Robert S. Maxwell and Robert D. Baker, *Sawdust Empire: The Texas Lumber Industry, 1830–1940;* Ruth Allen, *East Texas Lumber Workers: An Economic and Social Picture, 1870–1950;* Marilyn D. Rhinehart, "Underground Patriots: Thurber Coal Miners and the Struggle for Individual Freedom, 1888–1903," *SHQ* 92 (Apr., 1989): 509–42; Walter L. Buenger, "The Wonder Age: The Economic Transformation of Northeast Texas, 1900–1930," *SHQ* 98 (Apr., 1995): 519–49.

3. The two standard studies on railroads in Texas are S. G. Reed, *A History of the Texas Railroads and of Transportation Conditions under Spain and Mexico and the Republic and the State;* and C. S. Potts, *Railroad Transportation in Texas.* For a summary of early railroad building along the Upper Texas Gulf Coast, see Andrew Forest Muir, "Railroads Come to Houston, 1857–1861," *SHQ* 64 (July, 1960): 42–63; William D. Angel, Jr., "Vantage on the Bay: Galveston and the Railroads," *East Texas Historical Journal* 22, no. 1 (1984): 3–18; Vera L. Dugas, "A Duel with Railroads: Houston vs. Galveston, 1866–1881," *East Texas Historical Journal* 2, no. 2 (Oct., 1964): 118–27. Also see Ralph Traxler, Jr., "The Texas and Pacific Railroad Land Grants," *SHQ* 61, no. 3 (Jan., 1958): 357–70.

4. See Roger Olien and Diana Olien, *Wildcatters: Texas Independent Oilmen;* Roger Olien and Diana Olien, *Oil Booms: Social Change in Five Texas Towns;* James A. Clark and Michael Halbouty, *Spindletop;* Carl Coke Rister, *Oil! Titan of the Southwest;* Richard R. Moore, *West Texas after the Discovery of Oil: A Modern Frontier;* C. A. Warner, *Texas Oil and Gas since 1543;* Walter Rundell, Jr., *Early Texas Oil Photographic History, 1866–1936.*

5. Alwyn Barr, "Federal Aid for Texas Rivers and Harbors, 1867–1900," *Southern Studies* 16, no. 2 (1977): 233. For a discussion of various theories on the economic development of the Upper Texas Gulf Coast, see Feagin, *Free Enterprise City,* pp. 58–59; Pratt, *Growth of a Refining Region,* pp. 37–39; Buenger and Pratt, *But Also Good Business,* pp. 12–39; and Meyer, "Regional Economics," pp. 19–55.

6. Pratt, *Growth of a Refining Region,* pp. 37–39, 75, 81–82; Also Feagin, *Free Enterprise City,* pp. 58–59; Buenger and Pratt, *But Also Good Business,* pp. 12–39.

7. Pratt, *Growth of a Refining Region,* pp. 37–39.

8. Ibid., pp. 29, 51–52, 69–85.

9. Alwyn Barr, *Black Texans: A History of African Americans in Texas, 1528–1995,* pp. 147–49, 196–98.

10. In the years immediately following the Civil War, three distinct types of programs emerged to advance the cause of southern staple production. In the first, northern officials confiscated rebel land and reallocated it to freedmen as homesteads, which many used for farming. In the second, a system of year-long labor contracts allowed freedmen to remain on plantations while working in staple crop production in exchange for minimal wages. White planters also relied on convict leasing as a means to bolster crop production. Prisoners, many of whom were black, had their labor farmed out to the private sector as part of their criminal punishment. The state, in exchange, received payments from business people for the use of convicts. For example, see Nancy Lack-Cohen, "A Struggle for Sovereignty: National Consolidation, Emancipation, and Free Labor in Texas, 1865," *Journal of Southern History* 58 (Feb., 1992): 57–98; Barr, *Black Texans,* pp. 52–55, 88–90; Donald R. Walker, *Penology for Profit: A History of the Texas Prison System, 1867–1912;* Matthew J. Mancini, *One Dies, Get Another: Convict Leasing in the American South, 1866–1928,* especially chapter 10.

11. From the beginning of slavery until the start of the Civil War, the black population generally moved to the south and then to the west. From the end of the Civil War to the end of the World War I, the trend shifted northward. Nell Irvin Painter traces the forces leading to this change. See Painter, *Exodusters: Black Migration to Kansas after Reconstruction.* Peter Gottlieb examines the footsteps of southern blacks to Pittsburgh between 1916 and 1930. See Gottlieb, *Making Their Own Way: Southern Blacks' Migration to Pittsburgh, 1916–1930.* Also, see Florette Henri, *Black Migration: Movement North, 1900–1920;* Robert B. Grant, *The Black Man Comes to the City;* Hollis R. Lynch, comp., *The Black Urban Condition: A Documentary History, 1866–1971,* and R. H. Leavell, *Negro Migration in 1916–17.* The Upper Texas Gulf Coast, however, with its expanding industrial base, recorded a steady movement into the region following the Civil War.

12. U.S. Department of Commerce, Bureau of the Census, Population Census, 1870–1940.

13. Eric Arnesen, "Charting an Independent Course: African-American Railroad Workers in the World War I Era," in *Labor Histories: Class, Politics, and the Working-Class Experience,* ed. Eric Arnesen, Julie Greene, and Bruce Laurie; Arnesen, "Following the Color Line of Labor," pp. 53–87; Steven A. Reich, "Soldiers of Democracy: Black Texans and the Fight for Citizenship, 1917–1921," *Journal of American History* 82 (Mar., 1996): 1478–1504; Harris, *Harder We Run,* pp. 61, 63–68.

14. *Houston Informer,* June 14, 1919; Feb. 14, 1920.

15. Black interview.

16. Mack Middleton Merritt, interview by Ernest Obadele-Starks, Dec. 13, 1997, Houston, Texas, in possession of author.

17. U.S. Department of Commerce, Bureau of the Census, Population Census, 1870–1920.

18. Ibid., 1920–40.

19. U.S. Department of Commerce, Bureau of the Census, *Twelfth Census of the United States, 1900,* part I, pp. cxii, clxii., 52–53; U.S. Department of Commerce, Bureau of the Census, *Negro Population, 1790–1915* (Washington D.C.: Government Printing Office, 1918), p. 51.

20. Teel, "Discrimination Against Negro Workers in Texas"; James Martin Sorelle, "The Darker Side of 'Heaven': The Black Community in Houston, Texas, 1917–1945" (Ph.D. diss., Kent State University, 1980); Marshall, "Some Reflections on Labor History." On segregation and the discriminatory practices of union locals, see F. Ray Marshall, *The Negro Worker,* pp. 56–63, 117–19; F. Ray Marshall, "The Negro in Southern Unions," in *The Negro and the American Labor Movement,* ed. Julius Jacobson, pp. 128–55; F. Ray Marshall, "Unions and the Black Community," in *The American Labor Movement,* ed. David Brody, pp. 138–44; F. Ray Marshall, *The Negro and Organized Labor,* pp. 7, 44–45. Also, see Michael Honey, "Unionism and Racial Justice in Memphis," in *Organized Labor in the Twentieth-Century South,* ed. Zieger, pp. 135–44; Herbert Northrup, *Organized Labor and the Negro,* pp. 1–14; and Philip S. Foner, *Organized Labor and the Black Worker,* pp. 172–73, 204–205.

21. Harris, *Harder We Run,* pp. 26–28.

22. "Constitution of the General Assembly, District Assemblies, and Local Assemblies of the Order of the Knights of Labor of North America," Texas Company Collection, SC 3, Box 1, Folder 3, Houston Metropolitan Research Center, Houston, Texas (hereafter cited HMRC); Melton A. McLaurin, "Knights of Labor: Internal Dissensions of the Southern Order," in *Essays in Southern Labor History,* ed. Fink and Reed, pp. 3–17; Stephen Brier, "Interracial Organizing in the West Virginia Coal Industry: The Participation of Black Mine Workers in the Knights of Labor and the United Mine Workers, 1880–1894," in *Essays in Southern Labor History,* ed. Fink and Reed; Kenneth Kann, "The Knights of Labor and the Southern Black Worker," *Labor History* 18 (winter, 1977): 51–70; Marshall, *Negro and Organized Labor,* p. 11; Allen, *Chapters in the History,* pp. 20–21, 173–74, 187; Barr, *Black Texans,* p. 93.

23. Longshoremen Workers, Box 2E304, folder 4, Texas Labor Movement Collection, Eugene C. Barker Center for American History, University of Texas at Austin (hereafter cited TLMC). *Galveston Weekly News,* Nov. 5, 12, 1885; Kann, "Knights of Labor," p. 56; Allen, *Chapters in the History,* pp. 173–74.

24. *Austin Statesmen,* July 22, 1886; Allen, *Chapters in the History,* pp. 22, 24, 93, 97, 124, 126, 130; Mullenix, "History of the Texas State Federation of Labor"; Marshall, "Some Reflections on Labor History," p. 144.

25. Marshall, *Negro and Organized Labor,* p. 11.

26. Ibid., p. 15.

27. Proceedings of the 1904 Texas State Federation of Labor, p. 32 (hereafter cited TSFL Proceedings); 1905 TSFL Proceedings, p. 48; 1907 TSFL Proceedings, pp. 59–60; 1908 TSFL Proceedings, pp. 76–77; Allen, *Chapters in the History,* pp. 187–88, 199.

28. 1913 TSFL Proceedings, pp. 78–79; Allen, *Chapters in the History,* pp. 190–91; Marshall, *Labor in the South,* p. 52.

29. 1911 TSFL Proceedings, p. 79; 1913 TSFL Proceedings, pp. 88, 134; 1914 TSFL Proceedings, p. 113; Allen, *Chapters in the History,* pp. 190–92.

30. Allen, *Chapters in the History,* p. 173.

31. Ibid., pp. 130–35.

32. *Nation,* Oct. 30, 1890; Allen, *Chapters in the History,* p. 179; Barr, *Black Texans,* p. 151.

33. Allen, *Chapters in the History,* pp. 221–30, 238, 245, 246.

34. See V. O. Key, *Southern Politics: In State and Nation,* pp. 3–18; Chandler Davidson, *Race and Class in Texas Politics,* pp. 3–10. For more on Texas politics since the Civil War, see Alwyn Barr, *Reconstruction to Reform: Texas Politics, 1876–1906;* F. W. Winkler, ed., *Platforms of Political Parties in Texas;* Paul Douglas Casdorph, *A History of the Republican Party in Texas, 1865–1965;* Howard Beeth and Cary D. Wintz, eds., *Black Dixie: Afro-Texan History and Culture in Houston,* p. 27; Merline Pitre, *Through Many Dangers, Toils and Snares: The Black Political Leadership of Texas, 1868–1900,* pp. 166–73; Carl H. Moneyhon, "George T. Ruby and the Politics of Expediency in Texas," in *Southern Black Leaders of the Reconstruction Era,* ed. Howard N. Rabinowitz, pp. 379–80; James M. Smallwood, *Time of Hope, Time of Despair: Black Texans during Reconstruction,* pp. 91, 138–41.

35. See Paul Douglas Casdorph, "Norris Wright Cuney and Texas Republican Politics, 1883–1896," *SHQ* (Apr., 1965): 455–64; Virginia Neal Hinze, "Norris Wright Cuney" (M.A. thesis, Rice University, 1965); Maude Cuney-Hare, *Norris Wright Cuney: A Tribune of Black People,* pp. 42–49, 188–97; Pitre, *Through Many Dangers,* pp. 188–97.

36. "Longshoremen Workers," Box 2E304, folder 4, TLMC; Marshall, "Some Reflections on Labor History," p. 142; James V. Reese, "The Evolution of an Early Texas Union: The Screwmen's Benevolent Association of Galveston, 1866–1891," *SHQ* 75 (1971): 170, 180–81.

37. "Negro Longshoremen 1898–," Box 2E304, folder 4, TLMC; "History of Black Longshoremen," Box 2E304, folder 4, TLMC.

38. Smallwood, *Time of Hope, Time of Despair,* pp. 128–58; Also, see Jesse Dorsett, "Blacks in Reconstruction Texas, 1865–1877" (Ph.D. diss., Texas Christian University, 1981).

39. Maury Maverick to Forrest Bailey, Oct. 29, 1928, Box 2L45, Maury Maverick, Sr., Papers, Eugene C. Barker Center for American History, University of Texas at Austin; Doyle, "Maury Maverick and Racial Politics in San Antonio," p. 197.

40. Key, *Southern Politics,* pp. 254–55. Although Texas politics reflected the one-party system, as did most states in the South, issues having to do with the role of government in the distribution of income and wealth or with the status of racial groups, Chandler Davidson argues, divided the Texas voting constituency. See Davidson, *Race and Class in Texas Politics,* p. 18. For more on the establishment of Texas politics during the 1930s, see George N. Green, *The Establishment in Texas Politics: The Primitive Years, 1938–1957,* p. 7; George N. Green, *A Liberal View of Texas Politics since the 1930s;* and George N. Green, "The Far Right Wing in Texas Politics, 1930s–1960s" (Ph.D. diss., Florida State University, 1966).

41. Roosevelt created numerous New Deal agencies to provide jobs for the unemployed. The most important of these included the Employment Relief Administration, the National Recovery Administration, the Works Projects Administration, the Agricultural Adjustment Administration, the Tennessee Valley Authority, the National Youth Administration, and the Civilian Conservation Corps. Good studies on the New Deal include William R. Brock, *Welfare, Democracy, and the New Deal;* Thomas I. Emerson, *Young Lawyer for the New Deal: An Insider's Memoir of the Roosevelt Years;* Joseph J. Hutchmacher, *Senator Robert Wagner and the Rise of Urban Liberalism;* Albert U. Romasco, *The Politics of Recovery: Roosevelt's New Deal;* and Jordan Schwarz, *The New Dealers.* Leslie H. Fishel, "The Negro in the New Deal Era," *Wisconsin Magazine of History* 48 (winter, 1964–65):

112–26; Harvard Sitkoff, *A New Deal for Blacks: The Emergence of Civil Rights as a National Issue,* vol. 1, pp. 58–83; Raymond Wolters, *Negroes and the Great Depression: The Problem of Economic Recovery;* Jervis Anderson, *A. Philip Randolph: A Biographical Portrait,* p. 244. For more on Eleanor Roosevelt, see Russell Freedman, *Eleanor Roosevelt: A Life of Discovery;* John W. T. Youngs, *Eleanor Roosevelt: A Personal and Public Life;* and Tamara K. Hareven, *Eleanor Roosevelt: An American Conscience.*

42. *Houston Informer,* Mar. 21, 1936; *Negro Labor News,* Apr. 9, 1938; Nov. 12, 1938; Randy J. Sparks, "Heavenly Houston or Hellish Houston? Black Unemployment and Relief Efforts, 1929–1936," *Southern Studies* 25, no. 4 (winter, 1986): 353–67; Christie L. Bourgeois, "Stepping over Lines: Lyndon Johnson, Black Texans, and the National Youth Administration, 1935–1937," *SHQ* 91, no. 2 (Oct., 1987): 149–72; Eddie Simpson, Jr., *My Remembers: A Black Sharecropper's Recollections of the Depression.* General accounts of the Depression in Texas include S. S. McKay and O. B. Faulk, *Texas after Spindletop;* Robert C. Cortner, ed., *Texas Cities and the Great Depression;* Donald Whisenhunt, ed., *The Depression in the Southwest;* and Donald Whisenhunt, *The Depression in Texas: The Hoover Years.*

43. See Brock, *Welfare, Democracy, and the New Deal;* Romasco, *Politics of Recovery;* Schwarz, *New Dealers;* Emerson, *Young Lawyer,* p. 45.

44. Green, *Establishment in Texas Politics,* p. 62.

45. See Joseph McCartin, *Labor's Great War: The Struggle for Industrial Democracy and the Origins of Modern American Labor Relations, 1912–1921,* pp. 75, 114–18, 127, 149, 151–57; Joseph McCartin, "Abortive Reconstruction: Federal War Labor Policies, Union Organization, and the Politics of Race, 1917–1920," *Journal of Policy History* 9, no. 2 (1997): 158–65.

46. For a discussion on the formation of the NLRB, see James A. Gross, *The Making of the National Labor Relations Board: A Study in Economics, Politics and the Law, 1933–1937.*

47. "Our Inalienable Rights: A Brief History of Locals 229 and 243 Oil Workers International Union, 1937–1945," p. 2, Oil, Chemical and Atomic Workers (OCAW) Collection, Tyrrell Historical Library, Beaumont, Texas; National Labor Relations Board, *Decisions and Orders.*

48. "To Create a National Labor Board," Hearings before the Committee on Education and Labor, U.S. Senate, Congressional Record, 73rd Congress, 2nd Sess., part 3, Apr. 9, 1934, pp. 991–96.

49. Ibid., pp. 1020–22.

50. Ibid., p. 1022; Wolters, *Negroes and the Great Depression,* pp. 186–87.

51. Increasing interest in the role of the CIO in the American labor movement and the struggle for industrial unions during the 1930s has led to a flowering of recent literature. The most thorough treatment of the CIO is Robert H. Zieger, *The CIO, 1935–1955.* On the CIO in the South, see Zieger, *The CIO,* 74–78, 227–36; also, Rick Halpern, "Interracial Unionism in the Southwest: Fort Worth's Packinghouse Workers, 1937–1954," in *Organized Labor in the Twentieth-Century South,* ed. Zieger, pp. 158–69; Marshall, *Negro Worker,* pp. 23–29; Marshall, *Negro and Organized Labor,* pp. 34–41.

52. *Negro Labor News,* Sept. 11, 1937; Lee A. Lewis transcribed interview by George N. Green, Oct. 4, 1971, Texas Labor Archive Collection #14, University of Texas at Arlington (hereafter cited TLAC); Chris Dixie interview by Ernest Obadele-Starks, Apr. 22, 1995, Hous-

ton, Texas, Oral History Collection of the East Texas Economy (hereafter cited ETOH); 1938 Texas State Industrial Council (TSCIO) Convention Proceedings, p. 6; Marshall, *Negro Worker,* pp. 23–29; Marshall, *Negro and Organized Labor,* pp. 34–41. For discussions on the CIO's racial equality program see Michael Goldfield, "Race and the CIO: The Possibilities for Racial Egalitarianism during the 1930s and 1940s," *International Labor and Working-Class History* 44 (fall, 1993): 1–32; Judith Stein, "The Ins and Outs of the CIO," *International Labor and Working-Class History* 44 (fall, 1993): 53–63; Gary Gerstle, "Working-Class Racism: Broaden the Focus," *International Labor and Working-Class History* 44 (fall, 1993): 33–40; Robert Korstad, "The Possibilities for Racial Egalitarianism: Context Matters," *International Labor and Working-Class History* 44 (fall, 1993): 41–44.

53. *Negro Labor News,* Apr. 15, 1939.

54. *Negro Labor News,* July 17, Sept. 25, 1937; Nov. 6, 1937; July 30, 1938; Dixie interview. For a general look at the organizing years of the CIO in Texas, see Polakoff, "Development of the Texas State CIO Council."

55. *Negro Labor News,* July 31, 1937; June 27, 1939; Jan. 6, 1940; May 27, 1944. For more on the communist movement in the United States, see Albert Fried, ed., *Communism in America: A History in Documents;* Alex Lichtenstein, "Scientific Unionism and the 'Negro Question': Communists and the Transport Workers Union in Miami, 1944–1949," in *Southern Labor in Transition, 1940–1995,* ed. Robert H. Zieger; Harvey Klehr, *Secret World of American Communism;* Harvey A. Levenstein, *Communism, Anti-Communism, and the CIO;* Steve Rosswurm, ed., *The CIO's Left-Led Unions;* Kelley, *Hammer and Hoe;* Max M. Kampelman, *The Communist Party vs. the C.I.O.;* Zieger, *The CIO,* chapter 9.

56. *Negro Labor News,* Nov. 12, 1938; June 10, 1939; July 27, Oct. 19, 1940.

57. Ibid., Nov. 12, 1938; July 27, 1940; Oct. 19, 1940.

58. See Reich, "Soldiers of Democracy," pp. 1478–1504; Arnesen, "Charting an Independent Course," pp. 284–308; Harris, *Harder We Run,* pp. 67–76. Also, Tony Martin, *Race First: The Ideological and Organizational Struggles of Marcus Garvey and the Universal Negro Improvement Association.*

59. *Houston Informer,* June 28, 1919; Mar. 13, 1920; Dec. 23, 1922; Beeth and Wintz, eds., *Black Dixie,* p. 128. Martin, *Race First,* pp. 15, 367.

60. From 1910 to 1940 the population of Houston, the economic center of the Upper Texas Gulf Coast, nearly quintupled, a growth exceeded in this era by only one other major city, Los Angeles. By 1930, Houston led the South in the employment of blacks in the industrial workforce and employed more blacks in manufacturing jobs than its rival southern cities of Memphis, New Orleans, and Atlanta. It also ranked as the largest city in Texas, the second largest in the South, and the twenty-first largest in the nation. See U.S. Dept. of Commerce, Bureau of the Census, *The Labor Force: Parts I, II, III of the Fifteenth Census* (Washington, D.C.: Government Printing Office, 1940).

61. C. W. Rice was the principal owner of the *Negro Labor News.* To a large extent, the labor assessments of Rice reflected the polemics that passed between political opponents. Thus, Rice's publications could be considered subjective and partisan. See Hobart T. Taylor, "C. W. Rice: Labor Leader" (B.A. thesis, Prairie View State Normal and Industrial College, Prairie View, Tex., 1939); 1936–1954 Correspondence Folder, C. W. Rice Family and *Negro Labor News* Collection, RG MSS 242, HMRC (hereafter cited Rice Collection); For

more on Rice's position toward organized labor, see *Negro Labor News,* Apr. 9, Sept. 17, Oct. 29, 1938; June 24, Nov. 11, 13, 25, Dec. 9, 23, 1939; Apr. 22, 24, May 6, July 15, Sept. 2, 17, Aug. 19, Dec. 23, 1944. Also, Michael R. Botson, Jr., "Organized Labor at the Hughes Tool Company, 1918–1942: From Welfare to the Steel Workers Organizing Committee" (M.A. thesis, University of Houston, 1994), pp. 57–58.

62. Taylor, "C. W. Rice," chapter 3; *Negro Labor News,* Apr. 9, 1938; Nov. 13, Dec. 23, 1939.

63. *Negro Labor News,* Apr. 9, 1938; Nov. 13, Dec. 23, 1939.

64. *Negro Labor News,* May 27, Nov. 11, 1939; Mar. 16, 20, May 18, 1940; Jan. 9, 23, 1943; Barr, *Black Texans,* p. 136; Harvey O'Connor, *History of Oil Workers International Union-CIO,* p. 315; Maurice Easterwood interview by Ernest Obadele-Starks, Apr. 21, 1995, Houston, Texas, ETOH.

65. *Negro Labor News,* Nov. 25, Dec. 23, 1939.

66. Ibid., Nov. 25, Dec. 23, 1939; Mar. 30, 1940.

67. National Association of Industrial Labor for Colored People (NAIL) Business Proposal, MSS 285, Box 1, Folder 1, Reverend Bertron M. Jackson Family Collection, HMRC.

68. *Houston Informer,* July 12, Sept. 13, 1941; 1945 TSCIO Proceedings, Oct. 20, 1945, pp. 49–52; Beeth and Wintz, *Black Dixie,* pp. 112, 183.

69. Merline Pitre, "Black Houstonians and the 'Separate But Equal' Doctrine: Carter W. Wesley Versus LuLu B. White," *The Houston Review: History and Culture of the Gulf Coast* 12, no. 1 (1990): 23–36; Also, see Nancy Ruth Bessent, "The Publisher: A Biography of Carter W. Wesley" (Ph.D. diss., University of Texas, 1981).

70. Pitre, "Black Houstonians," pp. 23–36;

71. *Houston Informer,* Mar. 6, 9, 1940.

72. Allison "Bud" Alton, interview by Ernest Obadele-Starks, Apr. 21, 1995, Houston, Texas, ETOH; *Negro Labor News,* Mar. 16, 20, May 18, 1940; Jan. 9, 1943; *Houston Informer,* Mar. 9, 1940.

73. *Houston Informer,* Dec. 26, 1942.

74. *Negro Labor News,* Nov. 25, 1939; Dec. 26, 1942.

75. See Charles Flint Kellogg, *NAACP: A History of the National Association for the Advancement of Colored People, vol. 1, 1909–1920;* John Hope Franklin and Alfred A. Moss, Jr., *From Slavery to Freedom: A History of Negro Americans,* pp. 288–89; August Meier and Elliot Rudwick, *From Plantation to Ghetto,* pp. 87–89; Alan H. Spear, *Black Chicago: The Making of a Negro Ghetto, 1890–1920,* pp. 227–31.

76. *Negro Labor News,* Oct. 23, 1937; Nancy Dailey, "History of the Beaumont, Texas Chapter of the National Association for the Advancement of Colored People, 1918–1970" (M.A. thesis, Lamar University, 1971), pp. 23–46; Michael L. Gillette, "The NAACP in Texas, 1937–1957" (Ph.D. diss., University of Texas, 1984), pp. 1–5; Reich, "Soldiers of Democracy," pp. 1490–91;

77. See Merline Pitre, *In Struggle against Jim Crow: LuLu B. White and the NAACP, 1900–1957,* p. 70; Pitre, "Black Houstonians," pp. 23–36.

78. Richard M. Dalfiume, *Desegregation of the U.S. Armed Forces: Fighting on Two Fronts, 1939–1953;* Beth Bailey and David Farber, "The Double-V Campaign in World War II Hawaii: African Americans, Racial Ideology, and Federal Power," *Journal of Social History* 26 (summer, 1993): 817–43; John Modell, Marc Goulden, and Sigurdur Magnusson,

"World War II in the Lives of Black Americans: Some Findings and Interpretations," *Journal of American History* 76 (Dec., 1989): 838–48; Kenneth O'Reilly, "The Roosevelt Administration and Black America: Federal Surveillance Policy and Civil Rights during the New Deal and World War II," *Phylon* 48 (Mar., 1987): 12–25; Phillip McGuire, "Desegregation of the Armed Forces: Black Leadership, Protest, and World War II," *Journal of Negro History* 68 (fall, 1983): 147–58; Harvard Sitkoff, "Racial Militancy and Interracial Violence in the Second World War," *Journal of American History* 58 (Dec., 1971): 661–81; Karen Tucker Anderson, "Last Hired, First Fired: Black Women Workers during World War II," *Journal of American History* 69 (June, 1982); Lee Finkle, "The Conservative Aims of Militant Rhetoric: Black Protest during World War II," *Journal of American History* 60, no. 3 (Dec., 1973): 692–13; Richard M. Dalfiume, "The Forgotten Years of the Negro Revolution," *Journal of American History* 55 (1968): 90–106; James S. Olson, "Organized Black Leadership and Industrial Unionism: The Racial Response, 1936–1945," *Labor History* 10 (summer, 1969): 475–86. Also, see Neil A. Wynn, *The Afro-American and the Second World War.*

79. *Negro Labor News,* June 17, 1944.
80. *Houston Informer,* Dec. 13, 1941; *Negro Labor News,* Dec. 20, 1941; June 17, Dec. 23, 1944.
81. For specific discussions on the origins and development of the FEPC, see Merl E. Reed, *Seedtime for the Modern Civil Rights Movement: The President's Committee on Fair Employment Practice, 1941–1946;* Louis C. Kesselman, *The Social Politics of the FEPC: A Study in Reform Pressure Movements;* Louis Ruchames, *Race, Jobs, and Politics: The Story of FEPC;* Herbert Garfinkel, *When Negroes March: The March on Washington Movement in the Organizational Politics for FEPC;* Frances Anne Hardin, "The Role of Presidential Advisors: Roosevelt Aides and the FEPC, 1941–1943" (M.A. thesis, Cornell University, 1975).

CHAPTER 2

1. Spero and Harris, *Black Worker,* pp. 182–205, quotes found on pp. 183 and 199.
2. Gilbert Mers, *Working the Waterfront: The Ups and Downs of a Rebel Longshoreman,* pp. ix–x; Arnesen, *Waterfront Workers of New Orleans,* pp. 21, 126.
3. Reese, "Evolution of an Early Texas Union," pp. 158–85; Allen Clayton Taylor, "A History of the Screwmen's Benevolent Association from 1865 to 1924" (M.A. thesis, University of Texas, 1968), p. 71; James C. Maroney, "The International Longshoremen's Association in the Gulf States during the Progressive Era," *Southern Studies* 16, no. 2 (summer, 1977): 225–32.
4. Arnesen, "It Aint Like They Do in New Orleans," in *Racism and the Labour Market,* ed. van der Linden and Lucassen, pp. 57–64.
5. Reese, "Evolution of an Early Texas Union," pp. 160–61.
6. Longshore Workers, Box 2E304, folder 1, TLMC.
7. "Negro Longshoremen 1898–," Box 2E304, folder 4, TLMC; "History of Black Longshoremen," Box 2E304, folder 4, TLMC; Pitre, *Through Many Dangers,* pp. 188–97; Casdorph, "Norris Wright Cuney," pp. 455–64; Hinze, "Norris Wright Cuney"; Hare, *Norris Wright Cuney,* pp. 42–49.
8. "Longshoremen Workers," Box 2E304, folder 4, TLMC; "History of Screwmen's Be-

nevolent No. 2," Box 2E304, folder 1, TLMC; "Longshoremen Workers," Box 2E304, folder 1, TLMC; "Negro Longshoremen 1898—Federal Labor Union #7174," Box 2E304, folder 1, TLMC; *Galveston Daily News,* Nov. 5, 12, 1885; Reese, "Evolution of an Early Texas Union," pp. 158–85; Allen, *Chapters in the History,* pp. 173–74; Kann, "Knights of Labor," p. 56.

9. "Longshoremen Workers," Box 2E304, folder 4, TLMC; "History of Screwmen's Benevolent No. 2," Box 2E304, folder 1, TLMC; Longshoremen Workers, Box 2E304, folder 1, TLMC; "Negro Longshoremen 1898—Federal Labor Union #7174," Box 2E304, folder 1, TLMC.

10. "Negro Longshoremen 1898–," Box 2E304, folder 1, TLMC; "History of Black Longshoremen," Box 2E306, folder 6, TLMC; "An Account of the Mallory Line Strike of 1898," Box 2E304, folder 6, TLMC.

11. "Negro Longshoremen 1898–," Box 2E304, folder 1, TLMC; "History of Black Longshoremen," Box 2E306, folder 6, TLMC; "An Account of the Mallory Line Strike of 1898," Box 2E304, folder 6, TLMC.

12. "An Account of the Mallory Line Strike of 1898," Box 2E304, folder 6, TLMC; "Negro Longshoremen, 1898–," Box 2E304, folder 1, TLMC; *Galveston Daily News,* Aug. 31, Sept. 1–4, 1898; Jan. 25, 1919.

13. "An Account of the Mallory Line Strike of 1898," Box 2E304, folder 6, TLMC; "Negro Longshoremen, 1898–," Box 2E304, folder 1, TLMC.

14. "An Account of the Mallory Line Strike of 1898," Box 2E304, folder 6, TLMC; "Negro Longshoremen, 1898–," Box 2E304, folder 1, TLMC; "Longshoremen Workers: Union Organizing, 1866–1910," Box 2E304, folder 1, TLMC.

15. "Longshore Workers: Sabine District, 1897–1937," Box 2E305, folder 3, TLMC.

16. Ibid.

17. "Longshore Workers: Sabine District, 1897–1937," Box 2E305, folder 3, TLMC; interview notes of H. F. Gildersleve, July 29, 1936, Box 2E308, folder 2, TLMC.

18. 1914 District Proceedings of the Gulf Coast International Longshoremen's Association (DILA); "Longshore Workers," "Union Organizing," Box 2E304, folder 1, TLMC. The National Longshoremen's Association (NLA) of the United States was founded in 1892 by representatives of ten lumber handlers unions from the Great Lakes. Historians debate the year that the ILA was founded. Some historians suggest 1892, while others claim the union was first formed in 1877. The NLA joined the AFL in 1893 and changed its name to the International Longshoremen's Association (ILA). By 1901 the ILA's strength centered on the Great Lakes region, though by the 1910s, a Southern Gulf District of the ILA had joined Galveston, New Orleans, Mobile, and several other smaller ports. Not until World War I did the ILA have a significant impact on labor issues along the Upper Texas Gulf Coast. On the early history of the ILA see John R. Commons, "The Longshoremen of the Great Lakes," in *Labor and Administration,* pp. 267–68; Maud Russell, *Men along the Shore: The I.L.A. and its History,* pp. 62–74.

19. Quotes are from "Longshore Workers: Texas City and Port Arthur Lockout, 1914–1915," Box 2E305, folder 5, TLMC.

20. Interview notes of H. F. Gildersleve, July 29, 1936, Box 2E308, folder 2, TLMC; "Conflict and the Race Problem," Box 2E306, folder 5, TLMC; Gilbert Mers Report on Work

Conditions in the Gulf Coast," MSS 63, folder, 3, Gilbert Mers Collection, HMRC. Also, see Maroney, "International Longshoremen's Association," pp. 225–32.

21. Wendell P. Terrell, "A Short History of the Negro Longshoremen" (Senior thesis, Houston College for Negroes, 1936), Box 2E304, folder 1, TLMC; "Longshore Workers: Longshoremen in Texas, 1914–1923," Box 2E305, folder 6, TLMC.

22. "Longshore Workers: Longshoremen in Texas, 1914–1923," Box 2E305, folder 6, TLMC; Terrell, "Short History of the Negro Longshoreman"; "Anecdotal History of Local 1273," Box MSS 63, folder 9, Mers Collection, HMRC.

23. "Longshore Workers: Longshoremen in Texas, 1914–1923," Box 2E305, folder 6, TLMC; Terrell, "Short History of the Negro Longshoreman"; "Anecdotal History of Local 1273," Box MSS 63, folder 9, Mers Collection, HMRC.

24. James C. Maroney, "The Galveston Longshoremen's Strike of 1920," *East Texas Historical Journal* 16, no. 1 (1978): 34–38; Maroney, "The International Longshoremen's Association," pp. 231–32.

25. "Conflict and the Race Problem," Box 2E306, folder 5, TLMC; "Racial Conflicts," Box 2E306, folder 6, TLMC; Excerpts from the Proceedings of the Fourteenth Annual Convention of the South Atlantic and Gulf Coast District of the ILA, p. 9–12.

26. "Gilbert Mers Report on Work Conditions in the Gulf Coast," MSS 63, folder 3, Mers Collection, HMRC.

27. "Longshore Workers, Women, and the ILA, 1931–36," Box 2E306, folder 4, TLMC.

28. "Longshore Workers: Ship Channel Progressive Committee Newsletter, 1936–1937," Box 2E307, folder 1, TLMC.

29. "Negro Longshoremen," Box 2E306, folder 5, TLMC; "Black Longshoremen," Box 2E306, folder 5, TLMC; 1935 TSFL Proceedings.

30. LeRoy Hoskins interview by Ernest Obadele-Starks, Apr. 14, 1995, Galveston, Texas, ETOH.

31. *Negro Labor News,* Dec. 22, 1934; Oct. 23, 1937; *Houston Informer,* Jan. 4, 1936.

32. "Anecdotal History of Local 1273"; Gilbert Mers interview by Ernest Obadele-Starks, Apr. 15, 1995, Houston, Texas, ETOH; Bruce Nelson, *Workers on the Waterfront: Seamen, Longshoremen, and Unionism in the 1930s,* pp. 127–55, 223–49; Bruce Nelson, "Class and Race in the Crescent City: The ILWU, from San Francisco to New Orleans," in *CIO's Left-Led Unions,* ed. Rosswurm, pp. 19–45.

33. Don Willett, "The Galveston Bay Dock Wars, 1936–1937," *East Texas Historical Journal* 32, no. 1 (1994): 27–38.

34. "Political Activity," Box 2E306, folder 6, TLMC; "Racial Conflicts"; 1936 South Atlantic & Gulf Coast District, ILA Proceedings (hereafter cited ILA District Proceedings); 1937 ILA District Proceedings.

35. "Demands Agreed Upon in Joint Meetings of Committees on Contract Demands Representing All ILA Locals in the Port of Houston," July 22–23, 1937, MSS 63, folder 3, Mers Collection; 1935 TSFL Proceedings; 1936 ILA District Proceedings; *Negro Labor News,* Apr. 29, 1939.

36. 1942 and 1945 ILA District Proceedings; 1944 TSFL Proceedings; Hoskins interview; Russell, *Men along the Shore,* pp. 139–40; Paul T. Hartman, *Collective Bargaining and Productivity: The Longshore Mechanization Agreement,* pp. 34–35.

CHAPTER 3

1. Wright, *Old South, New South,* pp. 39, 43; Stanley Buder, *Pullman: An Experiment in Industrial Order and Social Planning;* Almont Lindsey, *The Pullman Strike: The Story of a Unique Experiment and of a Great Labor Upheaval;* Harris, *Harder We Run,* p. 41; John F. Stover, *The Railroads of the South, 1865–1900,* p. 58.

2. For railroad expansion in Texas see Muir, "Railroads Come to Houston," pp. 42–63; Angel, "Vantage on the Bay," pp. 3–18; Dugas, "A Duel with Railroads," pp. 118–27. Also Traxler, "Texas and Pacific Railroad Land Grants," pp. 357–70. The two standard studies on railroads in Texas are Reed, *History of the Texas Railroads,* and Potts, *Railroad Transportation in Texas.*

3. Harris, *Harder We Run,* pp. 40–41.

4. *Nation,* Oct., 1890; Allen, *Chapters in the History,* p. 179; Barr, *Black Texans,* p. 151; Don Hofsommer, *The Southern Pacific, 1901–1985,* pp. 5–7.

5. Memorandum for the Sub-Committee of the House Committee on Education and Labor in reference to H.R. 4453, "Discrimination Against Negro Railway Workers," 81st Congress, 1st Sess., 1917.

6. Ibid.

7. Ibid.

8. See Harris, *Keeping the Faith,* pp. 26–65, 226–28; Harris, *Harder We Run,* pp. 77–94; Florence Murray, *The Negro Handbook, 1942,* p. 136.

9. Mr. and Mrs. James H. Saunders transcribed interview by Carr Winn, Aug. 13, 1971, Oral History Collection #14, TLAC.

10. Saunders interview; Harris, *Keeping the Faith,* pp. 26–65, 226–28; Harris, *Harder We Run,* pp. 77–94. Also, see Anderson, *A. Philip Randolph.*

11. Harris, *Keeping the Faith,* pp. 26–65, 226–28; Harris, *Harder We Run,* pp. 77–94; Murray, *Negro Handbook,* p. 136.

12. See Paula F. Pfeffer, "The Women behind the Union: Halena Wilson, Rosina Tucker, and the Ladies' Auxiliary to the Brotherhood of Sleeping Car Porters," *Labor History* 36 (fall, 1995): 557–78; Melinda Chateauvert, *Marching Together: Women of the Brotherhood of Sleeping Car Porters.*

13. Arnesen, "Charting an Independent Course," pp. 294–96.

14. Damon McCrary to F. C. Caldwell, Mar. 30, 1939, Colored Trainmen of America (CTA) Collection, HMRC; Agreement between the Colored Brakemen and the Gulf Coast Lines, Jan. 1, 1929, CTA Collection; Agreement between International–Great Northern Railroad Company and the Order of Railway Conductors and the Brotherhood of Railroad Trainmen, Nov. 1, 1924, CTA Collection; Black interview; Murray, *Negro Handbook,* p. 138.

15. National Mediation Board Case Summary, Mar. 9, 1935, CTA Collection; Irving Bernstein, *The Lean Years: A History of the American Worker, 1920–1933,* pp. 215–20; Harris, *Harder We Run,* pp. 92–93.

16. Agreement between Missouri Pacific Lines, New Orleans–Texas–Mexico Railway Company, and the Brotherhood of Railroad Trainmen, May 1, 1935, CTA Collection.

17. W. G. Choate to Lloyd Allen, Oct. 22, 1937, CTA Collection.

18. George A. Cook to W. H. Jefferson, Dec. 13, 1935, CTA Collection.

19. Preliminary statement of Colored Trainmen of America to the Special Adjustment Board No. 24, Docket No. 141, CTA Collection.

20. *Negro Labor News,* Jan. 29, 1938.

21. "Resolution," of Colored Trainmen of America, Feb. 13, 1938, CTA Collection.

22. *Negro Labor News,* July 7, 1938.

23. W. H. Jefferson to L. A. David, Oct. 21, 1938, CTA Collection; W. H. Jefferson to L. A. Gregory, Sept. 19, 1938, CTA Collection; W. H. Jefferson to G. C. Kennedy, Sept. 27, 1938, CTA Collection; L. A. David to W. H. Jefferson, Oct. 24, 1938, CTA Collection.

24. Colored Trainmen of America Resolution, Feb. 14, 1939, CTA Collection.

25. Damon McCrary to F. C. Caldwell, Mar. 30, 1939, CTA Collection; Arnesen, "Charting an Independent Course," pp. 284–308; Harris, *Keeping the Faith,* p. 14.

26. Damon McCrary to F. C. Caldwell, Mar. 30, 1939, CTA Collection.

27. Colored Trainmen of America Constitution, Nov. 12, 1941, CTA Collection.

28. Damon McCrary to F. C. Caldwell, Mar. 30, 1939, CTA Collection; *Negro Labor News,* Oct. 9, 1937; Jan. 29, 1938.

29. Francis Wright to H. E. Roll, Apr. 20, 1943, CTA Collection; H. E. Roll to W. H Jefferson, Sept. 30, 1943, CTA Collection.

30. Damon McCrary to F. C. Caldwell, Mar. 30, 1939, CTA Collection; 1939 TSFL Proceedings, pp. 176–78; Mullenix, "History of the Texas State Federation of Labor," pp. 364–65. *Negro Labor News,* Oct. 9, 1937; Jan. 29, 1938; Harris, *Harder We Run,* pp. 71–72.

31. 1939 TSFL Proceedings, pp. 140–41; Afro American Railroad Employee Collection, RGD 004, Box 188, folder 13, HMRC; Harris, *Keeping the Faith,* p. 14.

32. J. D. Patrick to Office of Trainmaster, June 13, 1940, CTA Collection.

33. Moses LeRoy transcribed interview by George Green, Aug. 19, 1971, TLAC #20; *Negro Labor News,* May 13, 1939; Harris, *Keeping the Faith,* p. 170.

34. LeRoy interview; *Negro Labor News,* May 13, 1939; Harris, *Keeping the Faith,* p. 170.

35. *Negro Labor News,* Oct. 1, 15, 1938; Feb. 18, 1939; Harris, *Keeping the Faith,* pp. 2, 39.

36. *Negro Labor News,* Nov. 6, 1937; June 24, July 8, July 23, Nov. 25, 1939; Apr. 6, 1940; Dec. 23, 1944; Murray, *Negro Handbook,* pp. 139–40.

37. *Negro Labor News,* Apr. 9, 1938.

38. Ibid.

39. Ibid., Nov. 12, 1938.

40. Herman W. Simpson, *Hands of the Throttle: A Black Man's Struggle on the Road,* pp. 1–3.

41. *Negro Labor News,* May 13, 1939.

42. *Negro Labor News,* Nov. 13, 1939; Ira De A. Reid, *Negro Membership in American Labor Unions,* p. 33.

43. *Negro Labor News,* June 24, July 8, 23, Nov. 25, 1939; Apr. 6, 1940; Dec. 23, 1944; Murray, *Negro Handbook,* pp. 139–40.

44. *Negro Labor News,* June 1, 1940; Apr. 25, 1942; Murray, *Negro Handbook,* p. 138.

45. *Houston Informer,* July 21, 1945; Herbert Hill, *Black Labor and the American Legal System: Race, Work, and the Law,* p. 363; Arthur M. Ross and Herbert Hill, *Employment, Race, and Poverty,* p. 487.

CHAPTER 4

1. See Woodward, *Origins of the New South,* pp. 302–304; The best study to date on the refining industry in the American South is Pratt, *Growth of a Refining Region.* Also, see Olien and Olien, *Wildcatters;* Olien and Olien, *Oil Booms;* Clark and Halbouty, *Spindletop;* Rister, *Oil! Titan of the Southwest;* Moore, *West Texas after the Discovery of Oil;* Warner, *Texas Oil and Gas since 1543;* Rundell, *Early Texas Oil Photographic History.*

2. O'Connor, *History of Oil Workers International Union-CIO,* pp. 4–8, 205, 305.

3. O'Connor, *History of Oil Workers International Union-CIO,* pp. 1–4; Allen, *Chapters in the History,* pp. 221–22.

4. Pratt, *Growth of a Refining Region,* p. 164.

5. *Gulf Coast Oil News,* Oct. 20, 1917, pp. 12–13; O'Connor, *History of Oil Workers International Union-CIO,* pp. 4–6, 204, 221–28; James C. Maroney, "The Texas-Louisiana Oil Field Strike of 1917," in *Essays in Southern Labor History,* ed. Fink and Reed, pp. 161–72; Allen, *Chapters in the History,* pp. 222–24.

6. O'Connor, *History of Oil Workers International Union-CIO,* pp. 4–8.

7. Pratt, *Growth of a Refining Region,* pp. 164–65.

8. O'Connor, *History of Oil Workers International Union-CIO,* p. 15.

9. *Gulf Coast Oil News,* Nov. 10, 1917, p. 29; O'Connor, *History of Oil Workers International Union-CIO,* pp. 204, 359,

10. O'Connor, *History of Oil Workers International Union-CIO,* pp. 117–18.

11. *The Magpetco* was a monthly plant magazine published in the 1920s at Magnolia's Beaumont refinery. Quote is found in *The Magpetco* 1, no. 1 (Apr., 1921), p. 13; Pratt, *Growth of a Refining Region,* pp. 155–56.

12. *Houston Informer,* June 28, 1919; Mar. 13, 1920; Dec. 23, 1922; Beeth and Wintz, eds., *Black Dixie,* p. 128.

13. O'Connor, *History of Oil Workers International Union-CIO,* pp. 114–15, 18; Pratt, *Growth of a Refining Region,* p. 166.

14. Pratt, *Growth of a Refining Region,* pp. 172–73; Pratt, "The Oil Workers International Unions' Organization of the Upper Texas Gulf Coast: 1935–1945" (Senior thesis, Rice University, 1970), pp. 8, 19; Emilio Zamora, "The Failed Promise of Wartime Opportunity for Mexicans in the Texas Oil Industry," *SHQ* 95 (winter, 1992): 325–26; O'Connor, *History of Oil Workers International Union-CIO,* pp. 15, 29–35, 119, 305, 317.

15. "Early History of Port Neches Local 228," MS-129, Oil, Chemical, and Atomic Workers of America (OCAW) Collection, Tyrrell Historical Library, Beaumont, Texas, pp. 36–37, 52.

16. Oil Workers Interview Notes, Box 2E308, folder 2, TLMC.

17. "Our Inalienable Right," p. 2; O'Connor, *History of Oil Workers International Union-CIO,* p. 118.

18. "Our Inalienable Right," pp. 2–3.

19. Ibid.

20. *Houston Informer,* Mar. 13, 1943; O'Connor, *History of Oil Workers International Union-CIO,* p. 314.

21. National Labor Relations Board, *Decision and Order of the National Labor Relations Board,*

Dec. 16, 1939; O'Connor, *History of Oil Workers International Union-CIO,* pp. 221–22, 293–94.

22. *Negro Labor News,* Nov. 20, 1937.

23. *Houston Informer,* July 7, 1945; Clyde Johnson, "CIO Oil Workers' Organizing Campaign in Texas, 1942–1943," in *Essays in Southern Labor History,* ed. Fink and Reed, pp. 173–87.

24. John Crossland transcribed interview by George Green, Aug. 17, 1971, TLAC.

25. Jack Jones interview notes, July 31, 1936, Box 2E308, folder 2, TLMC.

26. *Negro Labor News,* June 18, 1938; May 27, Nov. 11, 1939; Jan. 9, 16, 23, 30, 1943; Dec. 23, 30, 1944; Zamora, "Failed Promise," p. 332.

27. Johnson, "CIO Oil Workers' Organizing Campaign in Texas, 1942–1943," pp. 173–87.

28. *Negro Labor News,* Jan. 16, 23, 1943; *Port Arthur News,* June 17, 1944; O'Connor, *History of Oil Workers International Union-CIO,* pp. 314–15; Ray Davidson, *Challenging the Giants: A History of the Oil Chemical and Atomic Workers International Union,* pp. 109, 150; Morris Akin, *Tales of a Texas Union Pioneer,* pp. 10–12.

29. "Our Inalienable Rights," pp. 9–10; O'Connor, *History of Oil Workers International Union-CIO,* pp. 119–22, 440–41.

30. O'Connor, *History of Oil Workers International Union-CIO,* pp. 9–10.

31. Ibid., p. 10.

32. "Our Inalienable Right," pp. 2–15; O'Connor, *History of Oil Workers International Union-CIO,* pp. 10, 15.

33. Figures on black workers in the Texas oil industry are taken from the U.S. Department of Commerce, Bureau of the Census, *Sixteenth Census of the Population,* vol. 2, part 6, Table 18a & 18b. On the Mexican figure, see Zamora, "Failed Promise," p. 326.

34. The Magnolia figures are derived from "Oil Workers Interview Notes," Box 2E308, folder 2, TLMC. Also, see U.S. Department of Commerce, Bureau of the Census, *Sixteenth Census of the Population;* Zamora, "Failed Promise," pp. 332, 336, 340; Pratt, "Oil Workers International Unions," p. 8. Zamora suggests a lower figure of 1200 for the workforce at Shell.

35. Zamora, "Failed Promise," pp. 326–27. For the national context of black workers in the oil industry, see Herbert Northrup, *Negro Employment in Basic Industries: A Study of Racial Policies in Six Industries,* pp. 529–38.

36. *Houston Informer,* Jan. 13, 1945.

CHAPTER 5

1. Hughes Tool also invested in the production of aircraft equipment, which became just as vital to its operation as oil drilling equipment.

2. Louie Enz interview by Mary Lyens, T. E. Parish, and Jim Clark, Jan. 16, 1968, The Hughes Tool Collection, Record Group 1005, HMRC; Botson, "Organized Labor at the Hughes Tool Company," pp. 3–4; Charles R. Hamilton, "Images of an Industry: The Hughes Tool Company Collection," *Houston Review: History and Culture of the Gulf Coast* 15 (1993): 45; David McComb, *Houston: The Bayou City,* p. 12; Pratt, *Growth of a Refining Region,* p. 140.

3. Botson, "Organized Labor at the Hughes Tool Company," pp. 7 12, 50–64. For more on the formation of the American Iron and Steel Institute (AISI) and its American Plan see William T. Hogan, *Economic History of the Iron and Steel Industry in the United States.* This study examines the economic history of the American steel industry and gives a detailed account of the AISI. Also, see Charles A. Gulick, *Labor Policy of the United States Steel Corporation.*

4. John S. Gray III, "Social Inequality of Hughes Tool Company Between 1928 and 1964," RGR-1, Box 1, file 17, Independent Metal Workers Union (IMWU) Collection, HMRC; Alton interview; Easterwood interview; Michael R. Botson, Jr., "Jim Crow Wearing Steel-Toed Shoes and Safety Glasses: Dual Unionism at the Hughes Tool Company, 1918–1942," *Houston Review: History and Culture of the Gulf Coast* 16 (1994): 101–16. Botson, "Organized Labor at the Hughes Tool Company," p. 50; *Negro Labor News,* Mar. 30, 1940.

5. Botson, "Organized Labor at the Hughes Tool Company," pp. 54–60; Botson, "Jim Crow Wearing Steel-Toed Shoes."

6. *Negro Labor News,* Feb. 18, 1939; Botson, "Organized Labor at the Hughes Tool Company," p. 56.

7. *Negro Labor News,* June 12, July 31, Sept. 25, 1937.

8. Botson, "Organized Labor at the Hughes Tool Company," pp. 59–60; "Summary of agreement arrived at by the Hughes Tool Company and its hourly employees," Oct. 1, 1937, pp. 1–11, IMWU, R-1, File 3, HMRC.

9. *Negro Labor News,* Feb. 18, 1939; Botson, "Organized Labor at the Hughes Tool Company," pp. 50–51.

10. "Summary of agreement arrived at by the Hughes Tool Company and its hourly employees," Oct. 1, 1937, IMWU.

11. *Negro Labor News,* Sept. 3, 1938.

12. Ibid., Feb. 4, 1939.

13. Alton interview.

14. Zieger, *The CIO,* pp. 34–41.

15. Botson, "Organized Labor at the Hughes Tool Company," p. 61; *Negro Labor News,* Jan. 2, 1943; Robert J. Norrell, "Caste in Steel: Jim Crow Careers in Birmingham, Alabama," *Journal of American History* 73 (Dec., 1986): 669–94; Bruce Nelson, "CIO Meant One Thing for the Whites and Another Thing for Us: Steelworkers and Civil Rights, 1936–1974," in *Southern Labor in Transition,* ed. Zieger, pp. 113–45.

16. *NLRB Decision and Order,* Case No. C-1494, Oct. 14, 1940; *Houston Informer,* Feb. 24, Mar. 9, Oct. 19, 1940; *Negro Labor News,* Oct. 19, 1940.

17. *Negro Labor News,* Mar. 30, 1940; Apr. 13, 1940; Jan. 9, 1943.

18. *Negro Labor News,* Feb. 18, 1939; Mar. 2, 1940; *Houston Informer,* Feb. 24, Mar. 9, 1940; Botson, "Organized Labor at the Hughes Tool Company," pp. 50–51.

19. *Negro Labor News,* Mar. 16, Apr. 20, 1940.

20. Ibid., Mar. 30, Apr. 20, 1940.

21. "Contract between The Employees Welfare Organization and the HTC Club of the Hughes Tool Company and the Hughes Tool Company, 1940–1941," IMWU, RGR-1, Box 1, file 1, HMRC; Botson, "Organized Labor at the Hughes Tool Company," pp. 50–64; Botson, "Jim Crow Wearing Steel-Toed Shoes," pp. 104–106.

22. Easterwood interview.
23. *NLRB Decisions and Orders,* Case No. R-2566, Nov. 13, 1941.
24. Botson, "Jim Crow Wearing Steel-Toed Shoes," pp. 112–16.
25. *Houston Informer,* Oct. 11, 1941; Botson, "Jim Crow Wearing Steel-Toed Shoes," p. 110.
26. *NLRB Decisions and Orders,* Case No. R-2566, Nov. 13, 1941; *Negro Labor News,* Apr. 25, May 30, 1942.
27. *NLRB Decisions and Orders,* vol. 45, pp. 824–25; Botson, "Jim Crow Wearing Steel-Toed Shoes," pp. 115–16.
28. *Houston Informer,* Aug. 1, 1942.
29. Ibid., July 18, Aug. 8, 29, 1942.
30. *NLRB Decisions and Orders,* vol. 56, p. 990; *Negro Labor News,* Dec. 26, 1942; Botson, "Jim Crow Wearing Steel-Toed Shoes," pp. 115–16.
31. *Negro Labor News,* Dec. 26, 1942; Jan. 2, 1943.
32. Ibid., Jan. 2, 30, 1943.
33. Ibid., Dec. 26, 1942; Jan. 2, 1943.
34. Ibid., Feb. 27, 1943.
35. Ibid., Jan. 23, 1943.
36. Ibid., May 13, 1939; Feb. 20, 1943.
37. "Contract Covering Wages, Hours and Conditions of Employment Between United Steel Workers of America CIO Locals 1742 and 2457 and the Hughes Tool Company," Apr. 6, 1943, IMWU; *Houston Informer,* Apr. 10, 1943; *Negro Labor News,* Feb. 19, 1944.
38. *Houston Informer,* Oct. 9, 1943; *Negro Labor News,* June 3, July 15, 22, 1944.
39. *Negro Labor News,* Apr. 15, June 3, 1944.
40. Ibid., July 1, 8, Aug. 19, 1944.
41. Ibid., Aug. 26, 1944.
42. Ibid., Sept. 9, Oct. 7, 1944.
43. Ibid., Oct. 14, 1944.
44. *Houston Informer,* Mar. 17, Sept. 1, 8, 1945.

CHAPTER 6

1. Most war contracts were awarded by four agencies: the army, the navy, the Maritime Commission, and Treasury Department. Memorandum, War Manpower Commission to all regional representatives, Nov. 14, 1942, Minutes and Decisions of the Regional and Essential Committees, Region VII, War Manpower Commission Records, RG 211, National Archives, Washington D.C.; Merl E. Reed, "The FEPC, the Black Worker, and the Southern Shipyards," *South Atlantic Quarterly* 74, no. 4 (autumn, 1975): 446–67.
2. McCartin, *Labor's Great War,* pp. 74, 80, 101, 115, 187; McCartin, "Abortive Reconstruction," pp. 155–83; Lester Rubin, *The Negro in the Shipbuilding Industry,* pp. 36–38, 40, 52–53.
3. William H. Harris, "Federal Intervention in Union Discrimination: FEPC and West Coast Shipyards during World War II," *Labor History* 22 (summer, 1981): 325–47; Alonzo Smith and Quintard Taylor, "Racial Discrimination in the Workplace: A Study of Two West Coast Cities during the 1940s," *Journal of Ethnic Studies* 8, no. 1 (spring, 1980);

Albert S. Broussard, *Black San Francisco: The Struggle for Racial Equality in the West, 1900–1954*, pp. 159–64; Rubin, *Negro in the Shipbuilding Industry,* pp. 46–49; Harris, *Harder We Run,* pp., 63–64; Northrup, *Organized Labor and the Negro,* pp. 210–31.

4. Reed, "FEPC, the Black Worker, and the Southern Shipyards," pp. 446–48; Rubin, *Negro in the Shipbuilding Industry,* pp. 41–45.

5. Reed, "FEPC, the Black Worker, and the Southern Shipyards," pp., 447–49; Bruce Nelson, "Organized Labor and the Struggle for Black Equality in Mobile during World War II," *Journal of American History* 80, no. 3 (Dec., 1993): 954.

6. Tillman Henderson to J. H. Morton, Sept. 26, 1944, Houston Todd file, FEPC Records; FEPC Complainant Form, Nov. 1943, Houston Todd file, FEPC Records; Henderson to Morton, Oct. 5, 1944, Houston Todd file, FEPC Records. Interview with C. B. Johnson by Ernest Obadele-Starks, Apr. 21, 1995, Houston, Texas; Final Disposition Report, Jan. 27, 1945, Houston Todd file, FEPC Records; Ellinger to Mitchell, June 2, 1945, Houston Todd file, FEPC Records. Correspondence on FEPC shipyard cases is from Entry 70, FEPC Records, National Archives, Fort Worth, Texas, unless otherwise noted.

7. Solomon R. Garrett to President Roosevelt, Sept. 23 1942, Houston Todd file, FEPC Records.

8. Albert Richard Spiller affidavit, May 10, 1944, Houston Todd file, FEPC Records; N. E. Waiters affidavit, Jan. 14, 1945, Houston Todd file, FEPC Records.

9. Richard Felder affidavit, May 19, 1942, Houston Todd file, FEPC Records.

10. Felix W. Ward affidavit, May 11, 1944, Houston Todd file, FEPC Records.

11. Thomas Scanton, "The Race Riots," *New Republic* 109 (July, 1943): 11; Julius A. Thomas, "Race Conflict and Social Action," *Opportunity* 21 (Oct., 1943): 165–67; Nelson, "Organized Labor and the Struggle for Black Equality," pp. 952–53, 978.

12. Marjorie Lawson to Malcom Ross, Oct. 25, 1943, Entry 37, Orange, Texas file, FEPC Records; Ellinger to Malloy, June 4, 1945, Houston Todd file, FEPC Records.

13. James Burran, "Violence in an 'Arsenal Of Democracy': The Beaumont Race Riot, 1943," *East Texas Historical Journal* (1975–76): 39–40; James S. Olson and Sharon Phair, "The Anatomy of a Race Riot: Beaumont, Texas, 1943," *Texana* 11 (1973): 64–72.

14. Burran, "Violence in an 'Arsenal of Democracy,'" p. 40.

15. Ike Ashburn to FEPC, May 31, 1944, Houston Todd file, FEPC Records; Charles J. MacGowan to Malcom Ross, May 23, 1944, Houston Todd file, FEPC Records; Ellinger to Ashburn, June 2, 1944, Houston Todd file, FEPC Records; Ellinger to Ashburn, June 16, 1944, Houston Todd file, FEPC Records; Ellinger to Ashburn, July 11, 1944, Houston Todd file, FEPC Records; Ellinger to Frank Liddell, Aug. 3, 1994, Houston Todd file, FEPC Records; Ellinger to Sam H. Benbow, Sept. 18, 1944, Houston Todd file. FEPC Records; Ellinger to Francis B. Dunn, Sept. 25, 1944, Houston Todd file, FEPC Records; Ellinger to Ashburn, Sept. 26, 1944, Houston Todd file, FEPC Records; Ellinger to Jeff Davis, Sept. 27, 1944, Houston Todd file, FEPC Records; Ashburn to Ellinger, Sept. 29, 1944, Houston Todd file, FEPC Records; Beall to Ellinger, Jan. 27, 1945, Houston Todd file, FEPC Records.

16. Ellinger to Mitchell, Feb. 6, 1945, Houston Todd file, FEPC Records; Walter K. Graham to Ellinger, Feb. 20, 1945, Houston Todd file, FEPC Records; J. S. Stevens to Graham, Feb. 26, 1945, Houston Todd file, FEPC Records.

17. Sam H. Benbow to Ellinger, Mar. 14, 1945, Houston Todd file, FEPC Records; Ellinger to Jeff Davis, May 16, 1945, Houston Todd file, FEPC Records; Davis to Ellinger, May 18, 1945, Houston Todd file, FEPC Records; Ellinger to Davis, May 24, 1945, Houston Todd file, FEPC Records.

18. Davis to Ellinger, May 20, 1944, Houston Brown file, FEPC Records; Final Disposition Report, Jan. 27, 1945, Houston Brown file, FEPC Records. An exact figure on black employment is not available. The figure is quoted from the FEPC Final Disposition Report.

19. Ellinger to Mitchell, Mar. 7, 1945, Houston Brown file, FEPC Records; Castañeda to Dunn, Sept. 12, 1944, Houston Brown file, FEPC Records.

20. Beall to Ellinger, Jan. 27, 1945, Houston Brown file, FEPC Records; Mitchell to Rear Admiral P. G. Crisp, Dec. 13, 1944, Houston Brown file, FEPC Records; Mitchell to Ellinger, Jan. 10, 1945, Houston Brown file, FEPC Records; Morton to Maslow, Jan. 1, 1945, Houston Brown file, FEPC Records; Weekly Report, Mar. 3, 1945, Houston Brown file, FEPC Records.

21. Weekly Report, Feb. 17, 1945, Galveston Yard file, FEPC Records; Final Disposition Report, Nov. 30, 1943, Galveston Yard file, FEPC Records; Ellinger to Mitchell, June 7 1945, Galveston Yard file, FEPC Records.

22. Ellinger to Mitchell, June 7, 1945, Galveston Yard file, FEPC Records.

23. Herman Hall affidavit, Oct. 27, 1944, Galveston Yard file, FEPC Records; Joel Millican affidavit, Feb. 15, 1945, Galveston Yard file, FEPC Records; Ezekiel Muse affidavit, undated, Galveston Yard file, FEPC Records; Alex Payton affidavit, undated, Galveston Yard file, FEPC Records; Alexander Pierce affidavit, June 5, 1945, Galveston Yard file, FEPC Records.

24. FEPC Data Sheet, undated, Galveston Yard file, FEPC Records; Singleton to FEPC, July 21, 1943, Galveston Yard file, FEPC Records; Johnson to Singleton, Aug. 11, 1943, Galveston Yard file, FEPC Records; Morton to Singleton, Sept. 11, 1944, Galveston Yard file, FEPC Records; Morton file memo, Sept. 26, 1944, Galveston Yard file, FEPC Records; Beall to Ellinger, Jan. 22, 1945, Galveston Yard file, FEPC Records. Ellinger to Singleton, Mar. 21, 1945, Galveston Yard file, FEPC Records; Ellinger to Major Walter Graham, Apr. 6, 1945, Galveston Yard file, FEPC Records; Vanderwende to Major Walter Graham, Apr. 13, 1945, Galveston Yard file, FEPC Records; Bi-Weekly Report, May 26, 1945, Galveston Yard file, FEPC Records.

25. McCollum to Ellinger, May 30, 1945, Galveston Yard file, FEPC Records; Ellinger to McCollum, June 7, 1945, Galveston Yard file, FEPC Records; Mitchell to Castañeda, Oct. 10, 1945, Galveston Yard file, FEPC Records; Weekly Report, Apr. 28, 1945, Galveston Yard file, FEPC Records.

CHAPTER 7

1. A. Philip Randolph, the well-known organizer of the BSCP, threatened to mobilize the black working class and stage a protest in Washington, D.C., in 1941 against racial discrimination in the country's workplaces. Randolph, along with numerous black leaders, persuaded President Roosevelt to establish the Fair Employment Practices Commission

(FEPC) to investigate complaints of discrimination. See Anderson, *A. Philip Randolph;* Harris, *Keeping the Faith;* Paula F. Pfeffer, *A. Philip Randolph, Pioneer of the Civil Rights Movement.*

2. Roosevelt was responding to A. Philip Randolph's threat of a nationwide boycott of defense industries that allowed discrimination to persist while blacks loyally supported the United States war effort home and abroad. See Reed, *Seedtime for the Modern Civil Rights Movement,* p. 345.

3. Over the past few years researchers have attempted to capture the essence and the meaning of the FEPC to black equality in American industries. The reactions to and outcomes of FEPC investigations differed between industries and by region. For discussions on these differences, see Dominic J. Capeci, Jr., "Wartime Fair Employment Practices Committees: The Governor's Committee and the First FEPC in New York City, 1941–1943," *Afro-Americans in New York Life and History* 9 (1985): 45–63; Reed, "FEPC, the Black Worker, and the Southern Shipyards," pp. 446–67; Merl E. Reed, "Pennsylvania's Black Workers, the Defense Industries, and the Federal Agencies, 1941–1945," *Labor History* 27 (1986): 356–84; Merl E. Reed, "FEPC and the Federal Agencies in the South," *Journal of Negro History* 65 (1980): 43–56; Harris, "Federal Intervention in Union Discrimination," pp. 325–47; Robert Bailey, "Theodore G. Bilbo and the Fair Employment Practices Controversy: A Southern Senator's Reaction to a Changing World," *Journal of Mississippi History* 52 (1980): 27–42; Louis C. Kesselman, "The Fair Employment Practice Movement in Perspective," *Journal of Negro History* 31 (1946): 30–46; John Beecher, "8802 Blues," *New Republic* (Feb., 1943): 249.

4. Harris, "Federal Intervention in Union Discrimination," pp. 325–47: Smith and Taylor, "Racial Discrimination in the Workplace," pp. 35–54; Broussard, *Black San Francisco;* Reed, *Seedtime for the Modern Civil Rights Movement,* pp. 273, 278.

5. Beecher, "8802 Blues," pp. 248–50; Reed, "FEPC and the Federal Agencies in the South," pp. 43–56; Reed, "FEPC, the Black Worker, and the Southern Shipyards," pp. 446–67; Reed, *Seedtime for the Modern Civil Rights Movement,* pp. 66–74.

6. Clay Cochran to Carlos Castañeda, Oct. 25, 1943, Administration Division, FEPC Records; Lawrence W. Cramer to M. C. Gonzales, Nov. 26, 1941, Division of Field Operations, FEPC Records; Will Alexander to W. G. Carnahan, Dec. 26, 1941, Division of Field Operations; Carlos Castañeda to Will Maslow, Jan. 26, 1944, Administrative Division. Also, see John Morton Blum, *V Was for Victory: Politics and American Culture during World War II;* Reed, *Seedtime for the Modern Civil Rights Movement,* pp. 205–208.

7. The Gulf Coast oil refineries investigated by the FEPC included Sinclair (Houston), Shell (Houston), Texas Company (Houston), Texas Company (Port Neches), Pure Oil (Port Neches), Republic (Texas City), Texas Company (Port Arthur), Gulf (Port Arthur), Humble (Baytown), and Magnolia (Beaumont). The figure on the black workforce in the Texas oil industry is taken from the U.S. Department of Commerce, Bureau of the Census, *Sixteenth Census of Population,* vol. 2, part 6, Table 18a & 18b; The estimated figure for the Mexican workforce is based on a total of 17,350 workers in twelve refineries reported by the FEPC. On the Mexican figure, see Zamora, "Failed Promise," pp. 326, 330–32. All FEPC oil case documents are from RG 228, Entry 70, National Archives, Fort Worth, Texas, unless otherwise noted. Clarence M. Mitchell to George M. Johnson,

Mar. 26, 1945, Entry 49, Shell file, FEPC Records; Data Form, Sept. 21, 1942, Humble file, FEPC Records; Humble refinery Final Disposition Report, Feb. 9, 1944, FEPC Records; Gulf refinery Final Disposition Report, Aug. 3, 1944, Gulf file, FEPC Records; Data Form, Sept. 1943, Sinclair file, FEPC Records; Final Disposition Report, Feb. 11, 1944, Sinclair file, FEPC Records. Clarence Mitchell to George M. Johnson, Mar. 26, 1945, Mitchell Office files, FEPC Records. For background on Castañeda, see Félix D. Almaráz, Jr., "Carlos Eduardo Castañeda, Mexican-American Historian: The Formative Years, 1896–1927," in *The Chicano,* ed. Norris Hundley, Jr., pp. 57–72.

8. See Clete Daniel, *Chicano Workers and the Politics of Fairness: The FEPC in the Southwest, 1941–1945,* p. 6.

9. Clarence M. Mitchell to George M. Johnson, Mar. 26, 1945, Entry 49, Shell file, FEPC Records; Otome Saito to Mitchell, Mar. 31, 1945, Entry 49, Shell file, FEPC Records; Zamora, "Failed Promise," pp. 330–32, 345.

10. Statement on Discrimination against Mexican Workers at the Baytown Humble refinery, signed by Andres Contreras, C. Beltran, J. Santana, Onofre Gonzalez, L. Herrera, and G. N. Ponce, Nov. 25, 1942, Humble file, FEPC Records; Clay Cochran to Castañeda, Dec. 29, 1943, Humble file, FEPC Records; Don Ellinger to Malcom Ross, May 1, 1945, Entry 49, Shell file, FEPC Records; Bloch to Castañeda, Dec. 7, 1944, Shell file, FEPC Records; Shell Case Summary, Entry 49, Division of Field Operations, Shell file, FEPC Records; Final Disposition Report, May 17, 1944, Shell file, FEPC Records; Mitchell to Johnson, Mar. 26, 1945, Shell file, FEPC Records; Otome Saito to Mitchell, Mar. 31, 1945, Entry 49, Shell file, FEPC Records; Ellinger to Mitchell, Mar. 31, 1945, Shell file, FEPC Records; Crossland interview; *Houston Informer,* May 12, 1945; Teel, "Discrimination against Negro Workers in Texas," pp. 30–41; Zamora, "Failed Promise," pp. 332, 341–42, 345–47.

11. FEPC Shell Case Stipulation, Dec. 30, 1944, Shell file, FEPC Records.

12. Mitchell to Bloch, Apr. 12, 1945, Entry 19, Legal Division, Correspondence file, FEPC Records. E. H. Walker to Malcom Ross, Apr. 19, 1945, Entry 49, Shell file, FEPC Records; Press Release, Entry 37, Review and Analysis Division, Tension files, FEPC Records; Ross to Walker, undated, Entry 49, Shell file, FEPC Records.

13. Ellinger to Ross, May 18, 1945, Entry 49, Tension file, FEPC Records; Ellinger to Ross, May 23, 1945, Entry 49, Tension file, FEPC Records; Zamora, "Failed Promise," pp. 330–32, 345; Clarence M. Mitchell to George M. Johnson, Mar. 26, 1945, Entry 49, Shell file, FEPC Records.

14. Ruth Ellinger interview by Ernest Obadele-Starks, Nov. 12, 1995, in possession of author; Zamora, "Failed Promise," p. 332.

15. Texas and New Orleans Railroad (TNO) Hearing Transcript, Headquarter Records, Entry 19, Legal Division, Case #82, FEPC Records; Ellinger to Scott, May 5, June 3, 1944 MKT file, FEPC Records; Pickett to Ellinger, June 15, 1944, MKT file, FEPC Records; Pickett to Ellinger, June 15, 1944, MKT file, FEPC Records.

16. Brin to Maslow, May 6, 1944, MKT file, FEPC Records; Maceo Hubbard to George M. Johnson, July 5, 1944, MKT file, FEPC Records; Ellinger to Simon Stickgold, Apr. 18, 1945, MKT file, FEPC Records; For more on the FEPC Birmingham hearings see Reed, *Seedtime for the Modern Civil Rights Movement,* pp. 90–91.

17. Ellinger to Harold Stafford, Aug. 15, 1944, MKT file, FEPC Records; Ellinger to J. H. Bond, Aug. 15, 1944, MKT file, FEPC Records; Ellinger to Mitchell, Mar. 6, 1945, MKT file, FEPC Records; Johnson to Mitchell, Mar. 23, 1945, MKT file, FEPC Records; Reed, *Seedtime for the Modern Civil Rights Movement,* pp. 90–92.

18. *Houston Informer,* Feb. 13, 1943.

19. Ellinger to Mann, Aug. 5, 1944, MKT file, FEPC Records; TNO Hearing, pp. 8, 10, 47–48.

20. TNO Hearing, pp. 47–48; Kenneth J. Lipartito and Joseph A. Pratt, *Baker & Botts in the Development of Modern Houston,* pp. 24–31.

21. FEPC data sheet, June 6, 1943, Hughes Tool file, FEPC Records; Ellinger to Brin, May 16, 1944, Hughes Tool file, FEPC Records; FEPC file memo, May 17, 1944, Hughes Tool file, FEPC Records; Ellinger to Thomas Mobley, July 12, 1944, Hughes Tool file, FEPC Records; FEPC to Major Arthur Krim, Oct. 31, 1944, Hughes Tool file, FEPC Records; Ellinger to Mobley, July 12, 1944, Hughes Tool file, FEPC Records; Maslow to Pressman, Oct. 17, 1944, Hughes Tool file, FEPC Records.

22. Harold Fatheree affidavit, July 16, 1942, Hughes Tool file, FEPC Records; Ezra Turner affidavit, Jan. 12, 1945, Hughes Tool file, FEPC Records; Easterwood interview; Alton interview.

23. Pressman to Maslow, Oct. 23, 1944, Hughes Tool file, FEPC Records; Maslow to Ellinger, Dec. 26, 1944, Hughes Tool file, FEPC Records; Ellinger to Maslow, Nov. 4, 1944, Hughes Tool file, FEPC Records.

24. Ellinger to Frank Hardesty, July 18, 1945, Hughes Tool file, FEPC Records.

25. Longshoremen Advertisement, Mar. 18, 1945, Entry 70, Longshoremen file, FEPC Records. Correspondence of Upper Texas Gulf Coast longshoremen is from entry 70 unless otherwise noted.

26. Ellinger to White, Apr. 9, 1945, Longshoremen file, FEPC Records; Everett to White, Apr. 13, 1945, Longshoremen file, FEPC Records.

27. Everett to White, Apr. 12, 1945, Longshoremen file, FEPC Records.

28. Ellinger to ILA Local 1273, Apr. 26, 1945, Longshoremen file, FEPC Records; Ellinger to Everett, Apr. 26, 1945, Longshoremen file, FEPC Records; Ellinger file memo, July 30, 1945, Longshoremen file, FEPC Records; Ellinger to White, Sept. 25, 1944, Apr. 9, 13, 1945, MKT file; *Houston Informer,* Apr. 14, 1945.

29. Ellinger to Mitchell, Apr. 17, 1945, MKT file, FEPC Records; Mitchell to Ellinger, Apr. 17, 1945, MKT file, FEPC Records; Ellinger to Quillian, Apr. 17, 1945, MKT file, FEPC Records; Ellinger to Quillian, Apr. 17, 1945, MKT file, FEPC Records.

30. Wesley to Ellinger, June 1, 1944, MKT file, FEPC Records; Ellinger to Wesley, Apr. 17, 1945, MKT file, FEPC Records.

31. Harold Shirley to L. A. Woods, Feb. 27, 1943, Houston Shipbuilding file, FEPC Records; Reed, *Seedtime for the Modern Civil Rights Movement,* p. 175.

32. Lawrence W. Cramer to S. D. Jones, Nov. 19, 1942, Houston Shipbuilding file, FEPC Records; Ellinger to Grovey, May 27, 1944, Houston Shipbuilding file, FEPC Records.

33. "Racial Tension," Box 454, 1943–45, Entry 37, Tension file, FEPC Records; *Houston Informer,* July 7, 1945; Beecher, "8802 Blues," p. 248; Bailey, "Theodore G. Bilbo and the Fair Employment Practices Controversy," pp. 27–42.

34. S. L. Davis to Coke Stevenson, June 14, 1944, FEPC folder, Coke Stevenson Papers, Texas State Library and Archives, Austin, Texas. J. H. Curtis, Jr., to Coke Stevenson, June 14, 1944, FEPC folder, Coke Stevenson Papers; P. M. Mckinley to Coke Stevenson, June 10, 1944, FEPC folder, Coke Stevenson Papers; F. M. Welch to Coke Stevenson, June 10, 1944, FEPC folder, Coke Stevenson Papers; Coke Stevenson to Leonard M. Brin, June 7, 1944, FEPC folder, Coke Stevenson Papers; Malcom Ross to Coke Stevenson, June 14, 1944, FEPC folder, Coke Stevenson Papers.

35. *Houston Informer,* Jan. 13, Oct. 27, 1945; 1945 ILA District Proceedings.

36. Garland Butler to Don Ellinger, May 16, 1945, Shell file, FEPC Records; Castañeda to Clarence Mitchell, Mar. 15, 1946, Shell file, FEPC Records; Clarence Mitchell office files, Entry 40, Box 461, FEPC Records; *Houston Informer,* May 12, June 9, 30, 1945.

37. *Houston Informer,* Apr. 26, 1947.

38. Reference file, July, 1941–Apr., 1941, Entry 33, Box 426, FEPC Records; *Negro Labor News,* Apr. 22, 24, May 6, June 17, July 8, Sept. 2, Nov. 4, Dec. 23, 1944; *Houston Informer,* June 6, 1945.

39. *Negro Labor News,* Sept. 2, 1944; Dec. 23, 1944; Apr. 24, 1944; May 6, 1944.

40. *Negro Labor News,* July 8, Nov. 4, 1944.

41. *Houston Informer,* Mar. 11, 1944; June 23, 30, 1945.

42. Ibid., June 30, 1945.

CONCLUSION

1. Irving McCann, *Why the Taft-Hartley Law,* pp. 1–5.

2. Ibid.

3. See Barbara S. Griffith, *The Crisis of American Labor: Operation Dixie and the Defeat of the CIO;* Michael Honey, "'Operation Dixie': Two Points of View," *Labor History* 31 (summer, 1990): 373–78; Solomon Barkin, "'Operation Dixie': Two Points of View," *Labor History* 31 (summer, 1990): 378–85.

BIBLIOGRAPHY

PUBLISHED SOURCES

Akin, Morris. *Tales of a Texas Union Pioneer.* Austin, Tex.: Morris Akin, 1993.

Allen, Ruth. *Chapters in the History of Organized Labor in Texas.* Austin, Tex.: The University, 1941.

———. *East Texas Lumber Workers: An Economic and Social Picture, 1870–1950.* Austin: University of Texas Press, 1961.

Almaráz, Félix D., Jr. "Carlos Eduardo Castañeda, Mexican-American Historian: The Formative Years, 1896–1927." In *The Chicano,* edited by Norris Hundley, Jr. Santa Barbara, Calif.: Clio Books, 1975.

Anderson, Jervis. *A. Philip Randolph: A Biographical Portrait.* New York: Harcourt Brace Javanovich, 1972.

Anderson, Karen Tucker. "Last Hired, First Fired: Black Women Workers during World War II." *Journal of American History* 69 (June, 1982).

———. *Wartime Women: Sex Roles, Family Relations, and the Status of Women during World War II.* Westport, Conn.: Greenwood Press, 1981.

Angel, William D., Jr. "Vantage on the Bay: Galveston and the Railroads." *East Texas Historical Journal* 22 (1984).

Arnesen, Eric. "The African-American Working Class in the Jim Crow Era." *International Labor and Working-Class History* 41 (spring, 1992).

———. "Charting an Independent Course: African-American Railroad Workers in the World War I Era." In *Labor Histories: Class, Politics, and the Working-Class Experience,* edited by Eric Arnesen, Julie Greene, and Bruce Laurie. Urbana: University of Illinois Press, 1998.

———. "Following the Color Line of Labor: Black Workers and the Labor Movement before 1930." *Radical History Review* 55 (1993).

———. *Waterfront Workers of New Orleans: Race, Class, and Politics, 1863–1923.* New York: Oxford University Press, 1991.

———. "'What's on the Black Worker's Mind?': African American Workers and the Union Tradition." *Gulf Coast Historical Review* 10 (1994).

———, ed. "It Aint Like They Do in New Orleans: Race Relations, Labor Markets, and Waterfront Labor Movements in the American South, 1880–1923." *Racism and the Labour Market: Historical Studies.* New York: Peter Lang, 1995.

Bailey, Beth, and David Farber. "The Double-V Campaign in World War II Hawaii: African Americans, Racial Ideology, and Federal Power." *Journal of Social History* 26 (summer, 1993).

Bailey, Robert. "Theodore G. Bilbo and the Fair Employment Practices Controversy: A Southern Senator's Reaction to a Changing World." *Journal of Mississippi History* 52 (1980).

Barkin, Solomon. "Operation Dixie: Two Points of View." *Labor History* 31 (summer, 1990).

Barr, Alwyn. *Black Texans: A History of Negroes In Texas, 1528–1995.* Austin, Tex.: Jenkins Publishing, 1973. Reprint, Norman: University of Oklahoma Press, 1996.

———. "Federal Aid for Texas Rivers and Harbors, 1867–1900." *Southern Studies* 16, no. 2 (1977).

———. *Reconstruction to Reform: Texas Politics, 1876–1906.* Austin: University of Texas Press, 1971.

Beecher, John. "8802 Blues." *New Republic* (February, 1943).

Beeth, Howard, and Cary D. Wintz, eds. *Black Dixie: Afro-Texan History and Culture in Houston.* College Station: Texas A&M University Press, 1992.

Bernstein, Irving. *The Lean Years: A History of the American Worker, 1920–1933.* Boston: Houghton Mifflin, 1972.

Blum, John Morton. *V Was for Victory: Politics and American Culture during World War II.* New York: Harcourt Brace Jovanovich, 1976.

Botson, Michael R., Jr. "Jim Crow Wearing Steel-Toed Shoes and Safety Glasses: Dual Unionism at the Hughes Tool Company, 1918–1942." *Houston Review* 16 (1994).

Bourgeois, Christie L. "Stepping over Lines: Lyndon Johnson, Black Texans, and the National Youth Administration, 1935–1937." *Southwestern Historical Quarterly* 91, no. 2 (October, 1987).

Brock, William R. *Welfare, Democracy, and the New Deal.* New York: Cambridge University Press, 1987.

Brody, David. "The Old Labor History and the New: In Search of an American Working Class." *Labor History* 20 (winter, 1979).

Broussard, Albert S. *Black San Francisco: The Struggle for Racial Equality in the West, 1900–1954.* Lawrence: University of Kansas Press, 1993.

Buder, Stanley. *Pullman: An Experiment in Industrial Order and Social Planning.* New York: Oxford University Press, 1967.

Buenger, Walter L. "The Wonder Age: The Economic Transformation of Northeast Texas, 1900–1930." *Southwestern Historical Quarterly* 98 (April, 1995).

———, and Joseph A. Pratt. *But Also Good Business: Texas Commerce Banks and the Financing of Houston and Texas, 1886–1986.* College Station: Texas A&M University Press, 1986.

———, and Robert A. Calvert. "The Shelf Life of Truth in Texas." In *Texas through Time: Evolving Interpretations,* edited by Walter L. Buenger and Robert A. Calvert. College Station: Texas A&M University Press, 1975.

Burran, James. "Violence in an 'Arsenal of Democracy': The Beaumont Race Riot, 1943." *East Texas Historical Journal* (1975–76).

Capeci, Dominic J., Jr. "Wartime Fair Employment Practices Committees: The Governor's Committee and the First FEPC in New York City, 1941–1943." *Afro-Americans in New York Life and History* 9 (1985).

Casdorph, Paul Douglas. *A History of the Republican Party in Texas, 1865–1965.* Austin, Tex.: Pemberton Press, 1965.

———. "Norris Wright Cuney and Texas Republican Politics, 1883–1896." *Southwestern Historical Quarterly* (April, 1965).

Cayton, Horace R., and George S. Mitchell. *Black Workers and the New Unions.* Chapel Hill: University of North Carolina Press, 1939.

Chateauvert, Melinda. *Marching Together: Women of the Brotherhood of Sleeping Car Porters.* Urbana: University of Illinois Press, 1998.

Clark, James A., and Michael Halbouty, *Spindletop.* New York: Random House, 1952).

Commons, John R. "The Longshoremen of the Great Lakes." In *Labor and Administration.* New York: The McMillan Company, 1913.

Cortner, Robert C., ed. *Texas Cities and the Great Depression.* Austin: Texas Memorial Museum, 1973.

Cummins, Light Townsend, and Alvin R. Bailey, eds. *A Guide to the History of Texas.* New York: Greenwood Press, 1988.

Cuney-Hare, Maude. *Norris Wright Cuney: A Tribune of Black People.* New York: Crisis, 1913; reprint, New York: G. K. Hall, 1995.

Dalfiume, Richard M. *Desegregation of the U. S. Armed Forces: Fighting on Two Fronts, 1939–1953.* Columbia: University of Missouri Press, 1969.

———. "The Forgotten Years of the Negro Revolution." *Journal of American History* 55 (1968).

Daniel, Clete. *Chicano Workers and the Politics of Fairness: The FEPC in the Southwest, 1941–1945.* Austin: University of Texas Press, 1991.

Davidson, Chandler. *Race and Class in Texas Politics.* Princeton: Princeton University Press, 1990).

Davidson, Ray. *Challenging the Giants: A History of the Oil Chemical and Atomic Workers International Union.* Lakewood, Colo.: Oil Chemical and Atomic Workers International Union, 1988.

Davis, Christopher S. "Life at the Edge: Urban and Industrial Evolution of Texas, Frontier Wilderness—Frontier Space, 1836–1896." *Southwestern Historical Quarterly* 89 (April, 1986).

Doyle, Judith Kaaz. "Maury Maverick and Racial Politics in San Antonio, Texas, 1938–1941." *Journal of Southern History* 53 (May, 1987).

Dugas, Vera L. "A Duel with Railroads: Houston vs. Galveston, 1866–1881." *East Texas Historical Journal* 2 (October, 1964).

Ellis, L. Tuffy. "The Revolutionizing of the Texas Cotton Trade, 1866–1885." *Southwestern Historical Quarterly* 73 (April, 1970).

Emerson, Thomas I. *Young Lawyer for the New Deal: An Insider's Memoir of the Roosevelt Years.* Savage, Md.: Rowman and Littlefield, 1991.

Feagin, Joe. *Free Enterprise City: Houston in Political-Economic Perspective.* New Brunswick, N.J.: Rutgers University Press, 1988.

Fink, Gary M., and Merl E. Reed, eds. *Essays in Southern Labor History: Selected Papers, Southern Labor History Conference, 1976.* Westport, Conn.: Greenwood Press, 1977.

———. *Race, Class, and Communities in Southern Labor History.* Tuscaloosa: University of Alabama Press, 1994.

Fink, Leon. "John R. Commons, Herbert Gutman, and the Burden of Labor History." *Labor History* 29 (summer, 1988).

Finkle, Lee. "The Conservative Aims of Militant Rhetoric: Black Protest during World War II." *Journal of American History* 60, no. 3 (December, 1973).

Fishel, Leslie H. "The Negro in the New Deal Era." *Wisconsin Magazine of History* 48 (winter, 1964–65).

Foley, Neil. *The White Scourge: Mexicans, Blacks, and Poor Whites in Texas Cotton Culture.* Berkeley: University of California Press, 1997.

Foner, Philip S. *Organized Labor and the Black Worker.* New York: International Publishers, 1982.

Franklin, John Hope, and Alfred A. Moss, Jr. *From Slavery to Freedom: A History of Negro Americans.* 6th ed. New York: Alfred A. Knopf, 1988.

Freedman, Russell. *Eleanor Roosevelt: A Life of Discovery.* New York: Clarion Books, 1993.

Fried, Albert, ed. *Communism in America: A History in Documents.* New York: Columbia University Press, 1997.

Garfinkel, Herbert. *When Negroes March: The March on Washington Movement in the Organizational Politics for FEPC.* Glencoe, Ill.: Free Press, 1959.

Gerstle, Gary. "Working-Class Racism: Broaden the Focus." *International Labor and Working-Class History* 44 (fall, 1993).

Goldfield, Michael. *The Color of Politics: Race and the Mainsprings of American Politics.* New York: The New Press, 1997.

———. "Race and the CIO: The Possibilities for Racial Egalitarianism during the 1930s and 1940s." *International Labor and Working-Class History* 44 (fall, 1993).

Gottlieb, Peter. *Making Their Own Way: Southern Blacks' Migration to Pittsburgh, 1916–1930.* Urbana: University of Illinois Press, 1987.

Granger, Lester B. "The Negro—Friend or Foe of Organized Labor." *Opportunity: Journal of Negro Life* 13 (May, 1935).

Grant, Robert B. *The Black Man Comes to the City.* Chicago: Nelson-Hall, 1972.

Green, George N. *The Establishment in Texas Politics: The Primitive Years, 1938–1957.* Westport, Conn.: Greenwood Press, 1979.

———. *A Liberal View of Texas Politics since the 1930s.* Boston: American Press, 1980.

Green, James R. *Grass-Roots Socialism: Radical Movements in the Southwest, 1895–1943.* Baton Rouge: Louisiana State University Press, 1978.

Greene, Lorenzo J., and Carter G. Woodson. *The Negro Wage Earner.* New York: Russell and Russell, 1930.

Griffith, Barbara S. *The Crisis of American Labor: Operation Dixie and the Defeat of the CIO.* Philadelphia: Temple University Press, 1988.

Griffler, Keith. *What Price Alliance?: Black Radicals Confront White Labor.* New York: Garland, 1994.

Gross, James A. *The Making of the National Labor Relations Board: A Study in Economics, Politics and the Law, 1933–1937.* Albany: State University of New York Press, 1974.

Gulick, Charles A. *Labor Policy of the United States Steel Corporation.* New York: Columbia University Press, 1924.

Halpern, Rick. "Interracial Unionism in the Southwest: Fort Worth's Packinghouse Workers, 1937–1954." In *Organized Labor in the Twentieth-Century South,* edited by Robert H. Zieger. Knoxville: University of Tennessee Press, 1991.

Hamilton, Charles R. "Images of an Industry: The Hughes Tool Company Collection." *Houston Review: History and Culture of the Gulf Coast* 15 (1993).

Hareven, Tamara K. *Eleanor Roosevelt: An American Conscience.* Chicago: Quadrangle Books, 1968.

Harris, William H. "Federal Intervention in Union Discrimination: FEPC and West Coast Shipyards during World War II." *Labor History* 22 (summer, 1981).

———. *The Harder We Run: Black Workers since the Civil War.* New York: Oxford University Press, 1982.

———. *Keeping the Faith: A. Philip Randolph, Milton P. Webster, and the Brotherhood of Sleeping Car Porters, 1925–37.* Urbana: University of Illinois Press, 1977.

Hartman, Paul T. *Collective Bargaining and Productivity: The Longshore Mechanization Agreement.* Berkeley: University of California Press, 1969.

Henri, Florette. *Black Migration: Movement North, 1900–1920.* Garden City, N.Y.: Anchor/Doubleday, 1975.

Hill, Herbert. *Black Labor and the American Legal System: Race, Work, and the Law.* Washington, D.C.: Bureau of National Affairs, 1977.

Hofsommer, Don L. *The Southern Pacific, 1901–1985.* College Station: Texas A&M University Press, 1986.

Hogan, William T. *Economic History of the Iron and Steel Industry in the United States.* Lexington, Mass.: D. C. Heath and Company, 1971.

Holbrook, Abigail Curlee. "Cotton Marketing in Antebellum Texas." *Southwestern Historical Quarterly* 73 (April, 1970).

Honey, Michael. "Labour Leadership and Civil Rights in the South: A Case Study of the CIO in Memphis, 1935–1955." *Studies in History and Politics* 6 (1986).

———. "Operation Dixie: Two Points of View." *Labor History* 31 (summer, 1990).

———. *Southern Labor and Black Civil Rights: Organizing Memphis Workers.* Urbana: University of Illinois Press, 1993.

———. "Unionism and Racial Justice in Memphis." In *Organized Labor in the Twentieth-Century South,* edited by Robert H. Zieger. Knoxville: University of Tennessee Press, 1991.

Hunter, Tera W. *To Joy My Freedom: Southern Black Women Lives and Labor after the Civil War.* Cambridge: Harvard University Press, 1997.

Hutchmacher, Joseph J. *Senator Robert Wagner and the Rise of Urban Liberalism.* New York: Atheneum, 1960.

Johnson, Clyde. "CIO Oil Workers' Organizing Campaign in Texas, 1942–1943." In *Essays in Southern Labor History: Selected Papers, Southern Labor History Conference, 1976,* edited by Gary M. Fink and Merl E. Reed. Westport, Conn.: Greenwood Press, 1977.

Kampelman, Max M. *The Communist Party vs. the C.I.O.* New York: Arno & The New York Times, 1971.

Kann, Kenneth. "The Knights of Labor and the Southern Black Worker." *Labor History* 18 (winter, 1977).

Kelley, Robin D. G. *Hammer and Hoe: Alabama Communists during the Great Depression.* Chapel Hill: University of North Carolina Press, 1990.

Kellogg, Charles Flint. *NAACP: A History of the National Association for the Advancement of Colored People, vol. 1, 1909–1920.* Baltimore: Johns Hopkins Press, 1967.

Kesselman, Louis C. "The Fair Employment Practice Movement in Perspective." *Journal of Negro History* 31 (1946).

———. *The Social Politics of the FEPC: A Study in Reform Pressure Movements.* Chapel Hill: University of North Carolina Press, 1948.

Key, V. O. *Southern Politics: In State and Nation.* New York: Knopf, 1950.

Kimeldorf, Howard. "Bringing Unions Back In (Or Why We Need a New Old Labor History)." *Labor History* 32 (winter, 1991).

Klehr, Harvey. *Secret World of American Communism*. New Haven: Yale University Press, 1995.

Korstad, Robert. "The Possibilities for Racial Egalitarianism: Context Matters." *International Labor and Working-Class History* 44 (fall, 1993).

————, and Nelson Lichtenstein. "Opportunities Found and Lost: Radicals and the Early Civil Rights Movement." *Journal of American History* 75 (September, 1988).

Lack-Cohen, Nancy. "A Struggle for Sovereignty: National Consolidation, Emancipation, and Free Labor in Texas, 1865." *Journal of Southern History* 58 (February, 1992).

Laswell, Mary. *John Henry Kirby: Prince of the Pines*. Austin, Tex.: Encino, 1967.

Leavell, R. H. *Negro Migration in 1916–17*. New York: Negro University Press.

Letwin, Daniel. *The Challenge of Interracial Unionism: Alabama Coal Miners, 1878–1921*. Chapel Hill: University of North Carolina Press, 1998.

Levenstein, Harvey A. *Communism, Anti-Communism, and the CIO*. Westport, Conn.: Greenwood Press, 1981.

Lichtenstein, Alex. "Scientific Unionism and the 'Negro Question': Communists and the Transport Workers Union in Miami, 1944–1949." In *Southern Labor in Transition, 1940–1995*, edited by Robert H. Zieger. Knoxville: University of Tennessee Press, 1997.

Lindsey, Almont. *The Pullman Strike: The Story of a Unique Experiment and of a Great Labor Upheaval*. Chicago: University of Chicago Press, 1942.

Lipartito, Kenneth J., and Joseph A. Pratt. *Baker & Botts in the Development of Modern Houston*. Austin: University of Texas Press, 1991.

Lynch, Hollis R., comp. *The Black Urban Condition: A Documentary History, 1866–1971*. New York: Thomas Y. Crowell, 1973).

McCann Irving. *Why the Taft-Hartley Law?* New York: Committee for Constitutional Government, 1950.

McCartin, Joseph. "Abortive Reconstruction: Federal War Labor Policies, Union Organization, and the Politics of Race, 1917–1920." *Journal of Policy History* 9, no. 2 (1997).

————. *Labor's Great War: The Struggle for Industrial Democracy and the Origins of Modern American Labor Relations, 1912–1921*. Chapel Hill: University of North Carolina Press, 1997.

McComb, David. *Houston: The Bayou City*. Austin: University of Texas Press, 1969.

McDaniel, Dennis K. "The C.I.O. Political Action Committee and Congressman Martin Dies' Departure from Congress: Labors Inflated Claims." *East Texas Historical Journal* 2 (fall, 1993).

McGuire, Phillip. "Desegregation of the Armed Forces: Black Leadership, Protest, and World War II." *Journal of Negro History* 68 (fall, 1983).

McKay, S. S., and O. B. Faulk, *Texas after Spindletop*. Austin, Tex.: Steck-Vaughn, 1965.

McMillen, Neil. *Dark Journey: Black Mississippians in the Age of Jim Crow*. Urbana: University of Illinois, 1989.

Mancini, Matthew J. *One Dies, Get Another: Convict Leasing in the American South, 1866–1928*. Columbia: University of South Carolina Press, 1996.

Maroney, James C. "The Galveston Longshoremen's Strike of 1920." *East Texas Historical Journal* 16, no. 1 (1978).

———. "The International Longshoremen's Association in the Gulf States during the Progressive Era." *Southern Studies* 16, no. 2 (summer, 1977).

Marshall, F. Ray. *Labor in the South.* Cambridge: Harvard University Press, 1967.

———. *The Negro and Organized Labor.* New York: John Wiley and Sons, 1965.

———. "The Negro in Southern Unions." In *The Negro and the American Labor Movement,* edited by Julius Jacobson. Garden City, N.Y.: Anchor Books, 1968.

———. *The Negro Worker.* New York: Random House, 1967.

———. "Some Reflections on Labor History." *Southwestern Historical Quarterly* 75 (1971).

———. "Unions and the Black Community." In *The American Labor Movement,* edited by David Brody. New York: Harper & Row, 1971.

Martin, Tony. *Race First: The Ideological and Organizational Struggles of Marcus Garvey and the Universal Negro Improvement Association.* Westport, Conn.: Greenwood Press, 1976.

Maslow, Will. "FEPC—A Case History in Parliamentary Maneuver." *University of Chicago Law Review* 13 (June, 1946).

———. "The Law and Race Relations." *The Annals of the American Academy of Political and Social Sciences* 244 (March, 1946).

Maverick, Maury. *A Maverick American.* New York: Covici, Friede, 1937.

Maxwell, Robert S., and Robert D. Baker. *Sawdust Empire: The Texas Lumber Industry, 1830–1940.* College Station: Texas A&M University Press, 1983.

Meier, August, and Elliot Rudwick. *From Plantation to Ghetto.* 3d ed. New York: Hill and Wang, 1976.

Mers, Gilbert. *Working the Waterfront: The Ups and Downs of a Rebel Longshoreman.* Austin: University of Texas Press, 1988.

Meyer, John. "Regional Economics: A Survey." *American Economic Review* 53 (March, 1963).

Modell, John; Marc Goulden; and Sigurdur Magnusson. "World War II in the Lives of Black Americans: Some Findings and Interpretation." *Journal of American History* 76 (December, 1989).

Moneyhon, Carl H. "George T. Ruby and the Politics of Expediency in Texas." In *Southern Black Leaders of the Reconstruction Era,* edited by Howard N. Rabinowitz. Chicago: University of Illinois Press, 1982.

Montgomery, David. "To Study the People: The American Working Class." *Labor History* 21 (fall, 1980).

Moore, Richard R. *West Texas after the Discovery of Oil: A Modern Frontier.* Austin, Tex.: Jenkins Press, 1971.

Muir, Andrew Forest. "Railroads Come to Houston, 1857–1861." *Southwestern Historical Quarterly* 64 (July, 1960).

Murray, Florence. *The Negro Handbook, 1942.* New York: Wendell Malliet and Company, 1942.

National Labor Relations Board. *Decisions and Orders.* Washington, D.C.: Government Printing Office, 1936–45.

Nelson, Bruce. "CIO Meant One Thing for the Whites and Another Thing for Us: Steelworkers and Civil Rights, 1936–1974." In *Southern Labor in Transition, 1940–1995,* edited by Robert H. Zieger. Knoxville: University of Tennessee Press, 1997.

———. "Class and Race in the Crescent City: The ILWU, from San Francisco to New Orleans." In *The CIO's Left-Led Unions,* edited by Steve Rosswurm. New Brunswick, N.J.: Rutgers University Press, 1992.

———. "Organized Labor and the Struggle for Black Equality in Mobile during World War II," *Journal of American History* 80, no. 3 (December, 1993).

———. *Workers on the Waterfront: Seamen, Longshoremen, and Unionism in the 1930s.* Urbana: University of Chicago Press, 1988.

Norrell, Robert J. "Caste in Steel: Jim Crow Careers in Birmingham, Alabama." *Journal of American History* 73 (December, 1986).

Northrup, Herbert. *Negro Employment in Basic Industries: A Study of Racial Policies in Six Industries.* Philadelphia: University of Pennsylvania, 1970.

Negro Employment in Southern Industry. Philadelphia: University of Pennsylvania, 1970.

———. *Organized Labor and the Negro.* New York: Harper, 1944. Reprint, New York: Kraus Reprint Company, 1971.

O'Connor, Harvey. *History of Oil Workers International Union-CIO.* Denver: International Oil Workers Union-CIO, 1950.

Olien, Roger, and Diana Olien. *Oil Booms: Social Change in Five Texas Towns.* Lincoln: University of Nebraska Press, 1982.

———. *Wildcatters: Texas Independent Oilmen.* Austin: Texas Monthly Press, 1984.

Olson, James S. "Organized Black Leadership and Industrial Unionism: The Racial Response, 1936–1945." *Labor History* 10 (summer, 1969).

———, and Sharon Phair. "The Anatomy of a Race Riot: Beaumont, Texas, 1943." *Texana* 11 (1973).

O'Reilly, Kenneth. "The Roosevelt Administration and Black America: Federal Surveillance Policy and Civil Rights during the New Deal and World War II." *Phylon* 48 (March, 1987).

Ozanne, Robert. "Trends in American Labor History." *Labor History* 21 (fall, 1980).

Painter, Nell Irvin. *Exodusters: Black Migration to Kansas after Reconstruction.* New York: Knopf, 1977.

Perloff, Harvey; Edgar Dunn, Jr.; Eric Lampard; and Richard Muth. *Regions, Resources, and Economic Growth.* Baltimore: Johns Hopkins University Press, 1960.

Pfeffer, Paula F. *A. Philip Randolph, Pioneer of the Civil Rights Movement.* Baton Rouge: Louisiana State University Press, 1990.

———. "The Women behind the Union: Halena Wilson, Rosina Tucker, and the Ladies' Auxiliary to the Brotherhood of Sleeping Car Porters." *Labor History* 36 (fall, 1995).

Pitre, Merline. "Black Houstonians and the 'Separate But Equal' Doctrine: Carter W. Wesley Versus LuLu B. White." *The Houston Review: History and Culture of the Gulf Coast* 12, no. 1 (1990).

———. *In Struggle against Jim Crow: Lulu B. White and the NAACP, 1900–1957.* College Station: Texas A&M University Press, 1999.

———. *Through Many Dangers, Toils and Snares: The Black Political Leadership of Texas, 1868–1900.* Austin, Tex.: Eakin Press, 1985.

Potts, C. S. *Railroad Transportation in Texas.* Temecula, Calif.: Reprint Services Corporation, 1909.

Pratt, Joseph A. *The Growth of a Refining Region.* Greenwich, Conn.: JAI Press, 1980.

"The Proposed Fair Employment Practice Act: Facts and Fallacies." *Virginia Law Review* 32 (December, 1945).

Rabinowitz, Howard N. *The First New South: 1865–1920.* Arlington Heights, Ill.: Harlan Davidson, 1992.

Randolph, A Philip. "The Trade Union Movement and the Negro." *Journal of Negro Education* 5 (January, 1936).

Reed, Merl E. "FEPC and the Federal Agencies in the South." *Journal of Negro History* 65 (1980).

———. "The FEPC, the Black Worker, and the Southern Shipyards." *South Atlantic Quarterly* 74, no. 4 (autumn, 1975).

———. "Pennsylvania's Black Workers, the Defense Industries, and the Federal Agencies, 1941–1945." *Labor History* 27 (1986).

———. *Seedtime for the Civil Rights Movement: The President's Committee on Fair Employment Practice.* Baton Rouge: Louisiana State University, 1991.

Reed, S. G. *A History of the Texas Railroads and of Transportation Conditions under Spain and Mexico and the Republic and the State.* Houston: St. Clair Publishing Company, 1941.

Reese, James V. "The Evolution of an Early Texas Union: The Screwmen's Benevolent Association of Galveston, 1866–1891." *Southwestern Historical Quarterly* 75 (1971).

Reich, Steven A. "Soldiers of Democracy: Black Texans and the Fight for Citizenship, 1917–1921." *Journal of American History* 82 (March, 1996).

Reid, Ira De A. *Negro Membership in American Labor Unions.* New York: Negro University Press, 1930.

Rhinehart, Marilyn D. "Underground Patriots: Thurber Coal Miners and the Struggle for Individual Freedom, 1888–1903." *Southwestern Historical Quarterly* 92 (April, 1989).

Richardson, Harry. *Regional Growth Theory.* New York: Wiley Publishers, 1973.

Rister, Carl Coke. *Oil: Titan of the Southwest.* Norman: University of Oklahoma Press, 1949.

Roediger, David R. *The Wages of Whiteness: Race and the Making of the American Working Class.* New York: Verso, 1991.

Romasco, Albert U. *The Politics of Recovery: Roosevelt's New Deal.* New York: Oxford University Press, 1983.

Ross, Arthur M., and Herbert Hill. *Employment, Race, and Poverty.* New York: Harcourt, Brace & World, Inc., 1967.

Rosswurm, Steve, ed. *The CIO's Left-Led Unions.* New Brunswick, N.J.: Rutgers University Press, 1992.

Rubin, Lester. *The Negro in the Shipbuilding Industry.* Philadelphia: University of Pennsylvania, 1970.

Ruchames, Louis. *Race, Jobs, and Politics: The Story of FEPC.* New York: Columbia University Press, 1953.

Rundell, Walter, Jr. *Early Texas Oil Photographic History, 1866–1936.* College Station: Texas A&M University Press, 1977.

Russell, Maud. *Men along the Shore: The I.L.A. and its History.* New York: Brussell & Brussell, Inc., 1966.

Scanton, Thomas. "The Race Riots" *New Republic* 109 (July, 1943).

Schwarz, Jordan. *The New Dealers.* New York: Knopf, 1993.

Simpson, Eddie, Jr. *My Remembers: A Black Sharecropper's Recollections of the Depression.* Denton: University of North Texas Press, 1995.

Simpson, Herman W. *Hands of the Throttle: A Black Man's Struggle on the Road.* Houston: Herman W. Simpson, 1995.

Sitkoff, Harvard. *A New Deal for Blacks: The Emergence of Civil Rights as a National Issue.* Vol. I. New York: Oxford University Press, 1978.

———. "Racial Militancy and Interracial Violence in the Second World War." *Journal of American History* 58 (December, 1971).

Smallwood, James M. *Time of Hope, Time of Despair: Black Texans during Reconstruction.* Port Washington, N.Y.: Kennikat Press, 1981.

Smith, Alonzo, and Quintard Taylor. "Racial Discrimination in the Workplace: A Study of Two West Coast Cities during the 1940s." *Journal of Ethnic Studies* 8, no. 1 (spring, 1980).

Sparks, Randy J. "Heavenly Houston or Hellish Houston? Black Unemployment and Relief Efforts, 1929–1936." *Southern Studies* 25, no. 4 (winter, 1986).

Spear, Alan H. *Black Chicago: The Making of a Negro Ghetto, 1890–1920.* Chicago: University of Chicago Press, 1967.

Spero, Sterling D., and Abram L. Harris. *The Black Worker: The Negro and the Labor Movement.* New York: Atheneum, 1966.

Spratt, John S. *The Road to Spindletop: Economic Change in Texas, 1875–1901.* Dallas: Southern Methodist University Press, 1955.

Stein, Judith. "The Ins and Outs of the CIO." *International Labor and Working-Class History* 44 (fall, 1993).

———. *Running Steel Running America: Race, Economic Policy, and the Decline of Liberalism.* Chapel Hill: University of North Carolina Press, 1998.

Stover, John F. *The Railroads of the South, 1865–1900.* Chapel Hill: University of North Carolina Press, 1955.

Thomas, Julius A. "Race Conflict and Social Action." *Opportunity* 21 (October, 1943)

Tindall, George B. *The Emergence of the New South, 1913–1945.* Baton Rouge: Louisiana State University Press, 1967.

Traxler, Ralph, Jr., "The Texas and Pacific Railroad Land Grants." *Southwestern Historical Quarterly* 61 (January, 1958).

Trotter, Joe William, Jr. *Coal, Class, and Color: Blacks in Southern West Virginia, 1915–32.* Urbana: University of Illinois Press, 1990.

U.S. Department of Commerce. Bureau of the Census, Population Census 1870–1950. Washington, D.C.: Government Printing Office, 1870–1950.

Vandiver, Frank E. *The Southwest: South or West?* College Station: Texas A&M University Press, 1975.

Vidrine, Eraste. "Negro Locals." *International Socialists Review* 5 (January, 1905).

Walker, Donald R. *Penology for Profit: A History of the Texas Prison System, 1867–1912.* College Station: Texas A&M University Press, 1988.

Warner, C. A. "Texas and the Oil Industry." *Southwestern Historical Quarterly* 50 (July, 1946).

———. *Texas Oil and Gas since 1543.* Houston: Gulf Publishing, 1939.

Wesley, Charles H. *Negro Labor in the United States 1850–1925: A Study in American Economic History.* New York: Vanguard Press, 1927.

Whisenhunt, Donald. *The Depression in Texas: The Hoover Years.* New York: Garland Press, 1983.

———, ed. *The Depression in the Southwest.* Port Washington, N.Y.: Kennikat Press, 1980.

Willett, Don. "The Galveston Bay Dock Wars, 1936–1937." *East Texas Historical Journal* 32, no. 1 (1994).

Winkler, E. W., ed. *Platforms of Political Parties in Texas.* Austin, Tex.: The University, 1916.

Wolters, Raymond. *Negroes and the Great Depression: The Problem of Economic Recovery.* Westport, Conn.: Greenwood Press, 1970.

Woodward, C. Vann. *Origins of the New South, 1877–1913.* Baton Rouge: Louisiana State University Press, 1951.

Woodward, C. Vann. *Strange Career of Jim Crow.* New York: Oxford University Press, 1955.

Wright, Gavin. *Old South, New South: Revolutions in the Southern Economy since the Civil War.* New York: Basic Books, 1986.

Wynn, Neil A. *The Afro-American and the Second World War.* London: Elek, 1976.

Youngs, John W. T. *Eleanor Roosevelt: A Personal and Public Life.* New York: Harper Collins, 1985.

Zamora, Emilio. "The Failed Promise of Wartime Opportunity for Mexicans in the Texas Oil Industry." *Southwestern Historical Quarterly* 95 (winter, 1992).

———. *The World of the Mexican Worker in Texas.* College Station: Texas A&M University Press, 1993.

Zieger, Robert H. *The CIO, 1935–1955.* Chapel Hill: University of North Carolina Press, 1995.

———. "'Which Side Are You On'—Workers, Unions, & Critics." *Labor History* 17 (spring, 1976).

———. "Workers and Scholars: Recent Trends in American Labor Historiography." *Labor History* 13 (spring, 1972).

———, ed. *Organized Labor in the Twentieth-Century South.* Knoxville: University of Tennessee Press, 1991.

———, ed. *Southern Labor in Transition, 1940–1995.* Knoxville: University of Tennessee Press, 1997.

UNPUBLISHED SOURCES

Afro American Photograph Collection. Houston Metropolitan Archive and Research Center, Houston, Texas.

Afro American Railroad Employee Collection. Houston Metropolitan Archive and Research Center, Houston, Texas.

Allen, Ruth. Papers. Texas Labor Archives, University of Texas, Arlington, Texas.

Association of Colored Trainmen Collection. Houston Metropolitan Archives and Research Center, Houston, Texas.

Banks, James Melvin. "The Pursuit of Equality: The Movement for first Class Citizenship Among Negroes in Texas." Ph.D. diss., Syracuse, 1962.

Bessent, Nancy Ruth. "The Publisher: A Biography of Carter W. Wesley." Ph.D. diss., University of Texas, 1981.

Botson, Michael R., Jr. "Organized Labor at the Hughes Tool Company, 1918–1942: From Welfare to the Steel Workers Organizing Committee." Master's thesis, University of Houston, 1994.

Brophy, William Joseph. "The Black Texan, 1900–1950: A Quantitative History." Ph.D. diss., Vanderbilt University, 1974.

Colored Trainmen of America (CTA) Collection. Houston Metropolitan Research Center, Houston, Texas.

Congressional Records. 73rd and 81st Congress.

Dailey, Nancy. "History of the Beaumont, Texas Chapter of the National Association for the Advancement of Colored People, 1918–1970." M.A. thesis, Lamar University, 1971.

Dorsett, Jesse. "Blacks in Reconstruction Texas, 1865–1877." Ph.D. diss., Texas Christian University, 1981.

District Proceedings of the Gulf Coast International Longshoremen's Association, 1914–45.

Evans, Patience. "A Political Mystery: Martin Dies' Withdrawal from the 1944 Texas Democratic Party." Master's thesis, University of Houston, 1984.

Fair Employment Practice Commission Records. National Archives, Fort Worth, Texas.

Fair Employment Practice Commission Records. National Archives, Washington, D.C.

Gillette, Michael L. "The NAACP in Texas, 1937–1957." Ph.D. diss., University of Texas, 1984.

Green, George N. "The Far Right Wing in Texas Politics, 1930s–1960s." Ph.D. diss., Florida State University, 1966.

Hardin, Frances Anne. "The Role of Presidential Advisors: Roosevelt Aides and the FEPC, 1941–1943." M.A. thesis, Cornell University, 1975.

Hinze, Virginia Neal. "Norris Wright Cuney." M.A. thesis, Rice University, 1965.

Honey, Michael. "Labor and Civil Rights in the South: The Industrial Labor Movement and Black Worker's in Memphis, 1929–1945." Ph.D. diss., Northern Illinois University, 1987.

Hughes Tool Collection. Houston Metropolitan Research Center, Houston, Texas.

Independent Metal Workers Union Collection. Houston Metropolitan Archives and Research Center, Houston, Texas.

International Longshoremen's Association. Atlantic and Gulf Coast District Convention Proceedings, 1936–46.

Jackson, Bertron M., Family Collection. Houston Metropolitan Research Center, Houston, Texas.

Korstad, Robert R. "Day Break of Freedom: Tobacco Workers and the CIO, Winston-Salem, North Carolina, 1943–1950." Ph.D. diss., University of North Carolina, Chapel Hill, 1987.

LeRoy, Moses. Papers. Houston Metropolitan Archives and Research Center, Houston, Texas.

Lewis, Lee A. Papers. Labor Archives, University of Texas, Arlington, Texas.

Mac Gibson, Charles. "Organized Labor in Texas from 1890 to 1900." M.A. thesis, Texas Tech University, 1973.

Maroney, James. "Organized Labor in Texas, 1900–1929." Ph.D. diss., University of Houston, 1975.

Maverick, Maury, Sr. Papers. Center for American History, University of Texas at Austin.

Mers, Gilbert. Papers. Houston Metropolitan Research Center, Houston, Texas.

Mullenix, Grady Lee. "A History of the Texas State Federation of Labor." Ph.D. diss., University of Texas at Austin, 1955.

National Association for the Advancement of Colored People. Papers. Labor Series. Library of Congress, Washington, D.C.

Negro Labor News Collection. Houston Metropolitan Research Center, Houston, Texas.

Oil, Chemical, and Atomic Workers Collection. Tyrrell Historical Library, Beaumont, Texas.

Payne, James Sutton. "Texas Historiography in the Twentieth-Century: A Study of Eugene C. Barker, Charles W. Ramsdell, and Walter P. Webb." Ph.D. diss., University of Denver, 1972.

Polakoff, Murray E. "The Development of the Texas State CIO Council." Ph.D. diss., Columbia University, 1955.

Pratt, Joseph A. "Oil Workers International Unions Organization of the Upper Gulf Coast, 1935–1945." Senior thesis, Rice University, 1970.

Sapper, N. G. "A Survey of the History of the Black People of Texas, 1930–1954." Ph.D. diss., Texas Tech University, 1972.

Shapiro, Harold. "The Workers of San Antonio, Texas, 1900–1940." Ph.D. diss., University of Texas at Austin, 1952.

Sorelle, James Martin. "The Darker Side of 'Heaven': The Black Community in Houston, Texas, 1917–1945." Ph.D. diss., Kent State University, 1980.

Stevenson, Coke, Papers. Texas State Library and Archives, Austin, Texas.

Taylor, Allen Clayton. "A History of the Screwmen's Benevolent Association from 1865 to 1924." M.A. thesis, University of Texas, 1968.

Taylor, Hobart. "C. W. Rice: Labor Leader." B.A. thesis, Prairie View State Normal and Industrial College, Prairie View, Texas, 1939.

Teel, Robert Eli. "Discrimination against Negro Workers in Texas: Extent and Effects." Master's thesis, University of Texas at Austin, 1947.

Terrell, Wendell P. "A Short History of the Negro Longshoremen." Senior thesis, Houston College for Negroes, 1936.

Texas Commission on Interracial Cooperation Collection. Houston Metropolitan Research Center, Houston, Texas.

Texas Company Collection. Houston Metropolitan Research Center, Houston, Texas.

Texas Labor Movement Collection. Center for American History, University of Texas at Austin.

Texas State Federation of Labor Convention Proceedings, 1936–47. Labor Archives. University of Texas, Arlington, Texas.

Texas State Industrial Union Council—CIO Convention Proceedings, 1936–46. Labor Archives. University of Texas, Arlington, Texas.

War Manpower Commission Records. National Archives, Washington, D.C.

Zeigler, Robert E. "The Workingman in Houston, Texas, 1865–1914." Ph.d. diss., Texas Tech University, 1972.

INTERVIEWS

Alton, Allison "Bud," by Ernest Obadele-Starks, April 21, 1995, Houston, Texas.

Black, Leona Mercedes, by Ernest Obadele-Starks, December 13, 1997, Houston, Texas.

Crossland, John, by George Green, August 17, 1971. Texas Labor History Collection. University of Texas, Arlington, Texas.

Dixie, Chris, by Ernest Obadele-Starks, April 22, 1995, Houston, Texas.

Easterwood, Maurice, by Ernest Obadele-Starks, April 21, 1995, Houston, Texas.

Ellinger, Ruth, by Ernest Obadele-Starks, November 12, 1995, Austin, Texas.

Hahs, Don, by Ernest Obadele-Starks, April 19, 1995, Houston, Texas.

Hoskins, LeRoy, by Ernest Obadele-Starks, April 14, 1995, Galveston, Texas.

Huddleston, O. J., by Ernest Obadele-Starks, April 14, 1995, Houston, Texas.

Johnson, C. B., by Ernest Obadele-Starks, April 21, 1995, Houston, Texas.

LeRoy, Moses, by George Green, September 19, 1971. Texas Labor History Collection. University of Texas, Arlington, Texas.

Lewis, Lee A., by George Green, October 4, 1971. Texas Labor History Collection. University of Texas, Arlington, Texas.

Merritt, Mack Middleton, by Ernest Obadele-Starks, December 13, 1997, Houston, Texas.

Mers, Gilbert, by Ernest Obadele-Starks, April 15, 1995, Houston, Texas.

Nichols, R. C., by Ernest Obadele-Starks, April 19, 1995, Houston, Texas.

Saunders, Mr. and Mrs. James H., by Carr Winn, August 13, 1971. Texas Labor History Collection. University of Texas, Arlington, Texas.

Wilson, C. D., by Ernest Obadele-Starks, April 15, 1995, Houston, Texas.

INDEX

Pages containing illustrations appear in italics.